RESPONSES

RESPONSES: PROSE PIECES, 1953–1976

EXPANDED EDITION BY
RICHARD WILBUR

STORY LINE PRESS

2000

Printed in the United States of America

The essay "Shakespeare's Poems" was originally the Introduction to *The Narrative Poems: And Poems of Doubtful Authenticity* by William Shakespeare, edited by Richard Wilbur and Alfred Harbage, in "The Pelican Shakespeare," General Editor: Alfred Harbage (rev. ed., New York: Penguin Books, 1974), copyright © 1962 by Harcourt Brace Jovanovich, Inc. "The Narrative of Arthur Gordon Pym" appeared originally in The Narrative of Arthur Gordon Pym by Edgar Allen Poe, copyright © 1974 by David R. Godine, and is reprinted by permission of David R. Godine, Publisher. The words quoted from "It's Only a Paper Moon," by Billy Rose, E. Y. Harburg, and Harold Arlen, © 1933 by Warner Bros. Inc., copyright renewed, all rights reserved, are used by permission.

Library of Congress Cataloging-in-Publication Data

Wilbur, Richard, 1921-
    Responses : prose pieces, 1953-1976 / by Richard Wilbur.-- Expanded ed.
    p. cm.
    ISBN 1-885266-82-0
    I. Title.

PS3545.I32165 R4 1999
809.1--dc21

99-048578

For Ellen, Peter, Christopher, Christie, and Nathan

CONTENTS

In re-publishing this, my first collection of prose pieces, the Story Line Press has found room for two additional items not previously included in any book of mine. One is a little thank-you talk given at a recent awards ceremony, in which something is said about form and order in life and art. The other is a 1959 lecture called "The House of Poe."

Malcolm Cowley remarked, when Responses came out in 1976, that it was full of the scattered makings of a good book on Poe. He was quite right, and I am sorry never to have hammered my thoughts on the subject into a single, sustained argument. "The House of Poe" will be found to repeat (or anticipate, rather) some of the material in the book's other Poe pieces; yet it stands alone in its full inventory of Poe's central symbolism, and though it may not be my best Poe essay, it has been the most influential. What it said in 1959 had not been said before, and therefore it met with some resistance. When (after its debut at the Library of Congress) I read the lecture at the University of Virginia, an August Poe scholar said to me with gentle Southern malice, "Mr. Wilbur, I do not myself believe what you have told us about Edgar Allan Poe, and yet I can see how you might believe it." Well, I really do believe it, and I hope to have opened a door into Poe for some readers.

—RW
Cummington, 1997

Poets sometimes write verses in answer to a request or expectation, but most poems are wholly uncalled for. At any rate, that has been the case with me. I can bring to mind a birthday poem, a sonnet for the opening of Lincoln Center, a hymn for a Christmas concert, some trivial jingles, some lines for an anti-war newspaper, a few translations done at an author's or editor's instance, and a number of aborted efforts to please or oblige; but all else in the way of poetry has come about unprompted. When I turn, however, to the accumulated prose from which this book has been selected, I find almost nothing that I was not asked to do. It was on my own initiative, to be sure, that I began to translate Molière's verse comedies into English, and that made, in time, for the writing of several short interpretive essays. But the remainder of these pieces were done–by choice, of course–in response to invitations to give a lecture or speech, contribute to a symposium, compose a broadcast, introduce a work, interpret an author, or help mark an anniversary.

Having confessed so much, I had better make no ingenious claims of unity for this book: it consists of some prose by-products of a poet's life, and cannot therefore be innocent of spottiness and imbalance. If the contents somehow hang together for the reader, I hope it will be because the voice, though changing with age and occasion, seems that of one person with certain persistent concerns and a mind largely his own. The arrangement is chronological, save that for strategic reasons the two earliest pieces have been placed at the end of the book. Not wishing to insist too much upon an interest in my own poems, I have left out all questionnaires and interviews. Of book reviews I include only one, a survey of studies which approaches the scope of an essay. One or two items appear here, despite my uncertainties, because of the kind advocacy of people whom I respect. Where two essays dealt with much the same material, and were of equal worth, I have chosen the one least likely to have been encountered by the reader.

This last principle helped me to decide among a number of pieces on Poe, about whom I have been thinking for many years. As a Junior Fellow at Harvard, between 1947 and 1950, I gave a seminar on Poe, and discarded an all-but-finished book on his work because I had not yet discovered a stable and adequate vocabulary in which to discuss him. My introduction to a 1959 paperback edition of his poems reached a large public, and the Library of Congress lecture called "The House of Poe," given in the same year, has been several times reprinted here and abroad. Three less familiar efforts, here presented, have been pruned of some redundancies, though a measure of repetition could not be avoided. I include all three, at the risk of disproportion, because I regard my decodings of Poe with a frank satisfaction. They seem to me original and true, and the best excuse for this collection.

The last paragraph of a preface frequently consists of acknowledgments to mentors, sources, colleagues, and helpers. Such a collection as this would call for an interminable roll of names, and so I shall suppress my gratitude, thanking only the several fellow-writers who urged that the book be made, and my wife for her good counsel in its making.

—R.W.
Cummington, Massachusetts, 1976

In 1959, as part of the Town of Amherst's bicentennial celebration, Louise Bogan, Archibald MacLeish, and I were invited to speak at the College on Emily Dickinson. We said our says to an audience which filled the huge basketball cage, and which would have made the subject quite shy. Our papers were subsequently published by the Amherst College Press under the title of Emily Dickinson: Three Views.

"SUMPTUOUS DESTITUTION"

At some point Emily Dickinson sent her whole Calvinist vocabulary into exile, telling it not to come back until it would subserve her own sense of things. Of course, that is not a true story, but it is a way of saying what I find most remarkable in Emily Dickinson. She inherited a great and overbearing vocabulary, which, had she used it submissively, would have forced her to express an established theology and psychology. But she would not let that vocabulary write her poems for her. There lies the real difference between a poet like Emily Dickinson and a fine versifier like Isaac Watts. To be sure, Emily Dickinson also wrote in the meters of hymnody, and paraphrased the Bible, and made her poems turn on great words like Immortality and Salvation and Election. But in her poems those great words are not merely being themselves; they have been adopted, for expressive purposes; they have been taken personally, and therefore redefined.

The poems of Emily Dickinson are a continual appeal to experience, motivated by an arrogant passion for the truth. "Truth is so rare a thing," she once said, "it is delightful to tell it." And, sending some poems to Colonel Higginson, she wrote, "Excuse them, if they are untrue." And again, to the same respondent, she observed, "Candor is the only wile"–meaning that the writer's bag of tricks need contain one trick only, the trick of being honest. That her taste for truth involved a regard for objective fact need not be argued: we have her poem on the snake, and that on the hummingbird, and they are small masterpieces of exact description. She liked accuracy; she liked solid and homely detail; and even in her most exalted poems we are surprised and reassured by buckets, shawls, or buzzing flies.

But her chief truthfulness lay in her insistence on discovering the facts of her inner experience. She was a Linnaeus to the phenomena of her own consciousness, describing and distinguishing the states and motions of her soul. The results of this "psychic reconnaissance," as Professor Whicher called it, were several. For one thing, it made her articulate about inward matters which poetry had never so sharply defined; specifically, it made her capable of writing two such lines as these:

> A perfect, paralyzing bliss
> Contented as despair.

We often assent to the shock of a paradox before we understand it, but those lines are so just and so concentrated as to explode their meaning instantly in the mind. They did not come so easily, I think, to Emily Dickinson. Unless I guess wrongly as to chronology, such lines were the fruit of long poetic research; the poet had worked toward them through much study of the way certain emotions can usurp consciousness entirely, annulling our sense of past and future, canceling near and far, converting all time and space to a joyous or grievous here and now. It is in their ways of annihilating time and space that bliss and despair are comparable.

Which leads me to a second consequence of Emily Dickinson's self-analysis. It is one thing to assert as pious doctrine that the soul has power, with God's grace, to master circumstance. It is another thing to find out personally, as Emily Dickinson did in writing her psychological poems, that the aspect of the world is in no way constant, that the power of external things depends on our state of mind, that the soul selects its own society and may, if granted strength to do so, select a superior order and scope of consciousness which will render it finally invulnerable. She learned these things by witnessing her own courageous spirit.

Another result of Emily Dickinson's introspection was that she discovered some grounds, in the nature of her soul and its affections, for a personal conception of such ideas as Heaven and Immortality, and so managed a precarious convergence between her inner experience and her religious inheritance. What I want to attempt now is a rough sketch of the imaginative logic by which she did this. I had better say before I start that I shall often seem demonstrably wrong, because Emily Dickinson, like many poets, was consistent in her concerns but inconsistent in her attitudes. The following, therefore, is merely an opinion as to her main drift.

Emily Dickinson never lets us forget for very long that in some respects life gave her short measure; and indeed it is possible to see the greater part of her poetry as an effort to cope with her sense of privation. I think that for her there were three major privations: she was deprived of an orthodox and steady religious faith; she was deprived of love; she was deprived of literary recognition.

At the age of seventeen, after a series of revival meetings at Mount Holyoke Seminary, Emily Dickinson found that she must refuse to become a professing Christian. To some modern minds this may seem to have been a sensible and necessary step; and surely it was a step toward becoming such a poet as she became. But for her, no pleasure in her own integrity could then eradicate the feeling that she had betrayed a deficiency, a want of grace. In her letters to Abiah Root she tells of the enhancing effect of conversion on her fellow-students, and says of herself in a famous passage:

> I am one of the lingering bad ones,
> and so do I slink away, and pause
> and ponder, and ponder and
> pause, and do work without
> knowing why, not surely for this
> brief world, and more sure it is not
> for heaven, and I ask what this
> message means that they ask for
> so very eagerly: you know of this
> depth and fulness, will you try to
> tell me about it?

There is humor in that, and stubbornness, and a bit of characteristic lurking pride: but there is also an anguished sense of having separated herself, through some dry incapacity, from spiritual community, from purpose, and from magnitude of life. As a child of evangelical Amherst, she inevitably thought of purposive, heroic life as requiring a vigorous faith.

Out of such a thought she later wrote:

> The abdication of Belief
> Makes the Behavior small–
> Better an ignis fatuus
> Than no illume at all–

That hers was a species of religious personality goes without saying; but by her refusal of such ideas as original sin, redemption, hell, and election, she made it impossible for herself–as Whicher observed– "to share the religious life of her generation." She became an unsteady congregation of one.

Her second privation, the privation of love, is one with which her poems and her biographies have made us exceedingly familiar, though some biographical facts remain conjectural. She had the good fortune, at least once, to bestow her heart on another; but she seems to have found her life, in great part, a history of loneliness, separation, and bereavement.

As for literary fame, some will deny that Emily Dickinson ever greatly desired it, and certainly there is evidence, mostly from her latter years, to support such a view. She did write that "Publication is the auction / Of the mind of man." And she did say to Helen Hunt Jackson, "How can you print a piece of your soul?" But earlier, in 1861, she had frankly expressed to Sue Dickinson the hope that "sometime" she might make her kinfolk proud of her. The truth is, I think, that Emily Dickinson knew she was good, and began her career with a normal appetite for recognition. I think that she later came, with some reason, to despair of being understood or properly valued, and so directed against her hopes of fame what was by then a well-developed disposition to renounce. That she wrote a good number of poems about fame supports my view: the subjects to which a poet returns are those which vex him.

What did Emily Dickinson do, as a poet, with her sense of privation? One thing she quite often did was to pose as the laureate and attorney of the empty-handed, and question God about the economy of His creation. Why, she asked, is a fatherly God so sparing of His presence? Why is there never a sign that prayers are heard? Why does Nature tell us no comforting news of its Maker? Why do some receive a whole loaf, while others must starve on a crumb? Where is the benevolence in shipwreck and earthquake? By asking such questions as these, she turned complaint into critique, and used her own sufferings as experiential evidence about the nature of the deity. The God who emerges from these poems is a God who does not answer, an unrevealed God whom one cannot confidently approach through Nature or through doctrine.

But there was another way in which Emily Dickinson dealt with her sentiment of lack–another emotional strategy which was both more frequent and more fruitful. I refer to her repeated assertion of the paradox that privation is more plentiful than plenty; that to renounce is to possess the more; that "The Banquet of abstemiousness / Defaces that of wine." We all know how the poet illustrated this ascetic paradox in her behavior–how in her later years she chose to live in relative retirement, keeping the world, even in its dearest aspects, at a physical remove. She would write her friends, telling them how she missed them, then flee upstairs when they came to see her; afterward, she might send a note of apology, offering the odd explanation that "We shun because we prize." Any reader of Dickinson biographies can furnish other examples, dramatic or homely, of this prizing and shunning, this yearning and renouncing: in my own mind's eye is a picture of Emily Dickinson watching a gay circus caravan from the distance of her chamber window.

In her inner life, as well, she came to keep the world's images, even the images of things passionately desired, at the remove which renunciation makes; and her poetry at its most mature continually proclaims that to lose or forgo what we desire is somehow to gain. We may say, if we like, with some of the poet's commentators, that this central paradox of her thought is a rationalization of her neurotic plight; but we had better add that it is also a discovery of something about the soul. Let me read you a little poem of psychological observation which, whatever its date of composition, may logically be considered as an approach to that discovery.

Undue Significance a starving man attaches
To Food—
Far off—He sighs—and therefore—Hopeless—
And therefore—Good—
Partaken—it relieves—indeed—
But proves us
That Spices fly
In the Receipt—It was the Distance—
Was Savory—

This poem describes an educational experience, in which a starving man is brought to distinguish between appetite and desire. So long as he despairs of sustenance, the man conceives it with the eye of desire as infinitely delicious. But when, after all, he secures it and appeases his hunger, he finds that its imagined spices have flown. The moral is plain: once an object has been magnified by desire, it cannot be wholly possessed by appetite.

The poet is not concerned, in this poem, with passing any judgment. She is simply describing the way things go in the human soul, telling us that the frustration of appetite awakens or abets desire, and that the effect of intense desiring is to render any finite satisfaction disappointing. Now I want to read you another well-known poem, in which Emily Dickinson was again considering privation and possession, and the modes of enjoyment possible to each. In this case, I think, a judgment is strongly implied.

> Success is counted sweetest
> By those who ne'er succeed.
> To comprehend a nectar
> Requires sorest need.
>
> Not one of all the purple Host
> Who took the Flag today
> Can tell the definition
> So clear of Victory
>
> As he defeated–dying–
> On whose forbidden ear
> The distant strains of triumph
> Burst agonized and clear!

Certainly Emily Dickinson's critics are right in calling this poem an expression of the idea of compensation with the wretchedness of the dying soldier's lot, and an improved understanding of the nature of victory may seem small compensation for defeat and death; but the more one ponders this poem the likelier it grows that Emily Dickinson is arguing the superiority of defeat to victory, of frustration to satisfaction, and of anguished comprehension to mere possession. What do the victors have but victory, a victory which they cannot fully savor or clearly define? They have paid for their triumph by a sacrifice of awareness; a material gain has cost them a spiritual loss. For the dying soldier, the case is reversed: defeat and death are attended by an increase of awareness, and material loss has led to spiritual gain. Emily Dickinson would think that the better bargain.

In the first of these two poems I have read, it was possible to imagine the poet as saying that a starving man's visions of food are but wish fulfillments, and hence illusory; but the second poem assures us of the contrary–assures us that food, or victory, or any other good thing is best comprehended by the eye of desire from the vantage of privation. We must now ask in what way desire can define things, what comprehension of nectars it can have beyond a sense of inaccessible sweetness.

Since Emily Dickinson was not a philosopher, and never set forth her thought in any orderly way, I shall answer that question by a quotation from the seventeenth-century divine Thomas Traherne. Conveniently for us, Traherne is thinking, in this brief meditation, about food–specifically, about acorns–as perceived by appetite and by desire.

The services of things and their excellencies are spiritual: being objects not of the eye, but of the mind: and you more spiritual by how much more you esteem them. Pigs eat acorns, but neither consider the sun that gave them life, nor the influences of the heavens by which they were nourished, nor the very root of the tree from whence they came. This being the work of Angels, who in a wide and clear light see even the sea that gave them moisture: And feed upon that acorn spiritually while they know the ends for which it was created, and feast upon all these as upon a World of Joys within it: while to ignorant swine that eat the shell, it is an empty husk of no taste or delightful savor.

Emily Dickinson could not have written that, for various reasons, a major reason being that she could not see in Nature any revelations of divine purpose. But like Traherne she discovered that the soul has an infinite hunger, a hunger to possess all things. (That discovery, I suspect, was the major fruit of her introspection.) And like Traherne she distinguished two ways of possessing things, the way of appetite and the way of desire. What Traherne said of the pig she said of her favorite insect:

> Auto da Fe and Judgment—
> Are nothing to the Bee—
> His separation from His Rose—
> To him—sums Misery—

The creature of appetite (whether insect or human) pursues satisfaction, and strives to possess the object in itself; it cannot imagine the vaster economy of desire, in which the pain of abstinence is justified by moments of infinite joy, and the object is spiritually possessed, not merely for itself, but more truly as an index of the All. That is how one comprehends a nectar. Miss Dickinson's bee does not comprehend the rose which it plunders, because the truer sweetness of the rose lies beyond the rose, in its relationship to the whole of being; but she would say that Gerard Manley Hopkins comprehends a bluebell when, having noticed its intrinsic beauties, he adds, "I know the beauty of Our Lord by it." And here is an eight-line poem of her own, in which she comprehends the full sweetness of water.

> We thirst at first–'tis Nature's Act–
> And later–when we die–
> A little Water supplicate–
> Of fingers going by–
>
> It intimates the finer want–
> Whose adequate supply
> Is that Great Water in the West–
> Termed Immortality–

Emily Dickinson elected the economy of desire, and called her privation good, rendering it positive by renunciation. And so she came to live in a huge world of delectable distances. Far-off words like "Brazil" or "Circassian" appear continually in her poems as symbols of things distanced by loss or renunciation, yet infinitely prized and yearned for. So identified in her mind are distance and delight that, when ravished by the sight of a hummingbird in her garden, she calls it "the mail from Tunis." And not only are the objects of her desire distant, they are also very often moving away, their sweetness increasing in proportion to their remoteness. "To disappear enhances," one of the poems begins, and another closes with these lines:

> The Mountain–at a given distance–
> In Amber–lies–
> Approached–the Amber flits–a little–
> And That's–the Skies–

21

To the eye of desire, all things are seen in a profound perspective, either moving or gesturing toward the vanishing point. Or to use a figure which may be closer to Miss Dickinson's thought, to the eye of desire the world is a centrifuge, in which all things are straining or flying toward the occult circumference. In some such way, Emily Dickinson conceived her world, and it was in a spatial metaphor that she gave her personal definition of Heaven. "Heaven," she said, "is what I cannot reach."

At times it seems that there is nothing in her world but her own soul, with its attendant abstractions, and, at a vast remove, the inscrutable Heaven. On most of what might intervene she has closed the valves of her attention, and what mortal objects she does acknowledge are riddled by desire to the point of transparency. Here is a sentence from her correspondence: "Enough is of so vast a sweetness, I suppose it never occurs, only pathetic counterfeits." The writer of that sentence could not invest her longings in any finite object. Again, she wrote, "Emblem is immeasurable—that is why it is better than fulfillment, which can be drained." For such a sensibility, it was natural and necessary that things be touched with infinity. Therefore her nature poetry, when most serious, does not play descriptively with birds or flowers but presents us repeatedly with dawn, noon, and sunset, those grand ceremonial moments of the day which argue the splendor of Paradise. Or it shows us the ordinary landscape transformed by the electric brilliance of a storm; or it shows us the fields succumbing to the annual mystery of death. In her love poems, Emily Dickinson was at first covetous of the beloved himself; indeed, she could be idola-

trous, going so far as to say that his face, should she
see it again in Heaven, would eclipse the face of Jesus.
But in what I take to be her later work the beloved's
lineaments, which were never very distinct, vanish
entirely; he becomes pure emblem, a symbol of remote spiritual joy, and so is all but absorbed into the
idea of Heaven. The lost beloved is, as one poem
declares, "infinite when gone," and in such lines as
the following we are aware of him mainly as an instrument in the poet's commerce with the beyond.

> Of all the Souls that stand create–
> I have elected–One–
> When Sense from Spirit–flies away–
> And Subterfuge–is done–
> When that which is–and that which was–
> Apart–intrinsic–stand–
> And this brief Tragedy of Flesh–
> Is shifted–like a Sand–
> When Figures show their royal Front–
> And Mists–are carved away,
> Behold the Atom–I preferred–
> To all the lists of clay!

In this extraordinary poem, the corporeal beloved
is seen as if from another and immaterial existence,
and in such perspective his earthly person is but an
atom of clay. His risen spirit, we presume, is more
imposing, but it is certainly not in focus. What the
rapt and pounding lines of this poem portray is the
poet's own magnificence of soul–her fidelity to desire, her confidence of Heaven, her contempt of the
world. Like Cleopatra's final speeches, this poem is
an irresistible demonstration of spiritual status, in
which the supernatural is so royally demanded that
skepticism is disarmed. A part of its effect derives,

by the way, from the fact that the life to come is described in an ambiguous present tense, so that we half suppose the speaker to be already in Heaven.

There were times when Emily Dickinson supposed this of herself, and I want to close by making a partial guess at the logic of her claims to beatitude. It seems to me that she generally saw Heaven as a kind of infinitely remote bank, in which, she hoped, her untouched felicities were drawing interest. Parting, she said, was all she knew of it. Hence it is surprising to find her saying, in some poems, that Heaven has drawn near to her, and that in her souls' "superior instants" Eternity has disclosed to her "the colossal substance/Of immortality." Yet the contradiction can be understood if we recall what sort of evidence was persuasive to Emily Dickinson.

"Too much proof," she wrote, "affronts belief"; and she was little convinced either by doctrine or by theological reasoning. Her residual Calvinism was criticized and fortified by her study of her own soul in action, and from the phenomena of her soul she was capable of making the boldest inferences. That the sense of time is subject to the moods of the soul seemed to her a proof of the soul's eternity. Her intensity of grief for the dead, and her feeling of their continued presence, seemed to her arguments for the reunion of souls in Heaven. And when she found in herself infinite desires, "immortal longings," it seemed to her possible that such desires might somewhere be infinitely answered.

One psychic experience which she interpreted as beatitude was "glee," or, as some would call it, euphoria. Now, a notable thing about glee or euphoria is its gratuitousness. It seems to come from nowhere, and it was this apparent sourcelessness of the emotion from which Emily Dickinson made her inference. "The 'happiness' without a cause," she said, "is the best happiness, for glee intuitive and lasting is the gift of God." Having forgone all earthly causes of happiness, she could only explain her glee, when it came, as a divine gift–a compensation in joy for what she had renounced in satisfaction, and a foretaste of the mood of Heaven. The experience of glee, as she records it, is boundless: all distances collapse, and the soul expands to the very circumference of things. Here is how she put it in one of her letters: "Abroad is close tonight and I have but to lift my hands to touch the 'Hights of Abraham.'" And one of her gleeful poems begins,

> 'Tis little–I could care for Pearls–
> Who own the ample sea–

How often she felt that way we cannot know, and it hardly matters. As Robert Frost has pointed out, happiness can make up in height for what it lacks in length; and the important thing for us, as for her, is that she construed the experience as a divine gift. So also she thought of the power to write poetry, a power which, as we know, came to her often; and poetry must have been the chief source of her sense of blessedness. The poetic impulses which visited her seemed "bulletins from Immortality," and by their means she converted all her losses into gains, and all the pains of her life to that clarity and repose which were to her the qualities of Heaven. So superior did she feel, as a poet, to earthly circumstance, and so strong was her faith in words, that she more than once presumed to view this life from the vantage of the grave.

In a manner of speaking, she was dead. And yet her poetry, with its articulate faithfulness to inner and outer truth, its insistence on maximum consciousness, is not an avoidance of life but an eccentric mastery of it. Let me close by reading you a last poem, in which she conveys both the extent of her repudiation and the extent of her happiness.

The Missing All, prevented Me
From missing minor Things.
If nothing larger than a World's
Departure from a Hinge
Or Sun's extinction, be observed
'Twas not so large that I
Could lift my Forehead from my work
For Curiosity.

This lecture was given during a poetry festival at Johns Hopkins University in October, 1961, and was published, together with other festival lectures, in The Moment of Poetry, *edited by D. C. Allen, in 1962. Readers have informed me that the Housman poem which I centrally discuss did, as I suspected, have a specific occasion, and was published in the London Times on the third anniversary of one of the battles of Ypres; also that the Nash poem which I cite is entitled "Reflection on Ice-Breaking," and may not mean what I have lubriciously supposed it to mean. I agree with the correspondent who feels that the lecture is unfairly hard on Etonians.*

ROUND ABOUT A POEM OF HOUSMAN'S

In the spring of 1944 my division was withdrawn from action and assigned to a rest area not far from Naples. Once we had pitched our tents, painted our tent pegs white, cleaned and polished our equipment, and generally recovered the garrison virtues, we were allowed to make occasional excursions, in groups of one truckload, to nearby points of interest. I remember best our trip to Pompeii. One reason why I remember it so clearly is that, on the day of our visit, Vesuvius began its worst eruption in many decades. Our six-by-six truck approached Pompeii through a fine, steady fall of whitish flakes, and set us down in a square already carpeted with ash. Some of our party, not caring for archeology, headed directly for the bars and other comforts of the modern city; but the rest of us thought it more seemly to begin, at least, with a look at the ruins. We found a displaced Greek woman who offered to be our guide, and she took us through the greater part of the excavations, pointing out the wall paintings, deciphering inscriptions, explaining the water system–until at last, just as we reached the Greek Forum, there was a sudden darkening of the air, a thickening in the fall of ashes, and she took fright and left us.

We found our way back to the modern city and established ourselves in a bar, sitting near the window so that we could watch for the return of our truck. The street was now full of natives evacuating the place, wading through the ashes under the usual clumsy burdens of refugees. Sitting there with a brandy bottle and watching such a scene, we felt something like the final tableau of Idiot's Delight. There were jokes about how we had better look smart and sit straight, since we might have to hold our poses for centuries. And one bookish soldier said that he had never felt so close to Pliny the Elder.

Before we had exhausted that vein of nervous humor, the truck arrived, and our scattered party emerged or was extricated from all the bars and dives of the vicinity. Climbing over the tailgate, most of us had some trophy or memento to show or show around: one had a bottle of Marsala, another a bottle of grappa; one had an album of colored views of the ruins; another drew from that breast pocket which is supposed to carry a bulletproof New Testament a packet of French postcards. And then there were cameos from Naples, and salamis, and pure silk placemats marked Ricordo d'Italia. When everything had been shown and assessed, one slightly drunken soldier leaned forward on his bench and said, "All right, boys, now you look at this." He held out his fist, opened it, and then on his palm stood a small, good replica of the famous sculpture of the wolf nursing Romulus and Remus.

"How about that?" he said. "Man, ain't that the dirtiest got-damn statue you ever saw?"

I don't tell that in ridicule of the soldier who said it. He had been a good farmer in East Texas, and he was a good soldier in Italy; his talk had more verve, rhythm, and invention in it–more poetry in it–than one usually hears in the talk of cultured people; and I would not call him inferior, as a man, to the soldier who happened to know that Pliny the Elder was done in by Vesuvius. I tell the story because, in this hopeful democracy of ours, in which the most unpromising are coerced into a system of free public education, we must often remind ourselves that the art public is not coextensive with the population, or even with the voting population. Any poet would feel justified in referring to Romulus and Remus and the wolf–one could hardly find a classical allusion more safely commonplace; and yet there really are millions of Americans who would not understand the reference, and who really might, if they saw the Wolf of the Capitol, mistake it for a dirty statue. We must stubbornly remember this whenever polemicists begin to strike the Whitman note, and to ask for a poetry at once serious and universally understandable.

A young Japanese woman told me recently of a parlor game that she and her friends had often played: fragmentary quotations from haiku are written on slips of paper; the slips of paper are put into a box; and then each player draws in his turn, reads out the fragment, and attempts to say the complete seventeen-syllable poem from memory. When cultured young Japanese play such a game as that, they are drawing on a detailed acquaintance with a vast haiku literature reaching back more than seven hundred years. And this acquaintance has to do with far more than subject matter. Haiku literature is, for instance, full of plum blossoms; and in order to see the uniqueness of a fragment having to do with plum blossoms one would have to possess not only a sense of the total history of that motif in Japanese verse, but also an intimate familiarity with the norms of diction, the strategies of suggestion, and the modes of feeling that belong to the haiku convention and to its great practitioners. It goes without saying that any modern Japanese poet who writes a haiku can expect his best readers to grasp his every echo, variation or nuance.

It is both good and bad that for American poets and their clientele there exists no such distinct, subtle, and narrow tradition. Our cultural and literary traditions are longer and far more inclusive than the Japanese, but they shape our lives far less decidedly and are subject to perpetual revision. A professor planning the reading list for a freshman humanities course scratches his head and wonders whether Saint Augustine's conception of history is in any way relevant to our own; one critic decides that our present sense of the past can do without Milton and Shelley, while another discovers that the main line of poetic tradition does, after all, lead through Alexander Pope. Similarly, our poets have shifting and rival conceptions of what the "tradition" is, and this leads in practice to a constant renewal, modification, and blending of conventions. What's good about this situation is that our poetry is not conventionally inhibited from coping with modern life as it comes; the modern poem is an adaptable machine that can run on any fuel whatever. The obvious disadvantage is that our unstable sense of literary tradition, and our dissolving multiplicity of conventions, make it hard for the educated person not a devotee of poetry to develop tact.

A tactful person is one who understands not merely what is said, but also what is meant. In a spring issue of the New Republic, a correspondent described the melancholy experience of exposing a class of engineers to a well-known four-line poem by Ogden Nash–the one that goes

> Candy
> Is dandy
> But liquor
> Is quicker.

As I recall, the article said that only one student in the lot recognized that poem as humor. The others either had no response or took it to be a straight-faced admonitory poem about obesity, blood sugar, or some such thing. Now, it is true that contemporary poets, encouraged by the critical rediscovery of the seriousness of wit, have done much to confound the distinction between light verse and serious poetry. Think how light Robert Frost can be, even in a quite serious poem; and think how often Phyllis McGinely trespasses on the serious. Still, it is a terrible failure of tact to read Mr. Nash's poem with a long face. The little jingly lines, the essentially comic rhymes, and the slangy diction combine to require that we place it within the convention of light verse. From a certainty as to the convention we derive a certainty as to tone, and when we know the tone we know what the subject must be: Mr. Nash is writing about strategies of seduction, a topic on which Americans incline to be coy, and his leaving the subject unstated is equivalent to a wink and a dig in the ribs.

Even in poems where the subject is fully stated, there is a world of difference between what is said and what is meant, and this I should like to prove by a brief absurd example. There is a charming popular song called "It's Only a Paper Moon," the first lines of which go as follows:

> Say, it's only a paper moon
> Sailing over a cardboard sea
> But it wouldn't be make believe
> If you believed in me.

I want now to juxtapose those lines with a passage from Matthew Arnold's "Dover Beach." That poem begins, as you'll remember,

> The sea is calm tonight,
> The tide is full, the moon lies fair
> Upon the straits . . .

and then it proceeds toward this climactic passage:

> Ah, love, let us be true
> To one another! for the world, which seems
> To lie before us like a land of dreams,
> So various, so beautiful, so new,
> Hath really neither joy, nor love, nor light,
> Nor certitude, nor peace, nor help for pain. . . .

It would be possible, I submit, to compose a one-sentence paraphrase which would do for both "Paper Moon" and "Dover Beach." It might go something like this: "The lover begs his beloved to cleave to him, and thus alleviate through human love his painful sense of the meaninglessness of the modern world, here symbolized by the false beauty of the moon." What I have just done is scandalous, of course; but I hope you will agree that it proves something. It proves that if we consider statement only, and work upon it with the disfiguring tool of paraphrase, a frisky pop song and a tragic poem can be made to seem identical. From this one can see how much of the meaning of any poem resides in its sound, its pacing, its diction, its literary references, its convention–in all those things that we must apprehend by tact.

One of my favorite poems of A. E. Housman is called "Epitaph on an Army of Mercenaries," and because it is a soluble problem in tact I want to discuss it here. Let me say it to you a first time in a fairly flat voice, so as to stress by lack of stress the necessity, at certain points, of making crucial decisions as to tone:

> These, in the day when heaven was falling,
> The hour when earth's foundations fled,
> Followed their mercenary calling,
> And took their wages and are dead.
>
> Their shoulders held the sky suspended;
> They stood, and earth's foundations stay;
> What God abandoned, these defended,
> And saved the sum of things for pay.

Perhaps the main decision to be made is how to say those last two words, "for pay." Should they be spoken in a weary drawl? Should they be spoken matter-of-factly? Or should they be spat out defiantly, as if one were saying "Of course they did it for pay;

what did you expect?" Two or three years ago, I happened to mention Housman's poem to a distinguished author who is usually right about things, and he spoke very ill of it. He found distasteful what he called its easy and sweeping cynicism, and he thought it no better, except in technique, than the more juvenile pessimistic verses of Stephen Crane. For him, the gist of the poem was this: "What a stinking world this is, in which what we call civilization must be preserved by the blood of miserable hirelings." And for him, that last line was to be said in a tone of wholesale scorn:

And saved the *sum of things* for *pay*.

I couldn't accept that way of taking the poem, even though at the time I was unprepared to argue against it; and so I persisted in saying Housman's lines to myself, in my own way, while walking or driving or waiting for trains. Then one day I came upon an excellent essay by Cleanth Brooks, which supported my notion of the poem and expressed its sense and tone far better than I could have done. Mr. Brooks likened Housman's Shropshire lads, so many of whom are soldiers, to those Hemingway heroes who do the brave thing not out of a high idealism but out of stoic courage and a commitment to some personal or professional code. Seen in this manner, Housman's mercenaries–his professional soldiers, that is–are not cynically conceived; rather, their poet is praising them for doing what they had engaged to do, for doing what had to be done, and for doing it without a lot of lofty talk. If we understand the poem so, it is not hard to see what tones and emphases are called for:

These, in the day when heaven was falling,
The hour when earth's foundations fled,
Followed their mercenary calling,
And took their wages and are dead.

Their shoulders held the sky suspended;
They stood, and earth's foundations stay;
What God abandoned, *these defended,*
And saved the sum of things for pay.

That is how I would read it, and I suspect that Mr. Brooks would concur. But now suppose that the distinguished author who thought the poem wholly cynical should not be satisfied. Suppose he should say, "Mr. Brooks's interpretation is very enhancing, and makes the poem far less cheaply sardonic; but unfortunately Mr. Brooks is being more creative than critical, and the poem is really just what I said it was."

There are a number of arguments I might venture in reply, and one would be this: Housman was a great classical scholar, and would have been particularly well acquainted with the convention of the military epitaph. His title refers us, in fact, to such poems as Simonides wrote in honor of the Spartans who fell at Thermopylae, or the Athenians who fought at the Isthmus. Those poems are celebratory in character, and so is Housman's. The sound and movement of Housman's poem accord, moreover, with the mood of plain solemnity that the convention demands. The tetrameter, which inclines by its nature to skip a bit, and which we have already encountered in "Say, it's only a paper moon," is slowed down here to the pace of a dead march. The rhetorical balancing of line against line, and half-line against half-line, the frequency of grammatical stops, and the even placement of strong beats make a deliberate movement inescapable; and this deliberate movement releases the full and powerful sonority that Housman intends. It is not the music or sardony.

The distinguished author might come back at me here, saying something like this: "No doubt you've named the right convention, but what you forget is that there are mock versions of every convention, including this one. While Housman's mock use of the military epitaph is not broadly comic but wryly subtle, it does employ the basic trick of high burlesque. Just as Pope, in his mock epic *The Rape of the Lock*, adopts the tone and matter of Milton or Homer only to deflate them, so Housman sets his solemn, sonorous poem to leaking with the word 'mercenary,' and in the last line lets the air out completely. The poem is thus a gesture of total repudiation, a specimen of indiscriminate romantic irony, and it is what we might expect from the poet who counsels us to 'endure an hour and see injustice done,' who refers to God as 'whatever brute and blackguard made the world,' and who disposes of this life by crying, 'Oh, why did I awake? When shall I sleep again?' "

From now on I am going to play to win, and I shall not allow the distinguished author any further rebuttals. The answer to what he said just now is this: while Housman may maintain that "heaven and earth ail from the prime foundation," he consistently honors those who face up manfully to a bad world; and especially he honors the common soldier who, without having any fancy reasons for doing so, draws his mercenary "thirteen pence a day" and fights and dies. We find this soldier in such poems as "Lancer," and "Grenadier," and Housman always says to him,

dead or living, drunk or dry,
Soldier, I wish you well.

The mercenaries of the poem I've been discussing
are enlisted from all these other soldier poems, and
though their deaths exemplify the world's evil,
Housman stresses not that but the shining of their
courage in the general darkness.

The poem is not a mock version of the military
epitaph; however, the distinguished author was right
in feeling that Housman's poem is not so free of irony
as, for instance, William Collins's eighteenth-century
ode "How sleep the brave . . ." These eight short
lines do, in fact, carry a huge freight of irony, most
of it implicit in a system of subtle echoes and allusions; but none of the irony is at the expense of the
mercenaries, and all of it defends them against slight
and detraction.

If one lets the eye travel over Housman's lines,
looking for echo or allusion, it is probably line 4 that
first arrests the attention:

And took their wages and are dead.

This puts one in mind of Saint Paul's Epistle to the
Romans, Chapter 6, where the Apostle declares that
"the wages of sin is death." The implication of this
echo is that paid professional soldiers are sinful and
unrighteous persons, damned souls who have for-
feited the gift of eternal life. That is certainly not
Housman's view, even if one makes allowance for
ironic exaggeration; and so we are forced to try to
imagine a sort of person whose view it might be.
The sort of person we are after is, of course, self-

righteous, idealistic, and convinced of his moral superiority to those common fellows who fight, not for high and noble reasons, but because fighting is their job. Doubtless you have heard regulars of the American army subjected to just that kind of spiritual snobbery, and one readily finds analogies in other departments of life: think of the way professional politicians are condemned by our higher-minded citizens, while shiny-faced amateurs are prized for their wholesome incapacity. Spiritual snobs are unattractive persons under any circumstances, but they appear to especial disadvantage in Housman's poem. After all, they and their civilization were saved by the mercenaries–or professionals–who did their fighting for them, and that fact makes their scorn seem both ungrateful and hypocritical.

Housman's echo of Saint Paul, then, leads us to imagine a class of people who look down on Tommy Atkins, and it also prompts us to defend Tommy Atkins against their unjust disdain. Let me turn now to some other echoes, to a number of Miltonic reverberations that are scattered throughout the poem. They all derive from some ten lines of the sixth book of *Paradise Lost*. That is the book about the war in heaven, wherein the good angels and the rebel angels fight two great and inconclusive engagements, after which the Messiah enters and single-handedly drives the rebels over the wall of heaven. It is probably not irrelevant to mention that the ruling idea of Book VI, the idea that all the action illustrates, is that might derives from right, and that righteousness therefore must prevail. Here is a passage that comes at the end of the second battle, when the good and bad angels are throwing mountains at each other:

> . . . horrid confusion heapt
> Upon confusion rose: and now all Heav'n
> Had gone to wrack, with ruin overspread,
> Had not th' Almighty Father where he sits
> Shrin'd in his Sanctuary of Heav'n secure,
> Consulting on the sum of things, foreseen
> This tumult, and permitted all, advis'd.

"The sum of things" means here the entire universe, including heaven and hell, and God is about to save the sum of things created or contemplated by sending his son against the rebel angels. Otherwise heaven might fall, and earth's foundations might flee. When the Messiah drives Satan and his forces over heaven's edge, and they begin their nineday fall into hell, Milton gives us another passage that Housman has echoed:

> Hell heard the insufferable noise, Hell saw
> Heav'n ruining from Heav'n, and would have fled
> Affrighted; but strict Fate had cast too deep
> Her dark foundations, and too fast had bound.

It is quite plain that Housman is reminding his reader of Milton, and in particular of these two passages from Book VI, in which we find "the sum of things," fleeing foundations, and heaven in peril of falling. The ticklish question now is how much of Milton should we put into Housman's poem; how detailed a comparison should we draw between the war in Milton's heaven and the battle in which Housman's mercenaries died? Should we, for instance, compare Housman's sacrificial mercenaries, whose deaths have preserved the sum of things, to the Son of God, who won the war in heaven and later died on earth to save mankind? Housman is quite capable of implying such a comparison. In his poem "The Carpenter's Son," Christ is a Shropshire lad who dies on the gallows because he would not "leave ill alone." And in the poem "1887," Housman says this of the soldiers who have helped God save the Queen by dying in battle:

> To skies that knit their heartstrings right,
> To fields that bred them brave,
> The saviours come not home tonight:
> Themselves they could not save.

As Mr. Brooks points out in his essay, those last lines "echo the passage in the Gospels in which Christ, hanging on the cross, is taunted with the words: 'Others he saved; himself he cannot save.'" It appears, then, that in his "Epitaph on an Army of Mercenaries" Housman may be bestowing on his soldiers the ultimate commendation; he may be saying that their sacrifice, in its courage and in the scope of its consequences, was Christlike. For the rest, I should say that Housman's Miltonic allusions have a clear derogatory purpose, and that their function is once again to mock those who feel superior to the soldiers whom the poet wishes to praise. Housman mocks those who feel that they are on the side of the angels, that their enemies are devils, that God is their property and will defend the right, that heaven and earth depend upon their ascendancy and the prevalence of their lofty mores, yet who count in fact not on God or on themselves but on the courage of mercenaries whom they despise.

These smug people, whom the poem nowhere mentions but everywhere rebukes, are covertly attacked again in line 5 through an allusion to the eleventh labor of Heracles. In that enterprise, Heracles was out to secure the golden apples of the Hesperides, and he applied for the help of Atlas, the giant who supports the heavens on his shoulders. Atlas agreed to go and get the apples, if Heracles would temporarily take over his burden. When Atlas returned, he noticed that Heracles was supporting the heavens very capably, and it occurred to him that Heracles might well continue in the assignment. Had Heracles not then thought of a good stratagem, and tricked Atlas into reassuming the weight of the skies, he would have been the victim of the greatest buck-passing trick on record. What Housman is saying by way of this allusion is that the battle of his poem was won not on the playing fields of Eton but in the pastures of Shropshire, and that the Etonians, and the other pillars of the established order, transferred their burden in this case to the lowly professional army. Once we recognize Housman's reference, we can see again the extent of his esteem for the so-called mercenaries: he compares them to the great Heracles. And once we perceive that line 5 has to do with buck-passing, with the transference of a burden, we know where to place the emphasis. It should fall on the first word:

Their shoulders held the sky suspended.

It was they, the mercenaries, and not the presumptive upholders of the right, who saved the day.

It seems to me that quite enough allusions have now been found; there may be others, but if so we don't need them for purposes of understanding. Nor, I think, do we need to consider the possible fiscal overtones of the words "saved" and "sum." It is true that in conjunction with the words "wages" and "pay," the phrase "saved the sum" has a slight clink of money in it, and one could probably think up an appropriate meaning for such a play on words. But readers and critics must be careful not to be cleverer than necessary; and there is no greater obtuseness than to treat all poets as Metaphysicals, and to insist on discovering puns which are not likely to be there.

What I have been trying to illustrate, no doubt too exhaustively, is how a reader might employ tact in arriving at a sure sense of an eight-line poem. Probably I've gone wrong here or there: I am afraid, for one thing, that I've made the poem seem more English and less universal than it is. But I hope at any rate to have considered some of the things that need considering: the convention of the poem; the use of the convention; the sound, pace, and tone of the poem; its consistency with the author's attitudes and techniques in other poems; and the implicit argument of its allusions or echoes. Let me read it a last time:

> These, in the day when heaven was falling,
> The hour when earth's foundations fled,
> Followed their mercenary calling,
> And took their wages and are dead.
>
> Their shoulders held the sky suspended;
> They stood, and earth's foundations stay;
> What God abandoned, these defended,
> And saved the sum of things for pay.

Karl Shapiro has published in *Poetry* a prose outburst with which I greatly sympathize and yet thoroughly disagree. I will not aim to answer it as a whole, because, as he himself says, it is too inconsistent to constitute a clear target. You can, within limits, argue with a wild man; wild men are simple; but there's no arguing with a subtle and reasonable man who is bent on being wild. Let me, however, quote one passage from Mr. Shapiro which bears on what I've been saying. He objects to the fact that in our country

> the only poetry that is recognized
> is the poetry that repeats the past,
> that is referential. It relates back to
> books, to other poetry, to names in
> the encyclopaedia. It is the poetry
> of the history-inhibited mind only,
> and as such it is meaningless to
> people who lack the training to
> read it. The Little Magazine, the
> avant-gardist, the culture academi-
> cian base the esthetic experience
> on education. Whereas poetry
> needs not education or culture but
> the open perceptions of the
> healthy human organism.

Mr. Shapiro and I agree that a poem which refers to Romulus and Remus and the wolf will be meaningless, in part at least, to those who lack the training to read it. I disagree, however, with Mr. Shapiro's determination to hound that wolf out of poetry, to abolish the literary and historical past, to confine us to the modern city and declare the ruins off limits. It would not be worth it to make poetry more generally usable at the cost of abridging the poet's consciousness.

I will say, parenthetically, that I wish the category

of expertly made popular poetry had not all but disappeared in this century. In the last century, the best poets did not hesitate to write on occasion simple songs, hymns, or story-poems which were instantly possessed and valued by a larger public. The author of "In Memoriam" also wrote the ballad of "The Revenge." Though societies were formed to unravel the knottiest verses of Robert Browning, there are no knots in "The Pied Piper of Hamelin." I think, too, of James Russell Lowell's "Once to Every Man and Nation," and of Longfellow's "Paul Revere." These are all fine poems, and all of them are perfectly transparent. Perhaps it is their very transparency that has led critics and teachers to fall silent about them, there being no call for learned meditation; and perhaps that silence has helped many of our poets to forget that there is such a thing as a good popular poem.

But now let me take Housman's poem as a miniature specimen of what Mr. Shapiro calls "high art," and defend it against Mr. Shapiro. It is probably not Housman whom Mr. Shapiro is attacking, and yet the strictures might apply to him. Mr. Shapiro talks as if a poem could be either referential or humanly vital, but not both. Surely you will agree that Housman's poem is both: it is a passionate celebration of courage, prompted, one suspects, by an immediate occasion; at the same time, and without any dampening of its urgency, it recalls a convention as old as the Greeks, and defends its heroes against detraction through liberal allusions to literature and myth. Mr. Shapiro says that to be referential is to "repeat the past"; Housman most certainly does not do that. What he does is to confront the present with a mind and heart that contain the past. His poem does not knuckle under to a Green convention, it makes use of that convention and much modifies it. His allusions do not "repeat" Milton and Saint Paul. Milton's good angels are not, in Housman's poem, what they were in *Paradise Lost;* they are transformed by a fresh conjunction; and Housman implicitly quarrels both with the moral exclusiveness of Saint Paula and with Milton's idea that righteousness must prevail.

I would uphold Housman's poem as a splendid demonstration of the art of referring. The poem requires a literate reader, but given such a reader it is eminently effective. I selected the poem for discussion precisely because, unlike most of Housman, it is capable of misinterpretation; nevertheless, as I have pointed out, a reader can arrive at a just sense of its tone and drift without consciously identifying any of its references. It all but delivers its whole meaning right away. One reason why Housman's allusions can be slow in transpiring, as they were for me, is that the words that point toward Milton or Saint Paul–such words as "wages" or "earth's foundations"–are perfectly at home in the language of the poem as a whole; and this seems to me a great virtue. In a bad poem, there are often certain words that step out of line, wave their arms, and cry "Follow me! I have overtones!" It takes a master to make references, or what Robert Frost calls "displacements," without in any way falsifying the poem's voice, its way of talking. Now, as for the allusions proper, they are to the Bible, *Paradise Lost,* and Greek mythology, all of which are central to any version of our tradition, and in some degree familiar to every educated reader. So familiar are these sources that I am sure Housman's allusions must unconsciously affect almost everyone's understanding of the poem, even upon a casual first reading. And I would say that our familiarity with the things to which Housman is referring justifies the subtlety and brevity of his echoes. The poem assumes that the words "wages" and "dead" will suffice to suggest Saint Paul, and I think that a fair assumption. Housman's allusions, once one is aware of them, are not decorative but very hard-working. Their chief function is to supplement Housman's explicit praise of the mercenaries with implicit dispraise of their detractors, and so make us certain of the poem's whole attitude toward its subject. To achieve such certainty, however, one need not catch every hint, every echo; any one of Housman's references, rightly interpreted, will permit the reader to take confident possession of the poem. I like that. A poem should not be like a Double-Crostic; it should not be the sort of puzzle in which you get nothing until you get it all. Art does not or should not work that way; we are not cheated of a symphony if we fail to react to some passage on the flute, and a good poem should yield itself more than once, offering the reader an early and sure purchase, and deepening repeatedly as he comes to know it better.

This is what happens time and again as one reads and rereads Housman. In his poem "On the Idle Hill of Summer," an indolent young man hears the stirring and fatal music of a marching column, and decides to enlist. The final quatrain goes like this:

> Far the calling bugles hollo,
> High the screaming fife replies,
> Gay the files of scarlet follow;
> Woman bore me, I will rise.

"Woman bore me, I will rise." He will rise and enlist because "woman bore him"–that is, because he is a man and cannot resist the summons of the bugle. The last line is forceful and plain, and clinches the poem beautifully. We need no more. Yet there is more, and perhaps on the second reading, or the fifth, or the twentieth, we may hear in that last line a reverberation of the prayer that is said at the graveside in the Anglican burial service, and that begins: "Man, that is born of a woman, hath but a short time to live, and is full of misery. . . ."

If we do catch that echo, the line gains both in power and in point; but if we do not catch it, we are still possessed of a complete and trustworthy version of Housman's poem. And, to speak again of Milton, I think that most of the reverberations in *Paradise Lost* work in the same way. Satan, wakening in the fiery gulf of hell, says to Beelzebub, who is sprawled at his side:

> If thou beest he; But O how fall'n! how chang'd
> From him, who in the happy Realms of Light
> Cloth'd with transcendent brightness didst outshine
> Myriads though bright. . . .

There is a suggestion of Isaiah there which perhaps I might notice unassisted; but I lack the ready knowledge of Virgil that Milton reasonably expected of his reader, and so I am grateful for the scholar's footnote which directs me to Book II of the Aeneid. There the shade of Hector appears to Aeneas in a dream, mangled, blackened with dirt, and quantum mutatus ab illo Hectore–"how changed" from that Hector who once returned from battle clothed in the bright armor of Achilles! The Virgilian echo is enhancing; it helps to tune the voice of Satan, and the likening of Beelzebub to Hector poignantly stresses the rebel angels' fall from brightness and from heroic strength and virtue. But if there were no footnote to help me, if I never sensed the shade of Hector behind Milton's lines, I should not on that account be balked or misled. I should already have gathered from the surface of the lines one sure and adequate sense of their tone and meaning.

Let me now read you a more dubious example of the art of referring. The poem is by Yeats; it was written in 1909 or 1910, after the poet's reconciliation with Maud Gonne; and its title is "King and No King."

> "Would it were anything but merely voice!"
> The No King cried who after that was King.
> Because he had not heard of anything
> That balanced with a word is more than noise;
> Yet Old Romance being kind, let him prevail
> Somewhere or somehow that I have forgot,
> Though he'd but cannon–Whereas we that had thought
> To have lit upon as clean and sweet a tale
> Have been defeated by that pledge you gave
> In momentary anger long ago;
> And I that have not your faith, how shall I know
> That in the blinding light beyond the grave
> We'll find so good a thing as that we have lost?
> The hourly kindness, the day's common speech,
> The habitual content of each with each
> When neither soul nor body has been crossed.

A great many intelligent readers, including some professional poets of my acquaintance, have found this poem very troublesome. In order to fathom its sixteen lines, one must follow the suggestion of Yeats's title and read *A King and No King*, which is a five-act play by Beaumont and Fletcher first performed in 1611. The play tells how King Arbaces of Iberia conceives an incestuous passion for his sister Panthea, and how his apparently hopeless situation is at last happily resolved by the discovery that Panthea is, after all, not his sister. Prior to this fifth-act clarification, Arbaces delivers a number of violent speeches expressing thwarted lust, and one of these Yeats has quoted. Speaking of the words "brother" and "sister," which are the obstacles to his seemingly guilty passion, Arbaces cries, "Let 'em be anything but merely voice"–meaning that if only they were not bodiless words, but concrete things like soldiers or cities, he could turn his cannon on them and destroy them.

Yeats is comparing King Arbaces's frustrated desires to his own, and he is also comparing the words "brother" and "sister," which so vex Arbaces, to some unshakeable pledge or vow made by the lady who is the addressee of his poem. If we look into Richard Ellmann's biography of Yeats, we find that Maud Gonne, in 1909, had informed Yeats "that their relations could be those of a spiritual marriage only," and that she had assured him, "You will not suffer because I will pray." Once we have this information, Yeats's poem becomes perfectly clear: it is a plea for physical as well as spiritual love, and in rereading it we must put a strong emphasis on the word "body" in the last line.

When one has managed to figure out some puzzling poem, it is natural to be a little foolishly proud; one feels like an insider, an initiate, and one is not inclined to be very critical of a work that has certified one's cleverness and industry. For a few heady weeks in 1954, I thought of myself as the only living

49

understander of Yeats's "King and No King." Since then, however, the number of insiders has grown considerably, and I now feel less proprietary toward the poem, and more objective. There is much to admire in "King and No King": the rhythmic movement is splendidly dramatic; the language slides deftly in and out of the common idiom; in respect of pacing and diction, the poem is a good specimen of that artful recklessness, that sprezzatura, which Yeats was aiming at in the first decade of this century. Yet what an inconsistency there is between the blurting, spontaneous manner of the opening lines and the poet's stubborn withholding of the theme! A good poet knows how, in referring to some little-known thing, to convey without loss of concision some sense of what the reference must mean; but Yeats, though he devotes almost seven lines to the Beaumont and Fletcher play, chooses to suppress any suggestion whatever that the play, and his poem, are concerned with frustrated sexual appetite. The consequence is that the reader stumbles badly on the sill of the poem, and never stops staggering until he is out the back door.

There are reasons, I suspect, for Yeats's having used a remote literary reference, not only as a source of analogies to his personal predicament, but also as a means of enshrouding his subject matter. The subject is, after all, inherently delicate, and there is also some danger of the ridiculous in an argumentative plea for physical favors, especially if one has known the woman since the late 1880's. But whatever Yeats's reasons for writing as he did–and I have no real business guessing at them–one must wonder about the public value of a poem that mutes its theme by a thoroughly reticent allusion to a little-known text.

One must also question the integrity, the artistic self-sufficiency, of any short poem that requires to be grasped through the reading of a bad five-act play and the consultation of a biography. As the English critic John Press has said, "There is a popular belief that what conservatives like to call real poetry was perfectly straightforward until some unspecified date, when poets suddenly changed into reckless bunglers or deliberately set out to bamboozle plain, honest readers with mumbo-jumbo." I hope that I do not seem to be offering aid and comfort to the holders of that unhistorical belief. What I do mean to say, in concession to Mr. Shapiro's view of things, is that the art of reference in poetry has become a very difficult art, owing to the incoherence of our culture, and that some poems refer more successfully than others. It is generally agreed, I hope, that one cannot sensibly describe a poem as a direct message from poet to public; but one can say that a poem addresses itself, in I. A. Richard's phrase, to some "condition of the language," and presupposes some condition of the culture. Every poem is based on an unformulated impression of what words and things are known and valued in the literate community; every poem is written, as it were, in some intellectual and cultural key. It is therefore possible to say of a poem that, in relation to its appropriate audience, it is tactful or not.

Housman's poem is a model of tact, both in its references and in its manner of referring. Yeats's poem is less tactful, because it cites an ancient play which the most eligible and cultured reader might not know, and which must be known if the poem is to be breached at all. As for the *Cantos* of Ezra Pound, they contain some of the finest passages in modern poetry, but they are supremely tactless. That is, they seem to arise from a despair of any community, and they do not imply a possible audience as Housman's poem does. It is all very well for Pound to claim that his *Cantos* deals "with the usual subjects of conversation between intelligent men"; but intelligent men, though they do talk of history and economics and the arts, do not converse in broken fragments of mythology, unattributed quotations, snatches of Renaissance correspondence, cryptic reminiscences, and bursts of unorthodox Chinese. Pound's presentational manner of writing, which developed out of Imagism, is the method least capable of turning his eccentric erudition into a consistently usable poetry. The advantage of the method is immediacy, and the investment of the idea in the thing, but the method does not work unless the reader knows what it is that is being so immediate. Because the *Cantos* lack any discursive tissue, because they refuse the reader any sort of intercession, even those whose learning exceeds Ezra Pound's cannot be said to be ready for them.

There are three things a reader might do about the Cantos. First, he might decide not to read them. Second, he might read them as Dr. Williams recommends, putting up with much bafflement for the sake of the occasional perfect lyric, the consistently clean and musical language, and the masterly achievement of quantitative effects through the strophic balancing of rhythmic masses. Or, thirdly, the reader might decide to understand the *Cantos* by consulting, over a period of years, the many books from which Pound drew his material. At almost every university, nowadays, there is someone who has undertaken that task: he may be identified by the misshapenness of his

52

learning and by his air of lost identity.

None of the three courses I have mentioned is a thoroughly happy one, and the *Cantos* are one proof of Mr. Shapiro's contention that poetry's relations with the past, on the one hand, and with its public, on the other, have become problematical. I will grant Mr. Shapiro that there are misuses of the past which can be hurtful to poetry. Antiquarianism is one: the rapt pedantry of Ezra Pound, and the bland, donnish pedantry of certain other poets, alike distract us from the uninterpreted fields and streets and rooms of the present, in which the real battles of imagination must be fought. I will grant, too, that the sense of history can be crippling to poetry if history is so interpreted as to impose some narrow limitation or imperative on the poet. The poet must not feel dwarfed by the literary past, nor should he listen too trustingly to those who say that poetry's role in society is inevitably diminishing. Nor should he adjust his concerns to what others consider the great thought currents of the times: the *Zeitgeist,* after all, is only a spook invented by the critics. Nor, finally, does poetry prosper when it puts itself wholly at the service of some movement, some institution. I think of Mayakovsky, who wrote, "I have subdued myself, setting my heel on the throat of my own song," and who said that he had "cancelled out his soul" the better to serve the socialist age. It may be true, as some say, that Mayakovsky was made by the Revolution; but surely the service of history broke him as well. In all these ways, historical consciousness can paralyze, trivialize, or enslave the poet's art; but I am not on that account moved to accept Mr. Shapiro's imperative, which is that poets must now secede from history and dwell in "biological time."

The past which most properly concerns the poet is, as T. S. Eliot has said, both temporal and timeless. It is, above all, a great index of human possibilities. It is a dimension in which we behold, and are beheld by, all those forms of excellence and depravity that men have assumed and may assume again. The poet needs this lively past as a means of viewing the present without provinciality, and of saying much in little; he must hope for the tact and the talent to make that past usable for the audience that his poems imply. My friend John Ciardi once said, "Pompeii is everybody's home town, sooner or later." I should add that for every poet, whatever he may say as critic or polemicist, Pompeii is still a busy quarter of the city of imagination.

The late Perry Miller, as general editor of the college text Major Writers of America *(1962), engaged me to edit and introduce the Poe section. The introductory essay that follows is a brief but comprehensive statement of my approach to Poe's life and works.*

EDGAR ALLAN POE

Edgar Poe was born in Boston, Massachusetts on January 19, 1809. His mother, Elizabeth Arnold Poe, was an actress of some talent and much charm, who in the year of Edgar's birth was to reach the peak of her career, playing Ophelia to the Hamlet of John Howard Payne. Her husband, David, an indifferent actor often humiliated by the critics, began in the same year to render himself unemployable through drink; at last, in July of 1810, he abandoned his family and vanished utterly from record. Soon after, Elizabeth Poe's fortunes and health declined, and in December of 1811, at the age of twenty-four, she died of consumption in a theatrical rooming house in Richmond, Virginia.

She left three children to the world. William Henry, the elder son, had long since been adopted by his grandfather, General David Poe, of Baltimore: gifted and unbalanced, he was to become a sailor, a poet, and a drunkard, and then to die at twenty-four of the disease that had carried off his mother. Rosalie, the youngest child, about whom there were rumors of illegitimacy, was taken into the charitable Richmond household of William MacKenzie: she would live into her sixties as a markedly eccentric spinster. Three-year-old Edgar, whose life was to be both better and worse than these, was also taken from his mother's death chamber into a charitable

Richmond family.

The charity seems to have been chiefly Frances Allan's; she was a soft-natured woman, and had no children of her own to love. John Allan, her husband, was a shrewd, handsome, ambitious merchant given to choler and self-righteousness, whose reception of Edgar must have been at best a matter of cold principle. But whatever the motives and intentions of his foster parents, the orphan boy found himself living, as a son, in the fine house of a family fast rising in Virginia's commercial aristocracy. When John Allan's business took him to England in 1815, Edgar was placed in the Manor House School at Stoke Newington, near London, where, as "master Allan," he studied until his eleventh year. On the family's return to Richmond, John Allan continued to provide his ward with the education of a young Virginia gentleman; moreover, the Allans gave polite parties for Edgar, to which the children of Richmond's best families were invited. The boy was also encouraged to learn the rudiments of the family business, so that, although his name had now reverted to "Master Poe," it became his and Richmond's presumption that he was, or would become, John Allan's adopted son and heir.

Nevertheless, there are indications that Richmond's acceptance of Edgar Poe was frankly provisional, and that the boy could never have felt a comfortable assurance as to his place in the world. In discussing Poe's school days, a Colonel Preston recalled that

> of Edgar Poe it was known that his parents had been players, and that he was dependent upon the

bounty that is bestowed upon an adopted son. All this had the effect of making the boys decline his leadership; and on looking backward on it since, I fancy it gave him a fierceness he would otherwise not have had.

It doubtless moved him to such feats as his Byronic seven-mile swim in the James River; insecurity may also have prompted, in some measure, his intense attachment to Mrs. Jane Stith Stanard, the mother of a schoolmate; and perhaps it was one cause of that growing moodiness which John Allan noted and disapproved.

As Edgar entered young manhood, there was a progressive collapse of sympathy between him and his guardian, who often accused him of idleness and a surly ingratitude. Too little is known of the substance of their differences to permit of any present adjudication, but certain things seem clear: John Allan was contemptuous of Edgar's developing literary ambition; he was disappointed by Edgar's want of interest in a mercantile career; and he was, for these and other reasons, impatient of supporting a troublesome ward with whom he had no temperamental affinity. This impatience was soon translated into action. When the respectable Royster family, in 1826, put an end to Edgar's courtship of their daughter Sarah Elmira, it was undoubtedly done on the basis of authoritative information that Edgar Poe was not to be John Allan's heir. And when Edgar, in that same year, entered the newly opened University of Virginia, it was with an allowance inadequate to his minimum needs. In an effort to escape the embarrassments that such malevolent parsimony made inevitable, he took to gambling, and in eight months lost some two thousand dollars. Since Allan then refused to pay both his legitimate debts and his "debts of honor," Edgar could not return to the university. After a violent quarrel with Allan, he left home and Richmond in March, 1827, with the vague project of "finding some place in the wide world."

In later years, Poe sometimes improved upon his life between 1827 and 1830 by tall tales of fighting in Greece, writing in Paris, or dueling in Spain. The truth is that the eighteen-year-old adventurer worked his way to Boston on a coal barge, under the alias of Henri le Rennet, found no employment there, and so enlisted in the U.S. army as Edgar A. Perry. During the early months of his enlistment, he published at Boston a small volume entitled *Tamerlane and Other Poems*. The poems were few, the edition extremely small, and the public impact negligible.

Poe had always done honorably as a scholar; he now did honorably as a soldier, and by January of 1829 reached the highest noncommissioned grade, that of sergeant major. However, the thought of completing a five-year hitch had already become intolerable to him ("the prime of my life would be wasted"), and he now sought to secure his discharge. This was finally effected, through the kind concern of his officers and the grudging consent of his guardian, on the understanding that Sergeant Major Perry would seek appointment to the U.S. Military Academy at West Point.

While waiting for his appointment to come through, Poe shared for a time the poverty of his grandmother Poe's household in Baltimore. Under that roof were his tubercular and dissipated brother, William Henry, his aunt Maria Clemm, and a seven-year-old cousin, Virginia, who six years thereafter was to become his "child-bride." In December Poe rejoiced in the publication of *Al Aaraaf, Tamerlane and Minor Poems* by the Baltimore house of Hatch and Dunning, and in its immediate favorable notice by the novelist and critic John Neal. This literary recognition, together with his ward's obedient intention of becoming a West Point officer, moved John Allan to permit him a visit to Richmond, and there Poe remained until yet another quarrel forced his return to Baltimore in May of 1830.

The appointment, however, had at last been wangled, and in June he went on to West Point. It is plain that Poe, who was overage for a cadet and had no relish for a military future, entered the academy in the desperate hope of recovering John Allan's favor and patronage. As always, he proceeded to distinguish himself in his studies; but Allan's refusal to write, or to send him any expense money, gave reason to doubt that diligence would be rewarded. Indeed, Poe was not even notified when his guardian–then nineteen months a widower–was married in October to a woman quite young enough to give him an heir. On learning of this fatal development, Poe relinquished his hopes of an inheritance and, lacking his guardian's permission to resign from the academy, sought and gained a prompt dismissal for "gross neglect of duty" and "disobedience of orders."

During his last days at West Point, Poe wrote Allan a letter which was full, as usual, of half-truth and self-pity, of alternate accusation and entreaty. "My future life," he said, "(Which thank God will not endure long) must be passed in indigence and sickness." The prophecy was correct, and the remaining eighteen years of his existence were–despite his more romantic biographers–a Sahara of dreariness, pain, and drudgery. To be sure, Poe's marriage, in 1836, to his girl-cousin Virginia secured him an oasis of affection and solicitude. If, as seems possible, Poe was sexually incapable, it was nevertheless a marriage; and Virginia's mother, Mrs. Clemm, who ran the always impoverished household until the end, was, as one lady visitor put it, "a sort of Universal Providence for her strange children." There was also the satisfaction of winning an occasional prize–fifty dollars for "Ms. Found in a Bottle," one hundred for "The Gold Bug"–and of publishing an occasional collection of poems or tales.

But Poe was never able to support his small family by his poetry and fiction–"Ligeia" sold for ten dollars–and it was not until the celebrity of "The Raven," in 1845, that he enjoyed any real reputation as an artist. Prior to that time he was known for, and subsisted by means of, his editorial and critical labors for a series of periodicals in Richmond, Philadelphia, and New York. He was a good editor. Among other achievements, he quintupled the circulation of the *Southern Literary Messenger*, and in six months built up the subscription list of *Graham's Magazine* from five thousand to twenty thousand–thus enriching his employers, but never, unfortunately, quite freeing his family from the necessity for supplemental begging. As a critic, Poe produced a great quantity of conscientious work, and in a period of puffery, chauvinism, and literary gang-warfare, was outstanding for his insistence on definite, high, and specifically aesthetic criteria. Because, as an editor of periodicals, he was obliged to review the books which came to his desk, Poe inevitably wasted much thought on unworthy subjects; it is lamentable that so fine a critical intellect had to concern itself, not only with Hawthorne and Bryant, but also, and mostly, with such titles as *The Canons of Good Breeding*, and *Poetical Remains of the Late Lucretia Maria Davidson*.

The romantic legend of Poe minimizes the hard-plugging professional writer and editor in favor of the drunkard whose excesses cost him the editorship of the *Messenger* and, later, of *Burton's*. What should be compassionately remembered is that Poe was always unstable, and often underfed and exhausted; his usual frame of mind, as his depression correspondence shows, was never very far from panic. Whenever his perilous balance was disturbed–as by the first signs of Virginia's fatal consumption, in 1842– he fell into a distraction of mind which, when it became insufferable, he blacked out by means of drink. It is doubtful that Poe consumed any great amount of alcohol in his lifetime, since his constitution would not tolerate it, even in modest quantities; and it seems best, as Poe himself advised, to refer the drink to the insanity, rather than the insanity to the drink.

Poe's last years were not without stable periods and literary achievements; out of them came "Ulalume," "The Domain of Arnheim," and the remarkable cosmological prose poem *Eureka*. But Virginia's decline and death robbed him of his one refuge from a world with which he could not steadily cope. It was not, as some have supposed, a burning-eyed libertine who conducted overlapping "affairs" with Mrs. Osgood, Mrs. Whitman, Mrs. Richmond, and his widowed childhood sweetheart, Elmira Royster Shelton. As W. H. Auden bluntly puts it, Poe was "an unmanly sort of man whose love-life seems to have been largely confined to crying in laps and playing house." What he sought from all these women, with the frantic anxiety of a lost child, was the equivalent of adoption.

A series of paranoid articles on Longfellow's "plagiarism," which Poe published in the *Broadway Journal* during 1845, would from a fully sane man have been dishonest, and Longfellow's decent and perceptive response was to say that the articles must have arisen from "the irritation of a sensitive nature, chafed by some indefinite sense of wrong." Thereafter the symptoms became clearer and more frequent: brain fever, fugue, persecutory hallucinations. . . . The circumstances which led to Poe's death are not fully known, and most scholars mistrust the story– eloquently evoked by Hart Crane in "The Bridge"– that Poe had been dragged, sick and drunk, from one polling place to another as a "repeater." But if his end, in October of 1849, was the result of foul play, those who left him dying in torn clothing, on a rainy Baltimore sidewalk, had only abetted an inevitable process of disintegration.

Poe's fiction is full of allusions to his own history, some of them relatively open, as when he assigns his birthday to William Wilson, and some of them– as when he borrows the name of Usher from an early benefactor of his mother–obscure both in reference and in point. Such personal allusions cannot well be ignored, but the reader should be warned against concluding from their frequency that Poe's fiction is nothing but murky autobiography or psychodrama. To say that Virginia Poe equals Ligeia, or that Ligeia equals Virginia Poe, is to shed little light on either. We shall not go wrong, however, if we take Poe's autobiographical references as indicative of a taste for covert significance, and approach him with the hypothesis that his meaning lies, where he said it should, in an "under current." It would also be safe to suppose, on the basis of so many private allusions, that Poe's vision of the world was personally come by, and that he is not to be explained as an American imitator of, for example, E. T. A. Hoffmann. The often terrible substance of his tales, as Poe himself said, is "not of Germany, but of the soul."

While detailed analogies between Poe's life and work are not of much use, there were constants in his life which, together with the prevalent literary influences, may be thought to have determined his themes and attitudes. For one thing, Poe at no time enjoyed a definite social identity. In childhood and youth, he was an orphan of "low" parentage, half-assimilated to the Virginia aristocracy. In manhood, despite his gentleman's training, he found himself doomed to a life of shabbiness, loan-begging, and hack work. One consequence was that he came to think of himself as a fallen aristocrat among "low ruffians and boobies . . . men . . . without a shadow . . . of caste." In politics, he grew aristocratic á outrance, hating the tyrant "Mob" and laying it down that "democracy is a very admirable form of government–for dogs." To a sense of fallen greatness we may also ascribe his continual fabrications about his family origins and European travels, and his pretensions to more linguistic knowledge than he possessed. (The knowledge of languages was still, in Poe's day, one mark of a gentleman; the Prince Regent had once asked regarding a stranger, "Is he a gentleman? Has he any Greek?")

But Poe's radical solution to the problem of his place in the world was, quite simply, to secede from it. "The sole unquestionable aristocracy," he announced, was that of the intellect, and by this he intended the poetic intellect only. Scientists, in his view, were mere "diggers and pedlars of minute facts," who belonged to the "sculleries" rather than the "parlors" of Mind. And since Poe thought of poetry as concerned, not with earthly and human things, but with the pursuit of unearthly beauty, the superiority of the poet, like that of the mystic, consisted in a rapt disrelation to other men. He was monarch of the domain of his own visions, as Crusoe of his desert island; his aristocracy was not social and comparative, but spiritual and absolute.

It was this Poe who told James Russell Lowell, in answer to a request for biographical data,

> I live continually in a reverie of the
> future. . . . You speak of "an
> estimate of my life,"–and, from
> what I have already said, you will
> see that I have none to give. . . .
> My life has been whim–impulse–
> passion–a longing for solitude–a
> scorn of all things present, in an
> earnest longing for the future.

It was this Poe who wrote to a lady admirer, "My existence has been the merest Romance–in the sense of the most utter unworldliness." And it was this Poe who embodied his isolate "real self," his poetic or visionary faculty, in such high-born, rich, solitary, and visionary figures as Roderick Usher and the hero of "The Assignation."

If Poe's galling sense of social anomaly inclined him toward a species of contemptus mundi, so also did his outrageous hunger to be loved and cared for.

"The want of parental affection," he wrote, "has been the heaviest of my trials," and his letters exhibit a lifelong effort to secure too late, and from almost any quarter, the various psychic benefits of a happy childhood. The world could not answer his exorbitant emotional demands, and he was therefore, one suspects, the more disposed to look for happiness beyond it–in the shadows of memory, in the valleys of dream, in glimpses of a past or future heavenly existence.

Another constant in Poe's life was extreme emotional conflict. This was manifested in the helpless ambivalence of his letters, and also, at times, of his criticism. Elizabeth Barrett noted how Poe, in a review of her poems, oscillated between "the two extremes of laudation and reprehension." "You would have thought," she told her husband-to-be, "that it had been written by a friend and foe, each stark mad with love and hate and writing the alternate paragraphs. . . ." In his conduct, as every biographer has observed, Poe was at all times his own worst enemy; he had a genius for self-defeat, and the imminence of any success, whether professional or amatory, led him to frustrate his apparent desires by doing or saying the fatal thing. He might have cried out with Saint Paul, "I do not understand my own actions. For I do not do what I want, but I do the very thing I hate." In his fiction, the theater of which was the individual soul, Poe sought to understand, and succeeded at least in portraying, that conflict and perversity from which all men have suffered, but few more fearfully than he.

That Poe was socially dislocated, emotionally starved, and torn in spirit does not explain his art. Yet these facts may help us to understand why, as a continuator of English and European romanticism, he could carry some of its tendencies to unprecedented extremes, demanding of poetry that it totally repudiate this earthly life and making, in his psychological fiction, a vast and original contribution to that movement which Erich Heller has called "the discovery and colonisation of inwardness."

From first to last, from "Al Aaraaf" to *Eureka,* Poe's vision of things was cosmic in extent, and any approach to his work must be prefaced by a brief synthetic account of that vision. The universe, as Poe conceived it, is a poetic or artistic creation, a "plot of God." It has come about through God's breaking up of His original unity, and His self-radiation into space; it is presently at the point of maximum diffusion, and will soon begin to contract toward a final reassembly in–and as–God. Since God, in creating the universe, fragmented Himself into His creatures, and now exists only in those "infinite individualizations of Himself," it is they who must, by some counterimpulse, restore the original oneness of things.

What must this counterimpulse be? Since "the source of all motion is thought," it must be intellectual or spiritual in character. And since the creation is a work of art, the counterimpulse that can reunify it must be imaginative. In short, the duty of God's creatures is to think God together again by discovering, through the fusing power of poetic imagination, the primal unity in the present diversity.

The one true response to the creation, then, is to take an imaginative delight in its beauty and harmony, seen and unseen. To deny the validity and holiness of poetic intuition, to prefer some other mode of knowledge, would be to deny God and fall away from Him. Unfortunately, the planet Earth has done just that, by succumbing to the spirit of scientific rationalism, and by preferring material "fact" to visionary truth. As a result, the souls of men have grown dark, diseased, and insensitive, and even physical nature has by contagion "fallen" from its original divine beauty and order. Before the earth can rejoin the cosmic process, and assist the other stars in reconstituting God, it will have to be redeemed from rationalism and materialism by that purifying fire which the Bible foretells.

Meanwhile, our fallen planet is not a happy environment for a poet. In him alone, of all the inhabitants of Earth, the divine spark of imagination still burns brightly; his soul alone vaguely remembers, from a previous existence, a divine harmony and beauty, and yearns to return thither. Yet everything around him conspires to reduce him to its own degraded level: the scientist and "utilitarian" discredit and abuse him, their corrupt and prosaic thought invades his consciousness, and nowhere in the human or natural environment can he find suitable objects for contemplation. His only means of escape is the suspension of outward consciousness, and a deliberate retreat from the temporal, rational, physical world into the visionary depths of his mind. There, in the immaterial regions of dream, he can purge himself of all earthly taint, and deliver himself to visions of that heavenly beauty which is the thought of God.

Poe's poet is thus at war with the external world. But he is also, unfortunately, at war within himself. As a pre-existent soul, or as a happy child, he once enjoyed a perfect psychic harmony; his consciousness was purely imaginative, and he knew the universe for the poem that it is. However, as he grew older on this corrupted Earth, and entered the society of men, it was unavoidable that his integrity of being should be compromised and destroyed. His intellect learned a respect for logic and prosaic fact; his awakening passions drew him toward the merely physical; conscience began its contests with desire; and there arose in him a mysterious spirit of perversity. Like Poe's university, the poet's soul has lost its original unity; and like that universe, it will not regain that unity save in death. Till then, the poet's imagination must struggle not only against the mundane and physical world around him, but also against the mundane and physical aspects of his divided nature; he will not now find it easy to disengage his spirit from earthly things, and commune with that heavenly harmony which he symbolized, in Poe's fiction, by such figures as the Lady Ligeia.

The Oxford Companion to American Literature summarizes "Ligeia" as follows:

> An aristocratic young man marries
> Ligeia, a woman of strange, dark
> beauty and great learning. They
> are deeply in love, and share an
> interest in the occult, until a
> wasting illness triumphs over
> Ligeia's passionate will to live,
> and she dies. In melancholy grief,
> her husband leaves his lonely
> home on the Rhine to purchase an
> English abbey, where he grows
> mentally deranged under the
> influence of opium. He marries

fair-haired Lady Rowena
Trevanion, although they are not
in love, and Rowena soon dies in a
strange manner. Her husband
watches by the bier, and sees signs
of returning life in the body, but
considers these to be hallucinations. At last she rises to her feet
and looses the cerements from her
head, so that masses of long black
hair stream forth. When she opens
her eyes, he realizes that the lost
Ligeia's will to live has triumphed,
for she has assumed what was
formerly the body of Rowena.

Considering its purpose and the difficulties involved, this summary is admirable, and yet it seems
ludicrously unrelated to the actual experience of
reading "Ligeia." It is as if some dark prophecy of
Nostradamus had been translated into the straightforward language of Walter Lippmann. An examination of the disparities between summary and story
may serve to set in relief some of Poe's characteris-
tics as a writer of fiction.

In the first place, the summary necessarily exaggerates the prominence of plot in Poe's story, the first
two-thirds of which consists mainly of rumination
and brooding description. Only with the onset of
Rowena's illness does narrative predominate, and
the effect of the whole is not to leave us with any
secure sense of fact or of causal sequence. Again, the
summary confers on the persons of the story a cred-
ibility of character, motive, and feeling which they
do not possess. We do not experience the narrator
as "an aristocratic young man," but as a monstrous

and unclassifiable sensibility. Ligeia does not strike us as a strangely beautiful and learned woman, but as an omniscient goddess. It does not seem adequate to say that the characters are "deeply in love" or "not in love," because their emotional frequencies are simply not ours: we cannot attune ourselves to a man who, looking into his beloved's eyes, is both "delighted and appalled," nor can we accept "mental alienation" as sufficient explanation of a perfectly motiveless remarriage. The fact is that Poe's characters escape our everyday understanding, and are meant to.

The main thing ignored in the summary is, of course, that "Ligeia" is not objectively told, but narrated–as so often in Poe–by a hero not quite in his ordinary mind. Such a narrative strategy has various effects, the chief one being this: that it encourages the reader to doubt that the ostensible story is the real or only one. Having come to doubt the ostensible story, the reader will perhaps decide to take it as a madman's misconstruction of doubtless prosaic events; but if he is familiar with Poe's criticism, he may more fruitfully decide to treat it as a cunning allegory, and look for some "mystic or secondary" meaning beneath it. Imaginative literature, Poe said, is "that class of composition in which there lies beneath the transparent upper current of meaning, an under or suggestive one." Since Poe thought "Ligeia" his best story, we may confidently sound it for an undercurrent.

The story begins with the narrator's confession that he "cannot remember how, when, or even precisely where" he first met Ligeia; moreover, he has never learned his beloved's surname, and cannot remember why not. Such a paroxysm of noninformativeness is potentially comic (and Poe later burlesqued the passage in "The Man Who Was Used Up"), but the intention here is serious. Vagueness and indefinitiveness were, in Poe's aesthetic theory, indispensable to the highest art, because they estrange the reader from mundane fact and meaning, and presumably set him adrift toward the spiritual and dim. This process of estrangement begins early and emphatically in "Ligeia," and is sustained throughout by the narrator's uncertainties, as well as by his repeated assertions that "words are impotent to convey" his subject matter.

But the more immediate effect of the opening paragraph is to detach Ligeia from the realm of actualities–from "when" and "where," from time and place–and, thus, to suggest that she is really an idea. The hero speculates that he may have forgotten his first meeting with Ligeia "because, in truth, the character of my beloved, her rare learning, her singular yet placid cast of beauty, and the thrilling and enthralling eloquence of her low musical language, made their way into my heart by paces so steadily and stealthily progressive, that they have been unnoticed and unknown." It is true that people may "grow on us," but so sourceless and insensible a process as the hero describes would better characterize the development of some taste, or faculty, or idea within the soul. Let us see what idea is embodied in Ligeia.

Poe borrowed her name–as so much else–from Milton: in *Comus*, when the Attendant Spirit summons the nymph Sabrina to free the chaste Lady from Comus's spell, he adjures her in the name of the siren Ligea (1. 880 ff.) and other sea-immortals. Poe first used the borrowed name in his cosmic poem "Al Aaraaf," where Ligeia is one of the two presiding spirits of a wandering star, the function of which is to mediate between Heaven and the scattered worlds of the universe, conveying to the latter a redemptive awareness of divine beauty and harmony. Like Milton's siren, she is associated with song; she governs, in fact, "the music of things" (II.127), and has properly been described as "the personified harmony of nature."

If one tries the experiment of identifying the heroine of "Ligeia" with her namesake in "Al Aaraaf," one finds that the story begins at once to make sense, and that all its apparent hyperbole becomes sober statement. If Ligeia is not a woman, but a mediatory spirit embodying the Platonic idea of harmony, she quite naturally has "the beauty of beings either above or apart from the earth," and speaks with "a melody more than mortal." Being immaterial, she might be expected to come and go "as a shadow," with a step of "incomprehensible lightness." And since she is the principle of harmony which pervades all things, it is understandable that the hero should discover "in the commonest objects of the universe, a circle of analogies" to the expression of her eyes.

Ligeia's eyes are her major feature, and hidden within them, the hero says, is a "something more profound than the well of Democritus." The nature of this mystery is readily discovered, since Poe was here quoting a passage that he attributed to Joseph Glanvill, and later used as the epigraph of "A Descent into the Maelström":

> The ways of God in Nature, as in
> Providence, are not as our ways;
> nor are the models that we frame
> in any way commensurate to the

72

vastness, profundity, and
unsearchableness of His works,
which have a depth in them
greater than the well of
Democritus.

It is now understandable why the narrator, looking into Ligeia's eyes, should be "delighted and appalled"; what he dimly glimpses there is nothing less
than "the ways of God."
   In short, Ligeia is not distinguishable from what
Poe called, in his review of R. H. Horne's *Orion*, "the
sentiment of the beautiful–that divine sixth sense
which is yet so faintly understood . . . that sense
which speaks of God through his purest, if not his
sole attribute–which proves, and which alone proves
his existence." Because the principle of harmony belongs to all those arts through which the spirit intu-
its supernatural beauty, Ligeia's attributes are not
merely musical: her hand is marble; her skin is ivory;
she resembles the Venus de' Medici; her hair inter-
prets the Homeric epithet "hyacinthine," and she
herself is a poet. She evokes Greek, Graeco-Roman,
or Hebrew art–as do all her many counterparts, including Helen and the Marchesa Aphrodite–because
such art was produced before the "fall" of Earth, in
a golden time when man's soul was attuned to universal beauty.
   The "gigantic" learning of Ligeia, which encompasses "all the wide areas of moral, physical, and
mathematical science," must be understood in some
mystic sense, because heavenly spirits cannot be supposed to study books. Here it is enlightening to recall a passage from "The Colloquy of Monos and
Una," in which Monos is lamenting the corruption

of Earth by the disease of rationalism. Alas, cries Monos, "alas for the pure contemplative spirit and majestic intuition of Plato! Alas for the Μουσικη [Music] which he justly regarded as an all sufficient education for the soul!"

In a footnote to this passage, Poe quotes the Republic twice, once to the effect that music is educationally all-sufficient, and again (from III.401) as follows:

> For this reason is a musical education most essential; since it causes Rhythm and Harmony to penetrate most intimately into the soul, taking the strongest hold upon it, filling it with *beauty* and making the man *beautiful-minded*. . . . He will praise and admire *the beautiful;* will receive it with joy into his soul, will feed upon it, and *assimilate his own condition with it.*

Poe then goes on to say:

> Music Μουσικη had, among the Athenians, a far more comprehensive significance than with us. It included not only the harmonies of time and of tune, but the poetic diction, sentiment and creation, each in its widest sense. The study of music was with them, in fact, the general cultivation of the taste–of that which recognizes the beautiful–in contradistinction from reason, which deals only with the true.

74

We may now interpret Ligeia's universal "learning" in this way: she is the inspirer and embodiment of a kind of knowledge, purely aesthetic and superior to the rational, which soars intuitively toward the Forms of things, and assimilates the soul to transcendental Beauty. Such knowledge is "all-sufficient" and all-inclusive, because it proceeds, by direct visionary means, toward those great answers which the trammeled reason will never reach. Such knowledge is also infallible because, the universe being an infinitely harmonious work of art, any perception of beauty or harmony must be true. The Keatsian idea that Beauty guarantees Truth was most boldly expressed by Poe in *Eureka,* where he argued that

> symmetry and consistency are
> convertible terms: –thus Poetry
> and Truth are one. A thing is
> consistent in the ratio of its truth–
> true in the ratio of its consistency.
> *A perfect consistency, I repeat, can be*
> *nothing but an absolute truth.*

So long as Ligeia is with him as his "wife," the hero's harmonious soul is untouched by his diseased Earthly environment, and devotes itself to unbroken poetic visions of ultramundane harmony and beauty. In the superficial story, this happy period belongs to his adult life, but there are strong hints of another chronology: as Ligeia bends over the hero at his studies, he "resigns himself, with a childlike confidence, to her guidance"; when she falls ill, he is "but as a child groping benighted"; and her death leaves him with "feelings of utter abandonment." It is, in fact, as a child that the hero dwells with Ligeia and the heavenly harmony she confers; he is Wordsworth's "Mighty prophet! Seer blest!" and the passing of Ligeia is the passing of childhood and its "visionary gleam." As Poe put it in his juvenile poem "Tamerlane,"

> . . . boyhood is a summer sun
> Whose waning is the dreariest one.
> For all we live to know is known,
> And all we seek to keep hath flown.

The remainder of the story is an allegory of the efforts of the poetic soul, once compromised and disrupted by exposure to the world, to overcome the world and itself, and recover the imaginative absolutism of childhood. The poet-hero's retreat into a "remote and unsocial" English abbey, his addiction to opium, and his "incipient madness" symbolize the retreat from waking consciousness–from bodily, moral, and intellectual consciousness–into the imaginative freedom of reverie and dream. Like "The Haunted Palace," the House of Usher, and all such edifices in Poe, the abbey represents the hero's isolated and self-absorbed mind. Its decay, like that of the Usher mansion, signifies that the consciousness within is disengaging itself from the material world and the material self, and will soon (in a subjective sense) destroy them. As for the interior, which the hero has decorated in a spirit of "child-like perversity," it is, like the apartment of the hero of "The Assignation," quite literally "a bower of dreams."

The abbey's bridal chamber–the one room fully described–is pentagonal in shape, but the angles are hidden by sarcophagi, and the walls are hung with a figured material continually agitated by an artificial current of wind. The effect, therefore, is generally circular, but there is a perpetual ambiguity of form. The room thus avoids–as all Poe's dream rooms do–that "rectangular obscenity" which Poe associated with the "harsh mathematical reason" now prevalent on Earth. The furnishings, like those of "The Assignation," reflect a scorn for "proprieties of place, and of time": the juxtaposition of Venetian, Saracenic, Druidical, and Egyptian objects exhibits the richness and daring of the hero's imagination, and very concretely expresses one idea of Poe's poem "Dream-Land," that in dreams we are "out of SPACE–out of TIME."

Entering dream, one escapes not only from local and temporal limitations, but also from external sensation. "It is as if," Poe says, "the five senses were supplanted by five others alien to mortality." Therefore Poe's dreamers lead a strictly indoor or sheltered existence, and their perceptions are wholly intramural. "Ligeia"'s bridal chamber has a window of "leaden hue," which denatures the daylight to a "ghastly lustre"; the wind which rushes behind the draperies is "artificial"; and the changeable figures of the agitated draperies suggest those vivid and ever-shifting images of the hypnagogic state which Poe took to be "glimpses of the spirit's outer world."

The bridal chamber is not only a dreaming mind, but a mind obsessed with a mournful longing for Ligeia. A vine–first in the hero's catalogue of natural objects reminiscent of his beloved–shadows the gray window; the walls, like Ligeia's intellect, are "gigantic"; the fires of the pendant censer "writhe" like Ligeia's fierce spirit; and the gold-and-black décor recalls her radiant eyes and jet-black hair. Plainly, the chamber does not contain a consciousness hospitable to Rowena.

What, on the allegorical plane, does the fair-haired Rowena stand for? She is beautiful, but, unlike Ligeia, she is earthly, temporal, material. She is, in fact, what Poe elsewhere calls "the type of physical beauty," and she stands also for that part of the hero's compromised nature which adheres to such beauty. The progressive wasting-away of Rowena enacts, therefore, a Platonic version of the art process, in which beauty is imaginatively extricated from the temporal and physical, and may at last be glimpsed in its bodiless essence. Rowena's decomposition is a progress toward the immateriality of Ligeia; her rigor mortis is an approach to the timeless and ideal condition of statuary; and when Rowena becomes Ligeia, and the hero is "chilled into stone" by the transformation, we perceive that he has momentarily purified his consciousness of everything earthly, attained once more to the Beautiful, and "assimilated his own condition with it."

Ostensibly, the transformation is effected by the "gigantic volition" of Ligeia, but the narrator is, in truth, the sole agent in the tale; the waning of Rowena and the waxing of Ligeia are governed by his mind's gradual movement from reverie to the visionary brink of sleep. "The night waned," he tells us, "and still, with a bosom full of bitter thoughts of the one only and supremely beloved, I remained gazing upon the body of Rowena." It is this remorseless and dematerializing gaze that alters Rowena—just as the bride of "The Oval Portrait" is withered by the gaze of her painter-husband.

Ligeia appears in proportion as Rowena fades, and we first see her as "a faint, indefinite shadow of angelic aspect" in the pool of light beneath the censer.

Of this censer, which hangs on its golden chain in the center of the chamber, something must be said. It derives ultimately from the *Iliad* (VIII.18-26), but Poe plainly found it in *Paradise Lost* (II.1004 ff., 1051 ff.), where the created universe depends from Heaven by a golden chain which serves also as the pathway of angels. In Poe's "Al Aaraaf" (II.20 ff.), Milton's chain is incorporated into the description of the palace of Nesace, spirit of Beauty:

A dome, by linkèd light from Heaven let down,
Sat gently on these columns as a crown–
A window of one circular diamond, there,
Looked out above into the purple air,
And rays from God shot down that meteor chain
And hallowed all the beauty twice again,
Save when, between th' Empyrean and that ring,
Some eager spirit flapped his dusky wing.

The golden chain reappears, as a chandelier, in a number of Poe's interiors, signifying always the linkage between poetic imagination and the divine mind. The particolored flames of the censer in "Ligeia" are the purifying fire of imagination, and consist of diffracted "rays from God." Because the golden chain is the pathway of angels, it is beneath the censer that we first spy Ligeia's "dusky wing"; and it is there, again, "in the middle of the apartment," that she at last reopens her profound eyes.

The foregoing discussion of "Ligeia" would be disproportionate were the story not so central to Poe's thought, so characteristic of his method, and so much an index of his symbolism, that it opens up the fiction in general. The typical Poe story is, in its action, an allegory of dream-experience: it occurs within the mind of the poet; the characters are not distinct personalities, but principles or faculties of the poet's divided nature; the steps of the action correspond to the successive states of a mind moving into sleep; and the end of the action is the end of a dream. Sometimes, as in "William Wilson," the narrative will have a strong admixture of realism and of credible psychology; elsewhere, as in "The Fall of the House of Usher," there will be no such admixture, and the one available coherence will be allegorical.

Generally, Poe offers the reader some suggestion that his characters are but aspects of a single personality: they will be bound together by marriage, or kinship, or old and intimate acquaintance; or perhaps they will share a common height, eye color, or birthday; or perhaps their names will have some obvious or sly similarity. In "Usher," which is essentially a retelling of "Ligeia," the narrator has been a boyhood companion of Roderick Usher and is now "his only personal friend," while Lady Madeline, the third character of the story, is Usher's twin sister and "sole companion for long years." The narrator's journey to Usher's domain is a dream-journey into his own mind, in the depths of which, and on the brink of sleep, he encounters in Roderick Usher his visionary soul. Usher embodies, in his tremulousness and in his variations of voice and mood, the incertitude of the hypnagogic state, that borderline condition wherein "the confines of the waking world blend with those of the world of dreams." Like the hero of "Ligeia," Usher is struggling to purge himself of waking and worldly consciousness, and Lady Madeline's "wasting-away," like Rowena's, enacts this process of purgation. Once dead and encoffined–once "death-refined"–Lady Madeline can rise again as a Ligeia-figure, climb to the turret room where

Roderick awaits her, and "in her violent and now final death-agonies, bear him to the floor a corpse." Grisly as their death-embrace may seem, it actually symbolizes the momentary reunion of a divided soul; and, since "by sleep and its world alone is Death imaged," it also symbolizes the final restoration and purification of that soul in the life to come.

The dematerialization of Usher's whirlwind-shaken house, and its collapse into its reflection in the tarn, express these same ideas; and they express as well the descent of the dreaming mind into unconscious sleep. "Ligeia" similarly ends, if not with a fall, at least with the vertigo that precedes and accompanies a fall. Its narrator's mind becomes "a helpless prey to a whirl of violent emotions," and the wind current that circles the vast room, agitating the lofty draperies, intensifies at the close, so that Ligeia's unbound hair "streams forth into the rushing atmosphere of the chamber."

The violent whirlings that conclude both "Ligeia" and "Usher" put one in mind of the dizzy windings and final plunge of "The Domain of Arnheim," and of the whirlpools of "Ms. Found in a Bottle" and "A Descent into the Maelström." The comparison is fruitful, because such tales prove, upon examination, to tell in their own way the essential "Ligeia" story. In them, the dreaming mind's movement toward unearthly visions is geared, not to the stages of a woman's dissolution, but to the stages of a journey. The visitor to Arnheim moves, during his river-journey, into an ever-increasing solitude and strangeness, leaving behind him first the city, and then the river-boat with its passengers and crew; transferred to a "fairy" canoe, he floats for a time in a circular basin which, in its perfect mirroring of nature, symbolizes the double consciousness of the hypnagogic state; then, drawn by the current, he glides down a dizzily winding stream until–a golden door swinging wide to the accompaniment of mysterious music–he plunges into "the circumscribed Eden of his dreams." The aspect of nature, during the journey, has undergone a gradual change from commonplace rustic charm to paradisal beauty, and this change corresponds precisely to the gradual transformation of the earthly Rowena into the heavenly Ligeia. "Ms. Found in a Bottle" tells the same story in terms of an ocean voyage, and in the key of terror.

Of all Poe's stories, those of detection seem most complete in their "upper current," and least in need of allegorical interpretation. They have on the face of it a clear point: the superiority of intuition to reason. In *Eureka*, following a denunciation of the Aristotlian and Baconian reasoning as "creeping and crawling," Poe asserts that Kepler's laws, from which Newton deduced the law of gravitation, were initially pure guesses, which Kepler then tailored into self-consistency and a consequent absolute truth.

> Yes!–these vital laws Kepler *guessed*–that is to say, he *imagined* them. Had he been asked to point out either the *de*ductive or *in*ductive route by which he attained them, his reply might have been– "I know nothing about *routes*–but I *do* know the machinery of the Universe. Here it is. I grasped it with *my soul*–I reached it through mere dint of *intuition*."

It is the Prefect of Police, in the three Dupin stories, who stands for that methodical reason which "creeps and crawls" and blinds itself with the "Scotch snuff of *detail*." Dupin, although Poe describes his mental operations as "analytic," and as based on a psychological calculus of probabilities, is actually representative of a pure poetic intuition bordering on omniscience. He dreams his solutions, and it sometimes appears that in solving a problem he can dispense, not only with reason, but with the problem itself. In "The Mystery of Marie Roget," Dupin sleeps in his armchair for seven or eight hours during the Prefect's recital of the evidence, his eyes hidden by green-glassed spectacles reminiscent of the tinted windows of Poe's dream-chambers. In "The Purloined Letter," Dupin invites the Prefect to give him the facts of the case—"or not"; just as he likes. The implication is that Dupin can somehow do without the mere facts; and indeed, within the first six speeches—well before the Prefect has told him anything—Dupin has intuitively solved the problem in all but its details. So confident is he of his principle of solution that he teases the Prefect by repeating it thrice.

It may be objected that Poe does also present Dupin as a reasoner, who offers his conclusions logically and at length. There are several answers to that objection, one being that a flat ascription of preterhuman powers, as in Superman Comics, makes for dull fiction. It is characteristic of Dupin that he first arrives at some conclusion, and then explains it logically to the narrator. In so doing, he is not reproducing his original mode of thought, any more than Poe, in his "Philosophy of Composition," gives a true account of the writing of "The Raven."

Rather, he is translating an ineffable process into lay terms; or demonstrating that intuition includes and obviates reason; or–like some Kepler–investigating the possibility that there was an implicit logic in his intuitive leap. This we know because, while Dupin's conclusions are always correct, the logic by which he claims to have reached them is generally faulty.* Readers would be more critical of Dupin's reasoning were they not disarmed by the correctness of his conclusions.

Insofar as Dupin has any method, it consists in identifying his intellect with that of another, and thereby divining what that person must think or do. Everyone has this power, in some degree, but with Dupin it is so strong that he can infallibly read the thoughts of a hypothetical Maltese sailor. In short, Dupin's power of divination is unlimited, and quite outflies the capabilities of his method; we are to see him not as a psychologist but as a seer. Poe said in his "Marginalia" that "poetic genius . . . in its supreme development, embodies all orders of intellectual capacity," and the statement applies to Dupin. He is a godlike genius who, possessing the highest and most comprehensive order of mind, includes in himself all possible lesser minds, and can therefore fathom any man–indeed, any primate–by mere introspection. How this omniscient solipsism is related to Poe's thought in general may be seen by a footnote to *Eureka,* in which Poe is remarking on his theory that the Universe, through its own imaginative efforts, is to be reabsorbed in God:

> The pain of the reflection that we
> shall lose our individual identity,
> ceases at once when we further

---

*See Denis Marion, *La Méthode Intellectuelle d'Edgar Poe* (1952).

reflect that the process, as above
described, is neither more nor less
than that of the absorption, by
each individual intelligence, of all
other intelligences (that is, of the
Universe) into its own. That God
may be all in all, each must
become God.

The poet-detective Dupin is in the vanguard of that movement.

"The Purloined Letter," despite its adequacy as a detective tale, and as a vindication of pure intuition, is also an allegory of conflict within a single soul. As allegory, it belongs to a class of tales–"The Man of the Crowd," "Murders in the Rue Morgue"–in which the soul of a poet "detects" and confronts the evil or brutal principle in itself. By hint upon hint, Poe invites the reader to play detective himself, and to discover that the Minister D– is the worldly, unprincipled "brother" or double of Auguste Dupin. And who is the queen, whom Dupin liberates from the Minister's power? Like the Lady Fortunato, like the Marchesa Aphrodite, like Di Broglio's wife, like Ligeia, she is that sense of beauty which must not be the captive of our lower natures.

The body of Poe's poetry is very small in proportion to his total work, partly because he had to neglect poetry in favor of better-paid literary labors, and partly because his conception of poetry, as it evolved, was so exclusive and extreme as to preclude any great productivity. Here are some random snippets from his criticism:

The phrase, "A long poem," is
simply a flat contradiction in

terms . . . didactic subjects are utterly *beyond,* or rather beneath, the province of true poesy . . . . A satire is, of course, no poem . . . we agree with Coleridge, that poetry and *passion* are discordant . . . . Poetry, in elevating, tranquilizes the soul. With the *heart* it has nothing to do . . . . With the Intellect or with the Conscience it has only collateral relations. Unless incidentally, it has no concern whatever with Duty or Truth . . . . Give it any undue decision–imbue it with any very determinate tone–and you deprive it, at once, of its ethereal, its ideal, its intrinsic and essential character. You dispel its luxury of dream.

To the short story, which Poe regarded as a lower form than poetry, "and more appreciable by the mass of mankind," he permitted some measure of verisimilitude, and a logical clarity of plot and idea. But the function of poetry being not to organize and interpret earthly experience, but to induce a mood in which the soul soars toward supernal beauty, Poe excluded from poetry anything that might detain the soul on Earth. Thus, poetry must be disembarrassed of that moral sense which involves us with humanity: it must throw overboard that factuality, and that narrative or logical clarity, which would render it compassable by the mundane intellect: and it must eschew all human emotions, since, when compared to the sense of beauty, they are–as Poe said in reviewing Horne's *Orion*–"vapid and insignificant" and "trammel the soul in its flight to an ideal Helusion."

In practice, these principles resulted in a remorseless elaboration of those techniques of "estrangement" which we have already noted in "Ligeia." We must not, Poe warns us in a review of Macaulay, "confound obscurity of expression with the expression of obscurity," and surely the best of his tales may be defended as illuminations of a subject matter essentially obscure. But the poems, with few exceptions, do not truly illuminate, and what brilliance they have is like that of a Fourth of July rocket destroying itself in the void.

When one of Poe's poems has a narrative basis, as in "The Valley of Unrest," the reader will often struggle in vain to derive it from the poem proper, and will arrive at a plot, if at all, by interpolation from related prose works. "The Haunted Palace" and "The Raven" are, among Poe's verse-narratives, relatively clear, yet even they have a tantalizing incompleteness which one does not find in the better tales. Although the "plots" of Poe's poems always bear on his inveterate concerns, they mostly seem to be there not for plot's sake, or for meaning's sake, but to furnish a substance which the poem may "waste away" and etherealize.

The celebrated vagueness of Milton's *Paradise Lost*, whereby he conveys the impression of shadowing-forth things unknowable in themselves, was appropriated by Poe for purposes fundamentally opposed to Milton's. Poe was not interested in giving a qualified concreteness to divine things, but, rather, in verbally destroying the concreteness of earthly things. From Milton's description of Chaos as a "dark Illimitable ocean without bound," Poe learned how to write of "seas without a shore" and "boundless floods"; likewise, Milton's "dark unbottomed infinite Abyss" begot the "bottomless vales" of Poe's "Dream-Land." In Poe, the effect of such paradoxes is quite simply to annihilate the words "seas," "floods," and "vales," as we understand them, and so magically to deprive the reader of a part of the world he knows. In so doing, Poe's paradoxes support his continual explicit stress on disappearance, silence, oblivion, and all ideas that suggest nonbeing. It was the notion of approximating nothingness that most excited him in his own poetry, and in that of others. As a critic, he quoted approvingly almost any use of such words as "dim" and "unseen," and in reviewing Joseph Rodman Drake's *Culprit Fay* he characteristically observed that "in the expression 'glimmers and dies' . . . the imagination is exalted by the moral sentiment of beauty heightened in dissolution."

In an 1843 review of Rufus Griswold's *Poets and Poetry of America*, Poe scanned the first line of his "Haunted Palace" as follows:

$$— \cup \quad — \cup \quad — \cup \quad — \cup$$
In the / greenest / of our / valleys.

This supports a considerable body of contemporary testimony to the effect that Poe's reading of his poems was metronomic. There are several explanations for this feature of his poetry, aside from the relative indelicacy of Poe's ear. Expressive rhythm in poetry derives either from the things and movements described, or from the emotions embodied. The first source of rhythm was not altogether denied to Poe; we have, for instance, the line "Down,

down that town shall settle hence." But the second was precluded by Poe's having banished from his poetry all emotion save that "tremulous delight" which attends an imaginary destruction of the physical world. Poe's rhythmic regularity is not, however, wholly the result of such exclusion. He thought of the poem not as an object for contemplation but as a means of engendering "sensations which bewilder while they enthrall–and which would not so enthrall if they did not so bewilder." In short, he thought of the poem as casting a spell, and accordingly endowed it with the brevity, repetitiveness, sonority, and the impressive rhythmic monotony of a charm or incantation. In a charm we are far less concerned with the sense than with the effect–nonsense will do, if it only works–and therefore Poe's incantatory techniques further the general effort of his poetry to nullify–in a logical and denotative sense–the words with which it is made.

Poe's poetry is pure negation; it does not and cannot acquaint us with supernal beauty, and the reader may well question whether there is anything very spiritual about a program of estranging us from the known by subverting the words through which we know it. A number of Poe's poems are enchanting in much the way they mean to be, but I reserve my respect for the major tales, which, for all the secretiveness of their allegory, are great and trail-blazing realizations of inner experience.

The commencement address is an extremely difficult form, so demanding in respect of clarity, animation, appropriateness, and wide pertinence that, having struggled with two for some weeks each, I should be wary of attempting a third. This one was given at Washington University, in Saint Louis, in the spring of 1964, and was published in the Washington University Magazine *that summer.*

A SPEECH AT A CEREMONY

Some people are very fond of ceremony. I think, for instance, of Benjamin Disraeli. Someone asked him, when he was a young man, what he thought life should be, and he unhesitatingly replied, "A continuous grand procession from the cradle to the grave." He required of life that the prose of every day be incessantly redeemed by pomp and drama, and anyone who reads his biography must marvel at how close he came to having his way. Disraeli always seemed an odd and flamboyant bird among the English, and I suppose he would have seemed even odder over here, in our unceremonious country. Pomp has never wholly caught on with us. Try as he might, John Adams never succeeded in setting a monarchical style for our republican way of life, and Americans ever since have been a little disrespectful of ceremonial grandeur. We recall the scandalous inaugural of Andrew Jackson and all that spilled whiskey on the White House carpets with a certain horror but also with a certain glee; and we like to hear stories, true or false, about Will Rogers calling the King of England "George," and Harry Truman addressing Princess Elizabeth as "dear."

To be sure, there are ceremonious Americans, and

we have all encountered a few. I recall one in particular. Toward the end of World War II, the U.S. Army established a number of temporary universities in Europe, in order to keep some of our troops out of trouble until it was time to go home. I was furloughed from Germany as a member of the first cycle at Shrivenham American University, which was housed in the buildings of a military school near London. Our university made a somewhat ragged start, because there was no library to speak of, because our textbooks were late in arriving, and because our classes consisted of men of all ages and degrees of culture; but once we got going, it was a splendid school, and I have never seen elsewhere such hunger for learning or such pleasure in teaching.

What I wanted to tell you, however, was this: before our university was two weeks old it possessed, by order of the general, a uniformed football squad, a football schedule, a corps of cheerleaders, a set of Shrivenham American University cheers, a glee club, and a nostalgic alma mater song which the glee club had already broadcast over the BBC. I think you'll agree that we had a truly ceremonious general: before we had a present, he gave us a tradition and a beloved past; in a time of confusion he offered his displaced charges, by means of songs and cheers and scheduled occasions, a certain sureness as to where we were, who we were, and what we were to feel.

The military profession is no doubt peculiarly aware of some of the uses of ceremony: our generals know how ceremony can convert bare discipline into a felt ritual, how it can dramatize routine, how it can promote that prompt simplicity of emotion which belongs to the soldierly nature. Yet in all professions some disposition toward ceremony can be found–even in my own calling of letters. Writers are thought to be impatient of pompous formalities, but I know some who are never so happy as at banquets, testimonials, and assemblies, where they can put on looks of simple greatness and bestow honors on each other.

Still, as I have said, we Americans are more skeptical than other peoples when it comes to the highfalutin, and it is common among us to feel that the thing to do about forms and observances is to see through them. If here and now we were to set about seeing through some formal occasion–a funeral, an inauguration, a confirmation, a commencement, a rally–I suppose we might say first that the function of any ceremony is to enable one to feel some appropriate emotion decisively–to feel it rightly and get it over with. In each man's private history, and in that part of public history which touches him, there occurs a number of moments or events to which he feels bound to respond. Very often he cannot, on his own hook, respond with any intensity, or with what seems to him a proper emotion, and this he finds troubling. He feels as if he were missing out on life; he feels as one might feel who had not looked up from the racing form as Man o' War went by, or who, at a New Year's Eve party, had dropped off to sleep in a chair and not awakened until 12:35. When we miss out on our emotional opportunities, we are upset at the moment of failure; and we are also nagged ever after by a sense of not having measured up, a sense of unfinished and unfinishable business.

It is from such remorse and regret that ceremony preserves us. The girl who awakens on her wedding day and finds that it seems like any other day; the shoe clerk who, after fifty years with the same store, can manage nothing but a dull wonder at the swiftness of time; the guilty man who wants to pray and cannot; for people like these–that is, for people like us–there are ceremonies that can demand and release a suitable emotion, persuade us that we are adequate to life, and so assist us to live some more. A prudent heart will not despise such aids.

And such aids are the more painfully needed the more our lives are formless, mannerless, traditionless, placeless, and private. There have been times and places in which men had ceremonious hearts and could respond unassisted to any circumstance, in a manner both fervent and orthodox. There are still such places and such men; but in most of our Western world, as the novelists have been telling us for decades, the ceremonious heart is rare. When Hans Castorp, in *The Magic Mountain,* is told of the manner in which the dead are brought down for burial from the higher sanatoria, he bursts into wild, uncontrollable laughter; it is a laugh, as the critic Eric Heller said the other day, that was never heard in ancient Greece. And think of the blank, intransitive hearts of the heroes of Albert Camus; think of the child in a Virginia Woolf novel who learns that her mother is dying and learns, too, that she does not care. There's no need to go on with such examples: in novel after novel of our times, we have been shown this peculiarly modern form of sickness or suffering: the inability to feel, or the inability to feel other than perversely.

Nor is it the novel alone that purveys this revelation about our times; surely the so-called sick humor that is now so popular in our night clubs and elsewhere tells the same story. With its cruelty, its callousness, its universal irreverence, sick comedy shocks us into laughter; it shocks us, however, not so much because we are conventional as because it exposes and caricatures the miserable indecorum of our own hearts. We have need, at times, of the benign coercion of ceremony.

There is another manner, I think, in which ceremony might be seen through and accounted for, and perhaps I can best approach the idea by quoting a much-anthologized poem of Carl Sandburg's. It is called "Limited," and it goes as follows:

> I am riding on a limited express, one of the crack trains of the nation.
> Hurtling across the prairie into blue haze and dark air go fifteen all-steel coaches holding a thousand people.
> (All the coaches shall be scrap and rust and all the men and women laughing in the diners and sleepers shall pass to ashes.)
> I ask a man in the smoker where he is going and he answers: "Omaha."

The poet is a little patronizing, it seems to me, toward the man in the smoker. Mr. Sandburg regards "Omaha" as a limited sort of answer, and it is. But surely Mr. Sandburg's jaw would have dropped if the man in the smoker had said, "I am hurtling into blue haze and dark air; I am passing to ashes; I am rushing toward death and infinite mystery." The fact is that the man answered naturally; we all prefer Omaha to death; we all prefer to move toward the unknown by short stages; and even monks and nuns, who have a special professional concern with last things, pass toward them by way of each day's duties, each day's canonical hours, and the feasts of the church year.

There are many pleasures and exhilarations in travel, but one of the greatest is the illusion that we are taking time and space into our own hands. We get on the train for Omaha, and soon by our own choice we are losing or gaining an hour; we are passing time, rather than being passed by it; no longer are we wholly subject to the earth's motion; we move purposively with or against it. And when we get down at Omaha, we feel that we have got somewhere. In our deepest consciousness we know that it is not true; that we have not mastered space and time; that the heart has gone on wearing out at the same rate; and that we are scarcely better or wiser than when we started out on the journey. We suppress that knowledge, however, because it is difficult to bear.

There is a great deal of knowledge that one would like to avoid. How unpleasant it is, for example, to be told in a statistical article how many glasses of milk one is expected to consume in a lifetime. Confronted with such a statistic, one sees oneself as a prisoner of appetite, helplessly consuming from birth until death, a creature wholly passive and repetitious. At such a moment the landscape of our life's journey lies before us like the desolate perspectives of di Chirico; we envision a desert prospect of unrelieved sameness, traversed only by a long line of milk glasses, dwindling toward a vanishing point which is also our own. Or consider a related kind of unpleasant awareness, the kind that comes when one realizes that for the fifth straight time one has failed to keep one's New Year's resolution to give up smoking. Much of the dignity of man consists, we think, in his power to choose, to decide, to exert his free will; yet every now and then one is forced to confess that, even in trifling matters, one does not have much volition.

"Once to every man and nation," says James Russell Lowell, "comes the moment to decide." One sometimes wonders whether, in the average life, a clear and crucial need to decide presents itself so much as once. We go to some school or other, we enter this line of work or that, we marry and beget, we vote and discuss, we move from one place to another place, we join this organization or that, and for all our striving after what Roy Fuller calls "the appearance of choice," there is always the secret suspicion that we have chosen nothing, but only drifted. There is a whole class of ceremonies which can be seen as allaying that suspicion, sustaining the appearance of choice, and nursing the illusion that each of us makes a purposive and decisive progress through life. All initiations are of that character, involving as they do a commitment to reshape one's life, to change oneself, or the supposition that one has already done so. A regular communicant of the church asks more than fifty times a year that the past be forgiven and resolves henceforward to lead a new life. But we do not change so often; indeed, if we had to show proof, on our birthdays, of having matured as well as aged, we would seldom clearly deserve the cake and candles.

It might be one function of ceremony, then, to punctuate our lives with what looked like significant choices and deliberate changes, and to hide from us the extent to which we are aimless and passive. And now let me venture a third and last explanation of the human weakness for the making of occasions. It has to do with the fact that, despite what the salesmen of easy chairs and annuities would have us be-

lieve, man is not capable of contentment. We are creatures of infinite hankering, and therefore we are
never satisfied, although we may dream of reaching
such a condition. I think of a poem of Stephen
Spender's, the opening lines of which are these:

> What I expected was
> Thunder, fighting,
> Long struggles with men
> And climbing.
> After continual straining
> I should grow strong;
> Then the rocks would shake
> And I should rest long.

But it doesn't work out that way; the long rest
never comes this side of the grave. To be sure, men
sometimes do arrive at their objectives; the point is
that the achievement never satisfies. A man who
solves a crossword puzzle, or fills the last gap in his
stamp collection, may feel a fleeting complacency,
but then there will be a letdown, and he will ask himself why he has given such time and thought to so
slight a thing. Or if the goal achieved does not disappoint us by its triviality, it is likely to appall us by
the revelation that we have not understood our own
desires. That is what happens in all those fairy stories where the hero is given three wishes, and it happens in life as well. Robert Penn Warren, in his essay
on Sam Houston, tells an astonishing thing; he tells
how Houston, at the battle of San Jacinto, saw his
officers riding up with four hundred prisoners; how
he knew by that that Santa Anna was utterly beaten,
and that he, Sam Houston, would soon realize his
ambition to be president of a vast southwestern republic; and how, at that moment of victory, instead

of rejoicing, Houston cried out, "Have I a friend in this world?" It is a strange story and an enigmatic cry, but I think that we would all explain it in the same way; we would guess that Houston, in the hour of his triumph, was suddenly free to know how his bitter ambition had estranged him from other men, and how the gaining of his goal would mean a lifetime of lonely eminence.

Some goals, when achieved, disappoint us because they turn out to be trivial; others, because the gain is attended by unforeseen loss. And even when the goal we reach is worthy and wholly desired, we are still not content. One evening, some twelve years ago, I fell into a deep depression because it occurred to me that I might very well die without having read Dante in the original. Shortly thereafter, by a stroke of luck, I found myself able to spend a year in Rome, and it was not long before I felt able to go beyond menus and billboards and newspapers and make an attempt on Italian poetry. On the day when I managed to get through a passage of the *Inferno* without consulting the dictionary, I was delighted both with the poem and with myself; and yet, remembering how I had once focused all my despair on the thought that I should never read Dante in his own tongue, I wondered a little at the moderation of my pleasure. Why did I not feel that I had arrived, once and for all? Why did I not cry *Nunc dimittis*, and die happy? The answer is simple: the self which desires a thing is not the self which at last possesses that thing. As one approaches any goal, it seems more and more reasonable that one should reach it, and desire commences to look beyond. Even as I delighted in my beginner's acquaintance with the *Inferno*, I was revising my despair and saying to myself, "You may very well die without ever having read Dante properly; and what's more, you know nothing about grand opera."

We are all like that, as Yeats said over and over in his poems. Some of you may know the little poem called "The Wheel" in which he says it most plainly:

> Through winter-time we call on spring,
> And through the spring on summer call,
> And when abounding hedges ring
> Declare that winter's best of all;
> And after that there's nothing good
> Because the springtime has not come—
> Nor know that what disturbs our blood
> Is but its longing for the tomb.

Yeats does not mean that men long to die, any more than Goethe's Faust, when he reaches for the poison goblet, longs to die. What Yeats and Goethe are talking about is the human craving for more life, for new life, for the compassing of all possibilities—for "life piled on life," as Tennyson's Ulysses said. We are all moved by that craving, even the laziest of us, and we value human discontent because of what it has driven men to accomplish; nevertheless, there are times when we weary of the fact that there is no such thing as a finished man, and wish that it were in us to rest and be satisfied. Perhaps it is a function of certain ceremonies to distract us for a moment from our own insatiable restlessness by saying to us: "Relax, you've made it; you've got what you wanted; you're a Nobel Prize chemist; you're a senior lifesaver; you're a Phi Beta Kappa; you're a bachelor of arts."

Which brings us to the present occasion. To hear me talk, as I have been doing for too long, you would think that a ceremony was nothing but a magical means of allaying individual anxieties. That is part of the truth, I think; but I don't think we are gathered here merely to enable the individual to discharge a timely and proper emotion or to furnish him with a charmed moment in which to feel purposive and realized. Nor have we come here in such numbers and such panoply to congratulate the individual on having made a good beginning of his personal career. For such a private happiness, private congratulations would suffice.

Insofar as this event is more than a sort of gaudy mail call, in which diplomas are delivered to their addresses, we are engaged in something corporate, something collective; for ceremonies are always of that character. Our corporate self is here to say something that, since commencements have persisted for so long, must seem to us true and important. And I think it is this: that learning and developed sensibility are real and excellent things, and vital to the society which it is their obligation to serve.

In order to feel entitled to make that affirmation and promise we need not believe that all members of this graduating class have done famously as scholars and sensibilities. Some, I am sure, have inwardly or outwardly more than fulfilled the requirements for the bachelor's degree; others, who graduate today by the skin of their teeth, may someday surprise us; still others, perhaps, will forever be scholars by imputation only. It does not matter; for the truth is that people and ceremonies are always more or less out of phase. Who knows when a man and a woman are truly married? Some, I think, are married before they ever come to the altar, while some, though pronounced man and wife, arrive at that condition late or never. But this does not invalidate the marriage ceremony. Ceremony becomes invalid only when it bears no relation to the facts; then it is dead and will not be tolerated, as Richard II learned to his sorrow. A ceremony is valid so long as the idea it celebrates is sometimes and in some measure achieved and embodied. What we celebrate in the marriage ceremony is marriage, and we can do so because Alcestis, Saint Joseph, and even some of our friends have managed to be married in fact. What we celebrate here today is the learned mind and the articulate spirit, and we can do so because, at this great university and elsewhere, such things have more than once been brought about.

I feel like a bit of an impostor this morning, because it is conventional nowadays for the commencement speaker to be a public man—a congressman, a general, an ambassador. And there is good reason for that convention. Sometimes these public men give addresses that are strangely wide of the mark: one will make a foreign-policy statement; another will take the occasion to run for office; and I have heard a prime minister of Canada inform a graduating class about the price of wheat. But whatever such public men may say, their mere presence on the platform is a dramatic reminder that our skills are prized and requisitioned by the community. We need that reminder, because the life of the mind is separate and lonely, and it is all too easy to come to feel that we do what we do merely for its own sake, for our career's sake, or for curiosity's sake, or for the pleasure of exercising a competence.

Belonging as I do to the world of the academy, I cannot polarize this occasion as a public man would do in my place; but the ritual will be accomplished if we all, as members both of the academy and of larger communities, remind ourselves that our gifts and skills are finally not our own. I need not elaborate on that idea because, as you have noticed, I am now saying what hundreds and thousands of commencement speakers have said. And this should not surprise or dismay us. It is characteristic of ceremonies that they can afford to mean the same thing again and again.

*Alfred Harbage kindly asked me to write an intro-
duction to the* Poems *volume of the Pelican
Shakespeare Series. It appeared in 1966.*

SHAKESPEARE'S POEMS

And Shakespeare, thou whose honey-flowing vein,
Pleasing the world, thy praises doth obtain;
Whose *Venus* and whose *Lucrece*, sweet and chaste,
Thy name in fame's immortal book have placed:
Live ever you, at least in fame live ever;
Well may the body die, but fame dies never.
–Richard Barnfield, 1598

Some poetic genera have survived our practice,
understanding, or both, and some have not. The sonnet, and even the sonnet-sequence, are still being
written, and the earliest English sonnets
(Shakespeare's among them) are still being read. We
have, in consequence, a going sense of what the sonnet can accomplish, and also of what subjects and
attitudes traditionally belong to it. But of the masque,
for instance, we have no corresponding natural
awareness; only the specialist in Stuart literature
could say whether Robert Frost's *A Masque of Reason*
is in any way a revival of the art form, and most
readers have enjoyed Milton's *Comus* without much
notion of its relation to the norms of courtly enter-
tainment. We can, of course, find an antique work
good without knowing precisely how it is "good of
its kind"; but much depends, in such cases, on the
simplicity of the convention and on the persistence
of analogous forms of poetry. The two long poems
that, in Barnfield's judgment, were to assure
Shakespeare's immortality are complex and confus-
ing in relation to a number of conventions, literary

103

and pictorial, and those conventions are dead; poems of the kind are no longer written, and few of them are still read. Since one cannot cheer without knowing what the game is, the reader of these poems today is likely to find himself wishing for some historical guidance.

The literature on the poems is extensive, but that vast machinery of mediation does not answer one's questions with the sure brevity of a computer. Some things are clear, however. The *Venus,* of which I shall speak first and most, is an Ovidian narrative poem which derives the greater part of its material from passages of the *Metamorphoses:* those on Venus and Adonis, on Narcissus, and on Salmacis and Heramphroditus. The epigraph, moreover, is taken from Ovid's *Amores.* Shakespeare was thus promising in some measure to emulate a witty, charming, and delicately sensual Latin poet. He was also choosing to retell a tale that every literate person knew in the original, and that had already been variously treated by English poets: by Golding in his moralizing translation of Ovid, by Spenser, by Lodge, and by several others.

The dedicatee of Shakespeare's poem was the Earl of Southampton, a young courtier who employed John Florio as his tutor in Italian and was presumably a sophisticate. Given such a first reader, Shakespeare would doubtless be inclined to make his poem not a moral allegory (as medieval Ovidian tradition would have urged) but lightly erotic and fashionably artificial, in the manner of Marlowe's *Hero and Leander.* If these were Shakespeare's desiderata, he cannot be said to have consistently achieved them; but that he aimed well enough at the tastes of Southampton and his like is indicated both by Gabriel Harvey's reference to *Venus's* rage among the "younger sort" and by the greater assurance of Shakespeare's dedication of *Lucrece* to Southampton one year later.

The poem has been praised for its quick, decisive beginning, and it is true that the first stanza provides the time, some sense of place, the persons, their motives, and the beginning of the action: Adonis is off to hunt, and the enamored Venus comes running to intercept him. But this sort of narrative urgency does not continue; indeed, it stops right there, and we see at once that Shakespeare is not plunging into his narrative but getting some part of it over with. As Venus begins her leisured and mannered importunities in stanza 2, it is clear that her much-told story will not be told here for story's sake. There is no question, of course, of any incapacity for narrative writing, as one may tell by this later stanza in which Venus, seeking Adonis, encounters his wounded and complaining hounds:

> When he hath ceased his ill-resounding noise,
> Another flap-mouthed mourner, black and grim,
> Against the welkin volleys out his voice.
> Another and another answer him,
> > Clapping their proud tails to the ground below,
> > Shaking their scratched ears, bleeding as they go.
> > > (919 ff.)

That is cleanly written, it is vivid for eye and ear, and it does not hover too much, but keeps the story in motion; the pack goes bleeding by, and Venus moves on with increased anxiety toward the discovery of Adonis. But when she does find him, when she "unfortunately spies / The foul boar's conquest of her fair delight," the event is almost parthetical, and the poem characteristically swerves from direct narrative into a cascade of similes, in which Venus's afflicted eyes are likened to fading stars, retracting snail horns, and the unnerved intelligence officers of a court.

Not only are the few happenings of the plot minimized in favor of such embroidery, but no depth or intelligible development can be found in the characters or relationship of Venus and Adonis. Adonis is a boy who likes hunting and is prodigiously insusceptible to love; sullenly, and on the whole mutely, he resists Venus's pleas and caresses from beginning to end. The one other thing we know about this rudimentary person is that he does have the decency to resuscitate a woman who has fainted. Venus, for her part, is at one moment moved by pity, but everything else she does and says—her wrestlings, her sophistries, her tricks, her reproaches—is traceable to her one allotted motive: a sometimes etherealized sensual passion. The death of Adonis saddens but does not chasten her, and though we leave her "immured" in Paphos she has not conceivably become a conventual type.

The poem differs from Ovidian poetry generally in containing a very high proportion of dialogue, but its many speeches do not serve, by characteristic cadence and lexicon, or by the betrayal of emotional pattern or conflict, to give the speakers any individual savor, or psychic volume. Their attitudes have been assigned in stanza 1, and whenever they sound unlike themselves we are dealing not with the emergence or revelation of a new quality but with inconsistency on the part of the author. For example, in her prophecy that sorrow shall hereafter attend on love (1135 ff.) Venus takes high moral ground and deplores jealousy, deceit, and unrestraint in a manner that is foreign to her but convenient for the poet's local purposes. Adonis asserts (409 ff.) that he "knows not love" and does not care to know it, but in the next stanza argues from a quite different and more knowing position that one may be spoiled for sexual love if one experiences it too early. The fine homily on Love and Lust (like the love-persuasions of Marlowe's Leander) comes oddly from one so innocent, and the inconsistency is not removed by the fact that Adonis admits it (806).

In addition to such distortions of character, which Shakespeare seems to have permitted himself for the sake of immediate effects, the reader must cope with apparent shifts in the poet's attitude toward his material. It will be granted, I am sure, that comedy enters the poem at the end of stanza 5, where Venus pulls Adonis from his horse and lugs him off under her arm, blushing and pouting. We are amused because a female is manhandling a male, and because the goddess of Love (though later she will stress her weightlessness) here seems not merely Rubenesque but grotesquely muscular. The occurrence is a sexual assault which, if described in a different key, might invite prurience and encourage perverse or passive fantasy. But there is no Swinburnian heavy breathing here; it is vaudeville, and it is vaudeville when Venus later falls flat not once but twice (463, 593).

If the presence of broad comedy forbids a prurient response to the early stanzas, the element of slapstick is in turn refined by the graceful artifice of Venus's entreaties, by her persistent high idealization of Adonis's beauty, by Shakespeare's stress on the loveliness of Adonis's "pretty ear" or Venus's "fair immortal hand," and by the benign ambience of summer dawn. We cannot take the word "lust" very seriously in an atmosphere of violets and divedappers; and when Venus "devours" Adonis as an eagle its prey, we are less likely to think of *Vénus tout entière à sa proie attachée* than of the amorous commonplace "I could eat you alive." The reader, in short, feels himself to be in that special literary preserve where the erotic may freely be enjoyed because taste and humor attend and control it. This is the domain of much of Herrick's poetry, and here as there it is understood that moral objections would be churlish.

A critic of 1823 described Venus and Adonis as "deficient in that delicacy which has happily been introduced by modern refinement." The eroticism of the poem, however, is never culpably gross. Venus's celebrated "deer park" speech (229 ff.) is far too clever for pornographic purposes, and such lines as the following have a Marlovian coolness and suavity:

> Who sees his true-love in her naked bed,
> Teaching the sheets a whiter hue than white,
> But, when his glutton eye so full hath fed,
> His other agents aim at like delight?
> (397-400)

There are also (in addition to the other alleviations I have mentioned) occasional maxims of this sort:

> Were beauty under twenty locks kept fast,
> Yet love breaks through and picks them all at last.
> (575-76)

This lacks the irony of Marlowe, but like his maxims in *Hero and Leander* it distances the action by amused generalization.

Nevertheless, Shakespeare's poem breaks its own contract with the reader. By line 551 Venus's eagle has become a vulture, her face "doth reek and smoke," and her "lust" is being denounced by the poet for its shamelessness and its subversion of reason. This passage endorses in advance Adonis's tirade (769 ff.) against "sweating Lust," in which that sweat which first seemed earthily matter-of-fact (25) and later erotically attractive (143-44) becomes wholly distasteful. Is the reader expected, at this point, to make such judgments retroactive, and to see the first part of the poem in a radically altered light? If so, it is too much to ask. One could no more do it than one could reconceive *Macbeth* as comedy. Shakespeare's (and Adonis's) distinctions between Love and Lust are in themselves eloquent and sound, but they have no place in such a poem as *Venus* started out to be, and one is forced to consider two possible explanations: either Shakespeare thought that he could jump, with aesthetic safety, from one Ovidian tradition to another; or the poet who was soon to write Sonnet 129 ("Th' expense of spirit in a waste of shame / Is lust in action") could not temperamentally sustain a blithe and amoral approach to sexual love.

Some critics, unwilling that Shakespeare should be imperfect even in "the first heir of his invention," have tried to read *Venus* as a coherent moral allegory. It is not hard to guess what sort of thing such attempts would entail: the identification of Adonis with reason and ideal beauty, Venus with lust; the assumption that hunting is here, as in *A Midsummer Night's Dream*, a metaphor for the conquest of the irrational; the interpretation of Adonis's horse as ungoverned appetite running mad; the placing of special emphasis on all passages (such as 889 ff.) having to do with the hierarchy of the faculties; and so on. The poem would thus become a myth (rather like Marlowe's digression, in *Hero and Leander,* on the enmity of Love and the Fates) of the flight of true Love and Beauty to heaven–a myth in which the imperfection of love on earth is explained as the result of passion's incapacity to defer to reason. Having come so far, an allegorical interpreter might dare to construe, in accordance with his view of the poem, that dense complex of repeated images or symbols which we encounter from the first stanza onward: suns and moons and faces red or pale, hot or cold; eyebeams or sunbeams commencing with the several elements, and with earth or heaven. By the time one finds the fatal boar being condemned for a "downward eye" imperceptive of beauty (1105 ff.) one is aware that these recurrent motifs may indeed be driving at something; but I am unable, thus far, to resolve them into any structure, and find that the chief result of so many burning faces, eyes, tears, and exhalations is an impression of close-up photography.

We are all, I hope, ambitious for Shakespeare, and would be pleased if the discovery of consistent moral allegory in his poem could be done in better conscience–with less suppression and inflation of evidence, and less disregard of tone. The moral and allegorical elements are really there; unfortunately, they are fitful and vague. It would please us, too, if the poem could be shown to have a clear pattern of attitudes embodied in its prevalent symbols; we might then hope to discover deep and powerful focal passages, as in the plays. The suns, moons, heads, and coins of Henry IV, Part I, and their attendant political conceptions, have such cumulative effect upon the reader's imagination that when, in Act IV, the Prince's troops are seen approaching Shrewsbury, "Glittering in golden coats, like images . . . and gorgeous as the sun at midsummer," those few words render the whole play simultaneous, and reverberate through all its architecture. But Venus is not architectural; there are no moments in which the entire work is many-dimensionally presented to the mind through a concentrative use of symbol or idea. The poem is additive, linear, spasmodic, opportunistic; it resembles a medieval episodic painting, or a series of tapestry panels deriving from one story but only tenuously related to each other. Or, to use a comparison nearer to our experience, it is like those musical comedies of the 1920's in which the "book" was a series of casual excuses for songs and dances, and the least mention of Chicago was sufficient to motivate a massive Chicago Number.

In order to enjoy Venus and Adonis, one must accept it as a lesser and looser thing than the more familiar plays, and not waste too much time in clucking one's tongue over its "frigid artificiality," its "remoteness from life," its deficiencies in story, character, and idea. The pleasures of the poem may be found anywhere at random, as in these lines from Venus's three-stanza vaunt about her conquest of Mars:

> Over my altars hath he hung his lance,
> His batt'red shield, his uncontrollèd crest,
> And for my sake hath learned to sport and dance,
> To toy, to wanton, dally, smile, and jest,
>   Scorning his churlish drum andensign red,

Making my arms his field, his tent my bed.

                                              (103-8)

That is part of an eighteen-line development of the
paradox that the God of War should surrender. Both
in *Venus* and in *Lucrece* Shakespeare sometimes employs brisk and arresting paradoxes ("O modest
wantons, wanton modesty!"), but the relish of this
passage lies in an eloquent expansion of the paradox, and a continually varied attack upon it. Wit is
not always brief; Venus offers Adonis "Ten kisses
short as one, one long as twenty," and Shakespeare
knows that in witty verse one must similarly divert
by unexpected proportion and duration. In the early
poems, where subtlety is chiefly of the surface, he
inclines to surprise more by excess than by concision, and we respond not with a jarred delight but
with that growing wonder we feel when the still-
strong miler lets himself out in the stretch, or the
jazz trumpeter sails on into yet another chorus. We
enjoy the display of resources, the prodigality, the
abundance. In the stanza above, there is a fairly full
inventory of Martial properties–lance, shield, helmet,
drum, ensign, field, and tent; but these things are so
variously tucked into the grammar as to give no impression of padding or of tiresome catalogue. And it
is precisely this handling of one enumeration that
permits another (the rather redundant infinitives of
lines 105 and 106) to be contrastingly presented in
bald sequence.

   No reader with an ear can fail to note that the vowel
progressions of the stanza are melodious, and that
the line, though end-stopped, is highly versatile in
pace and rhythm; the movement of the whole is ner-
vously fluent, as suits an extended poem so decora-

tively aloof from action and drama. It will be noticed here, as in the poem generally, that Shakespeare's lines tend to contain words, or groups of words, that balance upon some principle or other: very often, as in a line I have quoted ("The foul boar's conquest on her fair delight"), the balance involves antithesis. Line 104 above represents "balancing" at its most obvious, but in line 107 we have something subtler: a strong initial verb defers the seesaw effect, and the balanced words are inversely arranged as adjective-noun and noun-adjective. Line 108 then cleverly repeats the pattern with other grammatical elements.

Such talk is exceedingly dry, but it does bear upon the main and steadiest sources of pleasure in the poem–for us as for the artifice-loving Elizabethans: its elaborate inventiveness, its rhetorical dexterity, its technical *éclat*. There are numerous moments at which the poem creates a response to its subject, as in the beautiful stanza of the hands (361 ff.), but mostly one is reacting to an ostentatious poetic performance the artful variety of which I have scarcely begun to describe. Shakespeare has used an Ovidian story as the basis not for a narrative, dramatic, or philosophic poem, but of a concatenation of virtuoso descriptions, comparisons, apostrophes, essays, pleas, reproaches, digressions, laments, and what have you. The same is true of *Lucrece*, that "graver labor" which Shakespeare promised in his dedication of *Venus*, and which he published a year later, in 1594.

In this case the Ovidian source is the Fasti, and again Shakespeare was working with a story that English writers (among them Chaucer) had helped to make familiar. A prose "argument" and a first stanza that starts the action well along in the plot serve to curtail the narrative, and the 1,855-line poem will really tell or show us only this: the inner struggles of Tarquin as he approaches Lucrece's bed; his threatening proposal, and her pleas and refusals; her lamentations, once she has been dishonored; her revelation of Tarquin's guilt to Collatine and others; her suicide, and the banishment of the Tarquins. A large part of the poem consists of solitary lamentation by Lucrece, and it is undoubtedly true that Shakespeare was here creating a hybrid genre by combining a species of Ovidian narrative with the "complaint": it was probably from Daniel's *Complaint of Rosamond* (1593), in which the ghost of Henry II's unfortunate mistress asks our prayers and pity, that Shakespeare borrowed the stately seven-line stanza of *Lucrece*. At the same time, *Lucrece* greatly differs from *Rosamond*, the latter being a first-person account which offers neither scene nor dialogue until the poem is two-thirds done. Like *Venus*, *Lucrece* is narrated by the poet; it has access to the thoughts of its two principals, and consists in great part of rhetorical speeches which may at times suggest declamatory or Senecan drama, but seldom suggest that the poet has a future in the theater. Critics agree that among the few moments of dramatic potentiality are those in which Lucrece countermands her agitated orders to her maid (1289 ff.) and misunderstands the blushes of her groom (1338 ff.). One also feels that the reunion of Lucrece and her husband might be touching on the stage:

> Both stood, like old acquaintance in a trance,
> Met far from home, wond'ring each other's chance.
> (1595-96)

Action in *Lucrece* is smothered in poetry, as when

the concrete effect of Tarquin's lifted sword (505) is instantly blunted by a comparison; moreover, the action is given us in disjunct and unresolved tableaux. The sword is never lowered, and the hand remains indefinitely on the breast. Our mind's eye beholds not a cinematic continuity, but slides or tapestries which description may explore (as Lucrece explores her painting of Troy) or rhetoric at once forsake. Ideas are unimportant; the poet is not out to demonstrate the nature of chastity, or to confront the problem of evil in the world; his thought is conventional and can often be rendered by proverbs. Character in *Lucrece* is shallow, fixed, yet inconsistent, as in *Venus and Adonis*, and for the same reason: it is brilliance of the surface which has priority. Thus Tarquin is at first the "devil" to Lucrece's "saint" (85), but once alone and pondering he is provided with a better nature, so that he may be torn between conscience and lust; and this is done not for the sake of psychological revelation but for the provision of antithesis and rhetorical opportunity. Lucrece, when contemplating suicide, takes temporarily the Christian view of self-slaughter (1156 ff.) in order to divide herself for three stanzas. Divisions, vacillations, inward debates, anatomies of stimulus and response (426 ff.) and the psychic politics (288 ff.)–the poem is full of these things, and their main *raison d'être* is stylistic: they break down the characters and their thoughts into elements that can be balanced and elaborated.

The verse of *Lucrece* is even more obtrusively artificial than that of *Venus*, and its trickiness is somehow more difficult to like. Our first view of the heroine consists of a twenty-eight line description of the "war of lilies and of roses" in her complexion (50-

77), and its length and difficulty are exasperatingly disproportionate to the content. Perhaps the subject and initial tone of *Venus* made its extravagances–the egregious dimples of 241-48, for example–seem forgivably playful, while in a grave poem about rape and suicide such fiddling with red and white seems Neronian. There are, however, passages to admire, especially in the linked lamentations of Lucrece, which flow into each other with a smoothness worthy of Ovid. In contrast to Ovid and the Ovidians, Shakespeare makes little use, either in *Venus* or in Lucrece, of mythological reference, but when *Lucrece* invites Philomel to a duet (1128 ff.) a most obvious comparison of fates is made with the utmost freshness. And–to praise one passage more–Lucrece's contemplation of the painting of Troy is far more than a standard Elizabethan descriptive exercise, written to occupy the interval between the sending of the scroll and Collatine's return. It is, for one thing, full of explicit and implicit relationships between Troy and Lucrece's Rome. We are to liken Ardea's siege to Troy's; Helen in her "rape" resembles Lucrece, but in her infidelity contrasts with her; Paris, like Tarquin, is a king's son who puts his "private pleasure" before the public good; Sinon, like Tarquin, is a dissimulator, and the entry of the Greek horse into Troy is like Tarquin's ill-intentioned entry into Collatine's house. The description is also relevant to Tarquin's moral collapse, in its several contrasts between displays of passion (such as anger or cowardice) and examples of "government" or control. Finally, the passage dwells considerably on the clear depiction and ready perception of character or emotion in physiognomy, and so builds throughout toward Lucrece's bitter reflection that such a face as Tarquin's can yet "bear a wicked mind."

I have left myself scarcely any space in which to speak of that strange and masterly metaphysical poem "The Phoenix and the Turtle." Published in 1601, the poem is a celebration of ideal love between two people, its perfect lovers being presented as symbolic birds, the phoenix and the turtledove. Poets have often made *ad hoc* revisions of mythology or conventional symbolism, and Shakespeare has done so here: while the turtledove keeps its accepted meaning of Constancy, the phoenix is assigned the feminine gender and is made to stand not for Immortality, as would be traditional, but for Love. These initial attributions, however, are in no way limiting, for since the two birds accomplish a total fusion of their natures, they have at last the one joint meaning of pure and imperishable love. The poem is undoubtedly indebted to other literary bird-assembles, such as Chaucer's *Parliament of Fowls*, but given the chaste and world-forsaking character of the love whereby they are translated "In a mutual flame from hence," I think that the lovers must owe something of their wingedness to the *Phaedrus*. There Plato describes the highest love as an absolute spiritual union through which the lovers' souls recover their lost wings, and "when the end comes . . . are light and winged for flight."

The first part of the poem, in which the phoenix and turtle go unmentioned, is a summons to the celebrants and worthy witnesses of their funeral rite. The second part, which begins at the sixth stanza, is an anthem of praise in which those assembled "chaste wings" approach the transcendent truth of ideal love by demonstrating the powerlessness of reason to describe it: that two souls should be one is an idea that defeats mathematics and logic, and forces language into violent paradox. The collective reason of the mourners, convinced by self-defeat that "Love hath reason, reason none," proceeds then to compose a "threne" or dirge which is the poem's third movement. In it, reason affirms that the lovers have embodied a truth which lies beyond reason, and which with their death is lost to the world; at the same time, in response to the spirit of renewal which concludes all obsequies, and to the phoenix's association with the idea of rebirth, the "true or fair" are quietly made heirs of the lovers' example.

The language of this poem is intellectually strict and dry; the rhythm is abrupt and rugged in the tetrameter quatrains, like that of a nursery rhyme, and just a shade more serene in the triplets of the *Threnos*. The product of this precise abstract language and these spirited trochaic lines is, for one reader at least, an impression of complete vitality. We need not ask, in this poem, what and how much is meant by predatory birds or by burning eyes; the meanings are strong and ultimately plain. The Platonic conception of love, which in *Venus and Adonis* was inchoate and momentary, is here sharply realized, and the gift of paradox, which in *Venus* and *Lucrece* was exercised for its own sake, here serves a theme that cannot be expressed without it.

*In spring of 1966 there was a symposium of the
arts at the College of Wooster, in Wooster, Ohio.
My assigned topic was something like "Poetry and
the Pursuit of Significance," but I misheard it as
given on the telephone, and so wrote as follows,
scribbling in the first paragraph at the last minute.*

POETRY AND HAPPINESS

Frankly, the word "significance" gives me a chill,
and so the title of these remarks is not "Poetry and
Significance," but "Poetry and Happiness." I do fer-
vently hope, however, that happiness will turn out
to be significant.

I am not perfectly certain what our forefathers understood by "the pursuit of happiness." Of the
friends whom I have asked for an opinion, the ma-
jority have taken that phrase to mean the pursuit of
self-realization, or of a full humane life. Some darker-
minded people have translated "happiness" as material well-being, or as the freedom to do as you damn
please. I cannot adjudicate the matter, but even if
the darker-minded people are right, we are entitled
to ennoble the phrase and adapt it to the present
purpose. I am going to say a few things about the
ways in which poetry might be seen as pursuing
happiness.

There are, as I. A. Richards has said, two main ways
of understanding the word "poetry." We may think
of poetry as a self-shaping activity of the whole society, a collective activity by means of which a society
creates a vision of itself, arranges its values, or adopts
or adapts a culture. It is this sense of "poetry" that
we have in Wallace Stevens's poem "Men Made Out
of Words," where he says

119

The whole race is a poet that writes down
The eccentric propositions of its fate.

But "poetry" may also mean what we more usually mean by it; it may mean versus written by poets, imaginative compositions that employ a condensed, rhythmic, resonant, and persuasive language. This second kind of poetry is not unconnected
with the first; a poem written by a poet is a specific,
expert, and tributary form of the general imaginative activity. Nevertheless, I should like to begin by
considering poetry in the second and restricted sense
only, as referring to verse productions written by individuals whose pleasure it is to write them.

Back in the days of white saddle shoes and the
gentleman's grade of C, college undergraduates often found that they had an afternoon to kill. I can
remember killing part of one afternoon, with a literary roommate, in composing what we called "A
Complete List of Everything." We thought of ourselves, I suppose, as continuators of Dada, and our
list, as we set it down on the typewriter, amounted
to an intentionally crazy and disrelated sequence of
nouns. A section of our list might have read like this:
beauty, carburetor, sheepshank, pagoda, absence,
chalk, vector, Amarillo, garters, dromedary, Tartarus,
tupelo, omelet, caboose, ferrocyanide, and so on. As
you can imagine, we did not complete our list; we
got tired of it. As in random compositions of all
kinds–musical, pictorial, or verbal–it was possible
to sustain interest for only so long, in the absence of
deliberate human meaning. Nevertheless, there had
been a genuine impulse underlying our afternoon's
diversion, and I think that it stemmed from a primitive desire that is radical to poetry–the desire to lay

claim to as much of the world as possible through uttering the names of things.

This fundamental urge turns up in all reaches of literature, heavy or light. We have it, for example, in the eighteenth chapter of Hugh Lofting's *Story of Doctor Dolittle*, a chapter in which all children take particular joy. As you will remember, Doctor Dolittle and his animal friends, on their way back from Africa, come by chance into possession of a pirate ship, and find aboard her a little boy who has become separated from his red-haired, snuff-taking uncle. The Doctor promises to find the little boy's lost uncle, wherever he may be, and Jip the dog goes to the bow of the ship to see if he can smell any snuff on the North wind. Jip, it should be said, is a talking dog, and here is what he mutters to himself as he savors the air:

> Tar; spanish onions; kerosene oil,
> wet raincoats; crushed laurel-
> leaves; rubber burning; lace-
> curtains being washed–No, my
> mistake, lace-curtains hanging out
> to dry; and foxes–hundreds of
> 'em. . . .

These are the easy smells, Jip says; the strong ones. When he closes his eyes and concentrates on the more delicate odors which the wind is bringing, he has this to report:

> Bricks,–old yellow bricks, crum-
> bling with age in a garden-wall;
> the sweet breath of young cows
> standing in a mountain-stream; the
> lead roof of a dove-cote–or perhaps

a granary–with the mid-day sun on
it; black kid gloves lying in a
bureau-drawer of walnut-wood; a
dusty road with a horses' drinking-
trough beneath the sycamores;
little mushrooms bursting through
the rotting leaves. . . .

A catalogue of that sort pleases us in a number of
ways. In the first place, it stimulates that dim and
nostalgic thing the olfactory memory, and provokes
us to recall the ghosts of various stinks and fra-
grances. In the second place, such a catalogue makes
us feel vicariously alert; we participate in the extraordinary responsiveness of Doctor Dolittle's dog, and
so feel the more alive to things. In the third place,
we exult in Jip's power of instant designation, his
ability to pin things down with names as fast as they
come. The effect of the passage, in short, is to let us
share in an articulate relishing and mastery of phenomena in general.

That is what the cataloguing impulse almost always expresses–a longing to possess the whole
world, and to praise it, or at least to feel it. We see
this most plainly and perfectly in the Latin canticle
Benedicite, Omnia Opera Domini. The first verses of
that familiar canticle are:

O all ye Works of the Lord, bless ye the Lord: praise him,
and magnify him for ever.
O ye Angels of the Lord, bless ye the Lord: praise him,
and magnify him for ever.
O ye Heavens, bless ye the Lord: praise him and magnify
him for ever.
O ye Waters that be above the firmament, bless ye the Lord:
praise him and magnify him forever.

I need not go on to the close, because I am sure that you all know the logic of what follows. All the works of the Lord are called upon in turn–the sun, moon, and stars, the winds and several weathers of the sky, the creatures of earth and sea, and lastly mankind. There is nothing left out. The canticle may not speak of crushed laurel leaves and sycamores, but it does say more comprehensively, "O all ye Green Things upon the Earth, bless ye the Lord"; it may not speak of foxes and of young cows in a mountain stream, but it does say, "O all ye Beasts and Cattle, bless ye the Lord." What we have in the *Benedicite* is an exhaustive poetic progress from heaven, down through the spheres of the old cosmology, to earth and man at the center of things–a progress during which the whole hierarchy of creatures is cited in terms that, though general, do not seem abstract. It is a poem or song in which heaven and earth are surrounded and captured by words, and embraced by joyous feeling.

It is interesting to compare the strategy of the *Benedicite* to that of another and more personal poem of catalogue and praise, Gerard Manley Hopkins's "curtal sonnet" "Pied Beauty."

> Glory be to God for dappled things–
>   For skies of couple-colour as a brindled cow;
>   For rose-moles all in stipple upon trout that swim;
> Fresh-firecoal chestnut-falls; finches' wings;
>   Landscape plotted and pierced–fold, fallow, and plough;
>   And áll trádes, their gear and tackle and trim.
> All things counter, original, spare, strange;
>   Whatever is fickle, freckled (who knows how?)
>   With swift, slow; sweet, sour; adazzle, dim;
> He fathers-forth whose beauty is past change:

Praise him.

As in the old canticle, God is praised first and last; but what lies between is very different. Hopkins does not give us an inventory of the creation; rather, he sets out to celebrate one kind of beauty–pied beauty, the beauty of things that are patchy, particolored, variegated. And in his tally of variegated things there is no hierarchy or other logic: his mind jumps, seemingly at random, from sky to trout to chestnuts to finches, and finally, by way of landscape, to the gear and tackle of the various trades. The poem sets out, then, to give scattered examples of a single class of things; and yet in its final effect this is a poem of universal praise. Why does it work out that way?

It works that way, for one thing, because of the randomness which I have just pointed out; when a catalogue has a random air, when it seems to have been assembled by chance, it implies a vast reservoir of other things that might just as well have been mentioned. In the second place, Hopkins's poem may begin with dappled things, but when we come to "gear and tackle and trim," the idea of variegation is far less clear, and seems to be yielding to that of character. When, in the next line, Hopkins thanks God for "All things counter, original, spare, strange," we feel the poem opening out toward the celebration of the rich and quirky particularity of all things whatever.

The great tug-of-war in Hopkins's poetry is between his joy in the intense selfhood and whatness of earthly things, and his feeling that all delights must be referred and sacrificed to God. For Whitman, with whom Hopkins felt an uncomfortable affinity, there was no such tension. It is true that Whitman said, "I hear and behold God in every object," yet the locus of divinity in his poetry is not heaven but the mystic soul of the poet, which names all things, draws all things to unity in itself, and hallows all things without distinction. The divinely indiscriminate cataloguing consciousness of Whitman's poems can consume phenomena in any order and with any emphasis; it acknowledges no protocol; it operates, as Richard Lewis has said, "in a world . . . devoid of rank or hierarchy." In Section V of the "Song of Myself," Whitman describes an experience of mystic illumination, and then gives us these eight remarkable lines:

> Swiftly arose and spread around me the peace and
>   knowledge that pass all the argument of the earth,
> And I know that the hand of God is the promise of my
>   own,
> And I know that the spirit of God is the brother of my own,
> And that all the men ever born are also my brothers, and
>   the women my sisters and lovers,
> And that a kelson of the creation is love,
> And limitless are leaves stiff or drooping in the
>   fields,
> And brown ants in the little wells beneath them,
> And mossy scabs of the worm fence, heap'd stones, elder,
>   mullein and pokeweed.

That passage happens to proceed from God to man to nature, but there is nothing hierarchical in its spirit. Quite the contrary. This is the Whitman who said, "I do not call one greater and one smaller. . . . The Insignificant is as big to me as any." He speaks in the same rapt voice of men and women and moss and pokeweed, and it is clear that he might have spoken to the same purpose of ducks or pebbles or angels.

125

For Whitman, as for the Zen Buddhist, one thing is as good as another, a mouse is sufficient "to stagger sextillions of infidels," and any part, however small, includes by synecdoche the wonder of the whole.

I could go on to speak of still more list-making poets. I could quote the Rilke of the *Duino Elegies*, who asks

> Are we perhaps here merely to say, House, Bridge, Fountain, Gate, Jug, Fruit-tree, Window,
> Or Column, or Tower . . .

In our own immediate day there would be David Jones, Theodore Roethke, and Ruthven Todd in their later work; and indeed, there have been poets in all lands and ages who have sought to resume the universe in ordered categories, or to suggest its totality by the casual piling up of particulars.

But I have given enough examples already, and my aim here is not to make a catalogue of poetic catalogues, but to suggest by a few illustrations that the itch to call the roll of things is a major motive in the writing of poetry. Whether or not he composes actual catalogues like Whitman or Hopkins, every poet is driven by a compulsion to designate, and in respect of that drive the poet is not unlike people in general. We all want to be told, for no immediate practical reason, whether a certain column is Ionic or Corinthian, whether that cloud is stratus or cumulus, and what the Spanish word for "grocer" is. If we forget the name of a supporting actor in some film, or the roster of our Supreme Court bench, we are vexed and distracted until we remember, or look it up in some book of reference. If we travel to the tropics for the first time, and find ourselves surrounded not with oaks and maples but with a bristling wall of nameless flora, we hasten to arm ourselves with nature books and regain our control over the landscape.

The poet is like that, only more so. He is born, it appears, with a stronger-than-usual need for verbal adequacy, and so he is always mustering and reviewing his vocabulary, and forearming himself with terms he may need in the future. I recall the excitement of a poet friend when he discovered in a mushroom guide the word "duff," which signifies "decaying vegetable matter on the forest floor."

He was right to be excited, I think. Duff is a short, precise word which somehow sounds like what it means, and it is a word that poets must often have groped after in vain. My own recent discovery of that kind is the term for the depression in the center of one's upper lip. It had annoyed me, on and off, for many years that I had no word for something that was literally under my nose; and then at long last I had the sense to enquire of a dentist. He told me that the word is "philtrum," deriving from the Greek word for "love-potion," and implying, I should think, that the upper lip is an erogenous zone.

That sort of word-hunting and word-cherishing may sound frivolous to some, and it must be admitted that the poet's fascination with words can degenerate into fetishism and the pursuit of the exotic. More often, however, such researches are the necessary, playful groundwork for that serious business of naming which I have been discussing. Not all poets, especially in the present age, can articulate the universe with a *Benedicite*, or possess it by haphazard mysticism, but every poet is impelled to utter the whole of that world which is real to him, to respond to that world in some spirit, and to draw all its parts toward some coherence. The job is an endless one, because there are always aspects of life that we acknowledge to be real, but have not yet truly accepted.

For an obvious example, one has only to think of those machines which science has bestowed on us, and which Hart Crane said it was the great task of modern poetry to absorb. The iron horse has been with us for a century and a half, and the horseless carriage for eighty-odd years, but it is only in recent decades that "train" and "car" have consorted easily, in our verse, with "hill" and "ship" and "hawk" and "wagon" and "flower." And indeed there are still readers who think it unpoetic to bring a pickup truck into the landscape of a poem. The airplane has the aesthetic and moral advantage of resembling a bird and of seeming to aspire, but it took some hard writing in the thirties to install such words as "pylon" and "airfield" in the lexicon of modern verse. And for all our hard writing since, we have still not arrived at the point where, in Hart Crane's words, machinery can form "as spontaneous a terminology of poetic reference as the bucolic world of pasture, plow, and barn."

The urge of poetry is not, of course, to whoop it up for the automobile, the plane, the computer, and the space-ship, but only to bring them and their like into the felt world, where they may be variously taken, and to establish their names in the vocabulary of imagination. One perpetual task of the poet is to produce models of inclusive reaction and to let no word or thing be blackballed by sensibility. That is why I took a large pleasure, some years ago, in bringing off a line that convincingly employed the words "reinforced concrete." And that is why William Carlos Williams, with his insistence on noting and naming the bitterest details of the American urban scene, was such a hero of the modern spirit; he would not wear blinders in Rutherford and Paterson, but instead wrote beautifully of peeling billboards, wind-blown paper bags, and broken bottles in the gravel, claiming for poetry a territory that is part of our reality, and needs to be seen and said. For poetry, there is no such thing as no man's land.

The drive to get everything said is not merely a matter of acknowledging and absorbing the physical environment. The poet is also moved to designate human life in all its fullness, and it may be argued, for an extreme example, that the best of Henry Miller arises from a pure poetic compulsion to refer to certain realities by their real names. Mr. Miller's best is not very good, actually, and Aretino did it far better some centuries back; but there are passages in the *Tropics* that are clearly attempting, by means of an exuberant lyricism, to prove that the basic four-letter words are capable of augmenting our literary language without blowing it to pieces. I expressed this view not long ago, when testifying for Mr. Miller at an obscenity trial, and the judge replied only with a slow, sad shaking of the head. But I remain unshaken. I do not think that Mr. Miller succeeds very often in his aim, partly because the words he champions are what the theater calls bad ensemble players. But as for his aim, I recognize it as genuine and would call it essentially poetic.

Thus far I have been speaking of poetry as an inventory of external reality; now let me speak of poetry as discovery and projection of the self. The notion that art is self-expression, the expression of one's uniqueness, has provoked and excused a great deal of bad, solipsistic work in this century; nevertheless, the work of every good poet may be seen in one way or another as an exploration and declaration of the self.

In Emily Dickinson, for instance, we have a poet whose most electrifying work is the result of keen and dogged self-scrutiny. Having spied for a long time on her own psyche, she can report that "Wonder is not precisely knowing,/And not precisely knowing not." Or she can produce a little poem like this, about how anguish engrosses the sense of time:

> Pain has an element of blank;
> It cannot recollect
> When it began, or if there were
> A day when it was not.
> It has no future but itself,
> Its infinite realms contain
> Its past, enlightened to perceive
> New periods of pain.

Those lines are a pure trophy of introspection; they are not the rephrasing of something known, but the articulation of one person's intense inward observation. Yet because they are so articulate and so true, they light up both the poet's psychology and everyone else's.

Another version of self-discovery is implied in Edwin Muir's statement that "the task of a poet is to make his imaginative world clear to himself." What Muir meant was that every poet, owing to his character and early life, has a predisposition to project his sense of things by telling this or that story, by using this or that image or symbol. It may take a poet years to stumble on his destined story or symbol and set it forth, but for Muir they are always vaguely and archetypally there, at the back of the poet's mind.

When we say of a poet that he has found his subject, or found his voice, we are likely to be thinking about poetry in Muir's way, as a long struggle to objectify the soul. Marianne Moore sketching her first emblematic animal, Vachel Lindsay first attempting to catch the camp-meeting cadence, Frost first perceiving the symbolic possibilities of a stone wall–at such moments the poet is suddenly in possession of the formula of his feelings, the means of knowing himself and of making that self known. It was at such a moment that Rilke wrote in a letter, "I am a stamp which is about to make its impression."

As I have said, these moments of self-possession can be a long time in coming. Looking back at his early poems, and finding them cloudy and abortive, Yeats sadly wrote in his *Autobiography*, "It is so many years before one can believe enough in what one feels even to know what the feeling is." It was late in his life that a Scots poet whom I knew, while buckling his belt one morning, heard himself saying the Lord's Prayer, and concluded that he must be a Christian after all. Or to speak of a deconversion, there were eight years of silence between the clangorous, prophetic early books of Robert Lowell and the publication of *Life Studies*, in which a flexible, worldly voice suddenly speaks, with a whole personality behind it. What had happened to Lowell was, in Yeats's phrase, a "withering into the truth," and some such process must occur, I think, in the life of every poet.

It is Yeats above all, in the present age, who has preached and embodied the notion that poetry is self-projection; that the poet creates his world "lock, stock and barrel out of his bitter soul." "Revelation is from the self," he said; and though his way of putting it altered, he never ceased to think as he had done in 1893, when he wrote in his book *The Celtic Twilight,*

> What is literature but the expression of moods by the vehicle of symbol and incident? And are there not moods which need heaven, hell, purgatory and faeryland for their expression, no less than this dilapidated earth?

What's fundamental in poetry, according to that definition, is moods–that is, the poet's repertory of emotions, his spectrum of attitudes. All else is instrumental; persons, things, actions, and ideas are only means to externalizing the states of the poet's heart. Before Yeats was through, he had constructed a visionary system full of cycles and interpenetrating gyres which embraced all possible experience, all human types, all ages of man, all ages of history, this world and the next. It was a vision as inclusive as that of the *Benedicite,* but whereas the latter was for its poet an objective poem, Yeats's vision is all a deliberate ramification of his subjective life. The phases of the moon, the gong-tormented sea, the peacock's cry, hunchback and saint, Cuchulain–the ground of their reality is the various and conflicting spirit of the poet. When the young Yeats says

> Before us lies eternity; our souls
> Are love, and a continual farewell,

and when he later proclaims that "men dance on deathless feet," he is not expounding the doctrine of reincarnation, but exploiting that idea as a means of expressing his own heart's insatiable desire for life. The spirits who brought Yeats the substance of his system did not bring him an epitome of external truth; rather, they said, "We have come to give you metaphors for poetry." And when Yeats felt that certain of his expressive fictions were exhausted, he turned for a new start not to the world but to what he called, in a famous line, "the foul rag and bone shop of the heart."

I have said something now about two impulses of poetry–the impulse to name the world, and the impulse to clarify and embody the self. All poets are moved by both, but every poet inclines more to one than to the other, and a way of measuring any poet's inclination is to search his lines for moments of descriptive power. Description is, of course, an elaborate and enchanted form of naming, and among the great describers of the modern period are Hopkins, and Williams, and Lawrence in his animal poems, and Marianne Moore, who once described a butterfly as "bobbing away like wreckage on the sea." And then there is that thunderstorm in a poem of Elizabeth Bishop's, which moves away, as she tells it,

> in a series
> Of small, badly-lit battle scenes,
> Each in "Another part of the
> field."

Or there is the beautifully realized little sandpiper, in her latest book, who runs "in a state of controlled panic" along a beach which "hisses like fat."

Now, Yeats had his sea birds, too, and in his youthful novel *John Sherman* there were some puffins very accurately observed; but soon he became concerned, as he said, with "passions that had nothing to do with observation," and the many birds of his subsequent work are a symbolic aviary of no descriptive interest. Yeats rarely gives us any pictorial pleasure, in birds or in anything else, being little concerned in his naming of things to possess them in their otherness and actuality. Nevertheless, he, like all poets, is a namer; and Miss Bishop, for all her descriptive genius, is like all other poets a scholar of the heart. It is a matter of proportion only, a matter of one's imaginative balance.

And having said the word "balance," I want to offer a last quotation from Yeats, which speaks directly to the question of art and happiness. In a letter to Dorothy Wellesley, written sometime in the thirties, Yeats said,

> We are happy when for everything inside us there is a corresponding something outside us.

That is an observation about life in general, but above all it applies to poetry. We are happy as poets, Yeats says, when our thoughts and feelings have originals or counterparts in the world around us—when there is a perfect conversancy or congruence between self and world. In Yeats's poetry, the chief symbol for such happiness is the marriage bed, and his artful lovers Solomon and Sheba, each striving to incarnate the other's dream, represent the mutual attunement of imagination and reality. Keats's lovers Madeline and Prophyro, in "The Eve of St. Agnes," accomplish the same miracle and symbolize the same thing; each, without loss of reality, becomes the other's vision, and the poem is one solution to Keats's continuing enquiry into the right balance between vision and everyday experience. Elsewhere he employs or espouses other formulae, as in the poem "To Autumn," where imagination does not transmute and salvage the world, but, rather, accepts it in all its transient richness, and celebrates it as it is.

There is a similar quality of acceptance in Robert Frost's poems about imaginative happiness. Here is one called "Hyla Brook."

> By June our brook's run out of song and speed.
> Sought for much after that, it will be found
> Either to have gone groping underground
> (And taken with it all the Hyla breed
> That shouted in the mist a month ago,
> Like ghost of sleigh-bells in a ghost of snow)–
> Or flourished and come up in jewelweed,
> Weak foliage that is blown upon and bent
> Even against the way its waters went.
> Its bed is left a faded paper sheet
> Of dead leaves stuck together by the heat–
> A brook to none but who remember long.
> This as it will be seen is other far
> Than with brooks taken otherwise in song.
> We love the things we love for what they are.

It does not trouble him, Frost says, that the brook on his farm runs dry by June, and becomes a gulley full of dead leaves and jewelweed; it may not be Arethusa or smooth-sliding Mincius; it may not, like Tennyson's brook, go on forever; but it has real and memorable beauties that meet his desire. Loving it for what it is, the poet does not try to elevate his subject, or metamorphose it, or turn it into pure symbol; it is sufficient that his words be lovingly adequate to the plain truth. In another and comparable poem, called "Mowing," Frost builds toward a similar moral: "The fact is the sweetest dream that labor knows." One does not think of Wallace Stevens, who so stressed the transforming power of imagination, as having much in common with Frost, and yet Stevens would agree that the best and happiest dreams of the poet are those that involve no denial of the fact. In his poem "Crude Foyer," Stevens acknowledges that poets are tempted to turn inward and conceive an interior paradise; but that is a false happiness; we can only, he says, be "content,/At last, there, when it turns out to be here." We cannot be content, we cannot enjoy poetic happiness, until the inner paradise is brought to terms with the world before us, and our vision fuses with the view from the window.

Regardless, then, of subjective bias or of a reverence for fact, poets of all kinds agree that it is the pleasure of the healthy imagination to achieve what Stevens called "ecstatic identities with the weather." When the sensibility is sufficient to the expression of the world, and when the world, in turn, is answerable to the poet's mind and heart, then the poet is happy, and can make his reader so.

Now, if I were satisfied with my use of the word "world," which I have been saying over and over in an almost liturgical fashion, I might feel that I had come near to the end of my argument. But world, in contemporary usage, is a particularly sneaky and ambiguous term. I see that I must try to use it more precisely, and that once I have done so there will be more to say. What might I mean by world? I might mean what Milton meant when he spoke of "this pendant world"; that is, I might mean the universe. Or I might mean the planet Earth; or I might mean the human societies of Earth, taken together. Or if I defined world by reference to the soul or self, I might mean what a German philosopher called the "Non-Ego," or what Andrew Wyeth meant when he called one of his paintings "Christina's World." I am sure that you have all seen that touching painting of Wyeth's: it shows us a crippled girl sitting in a field of long grass, and looking off toward a house and barn; her "world" consists of what she can see, and the desolate mood in which she sees it.

Literary critics, nowadays, make continual use of the word "world" in this last sense. They write of Dylan Thomas's world of natural process, Conrad Aiken's world of psychic flux, John Ransom's gallant and ironic world of the South, or the boyish, amorous, and springtime world of E. E. Cummings. Any of us could assign a "world," in this sense, to any poet whose work we know; and in doing so, we would not necessarily be blaming him for any narrowness of scope. Robinson Jeffers on his mountaintop by the Pacific, writing forever of hawks and rocks and of the violent beauty of nature, was not prevented from speaking, through his own symbols and from his own vantage, of God and history and cities and the passions of men and women. Like any good poet of this American century, he found images and symbols that could manifest the moods of his heart, and elected a world of his own through which the greater world could someway be seen and accounted for.

And yet if one thinks back to the Italian fourteenth century, if one thinks of the "world" of Dante's imagination, how peripheral and cranky Jeffers seems! Dante's poetry is the work of one man, who even at this distance remains intensely individual in temper and in style; and yet the world of his great poem was, for his first readers, quite simply the world. This was possible because he was a poet of genius writing from the heart of a full and living culture. He lived and wrote, in Steven's phrase, "at the center of a diamond."

I bring up Dante not merely to belabor the present with him, but because there is something that needs to be explained. We are talking of poetry as a mode of pursuing happiness; we live in a century during which America has possessed many poets of great ability; nevertheless, it is no secret that the personal histories of our poets, particularly in the last thirty years, are full of alcoholism, aberration, emotional breakdowns, the drying up of talent, and suicide. There is no need to learn this from gossip or biography; it is plainly enough set down in the poetry of our day. And it seems to me that the key to all this unhappiness may lie in the obligatory eccentricity, nowadays, of each poet's world, in the fact that our society has no sufficient cultural heart from which to write.

Alberto Moravia, in a recent article on a great American writer and suicide, Ernest Hemingway, describes our country as "a minor, degraded and anti-humanistic culture," and observes that our typical beginning novelist, lacking any faith in the resources of culture, "confines himself to recounting the story of his youth." Having done so once successfully, the novelist proceeds, for lack of any other subject, to do it again and again, and, as Moravia puts it, "mirrors increasingly, in the mechanization of his own work, the mechanization of the society for which he is writing." I am sorry to say that I cannot brush aside Signor Moravia's general judgment

138

upon us. I wish that I could.

One can protest that not all of our novelists are the prisoners of their own early lives, and that most of our poets are cultured in the sense of being well schooled in the literary and artistic tradition. But one cannot deny that in the full sense of the word "culture"–the sense that has to do with the humane unity of a whole people–our nation is impoverished. We are not an articulate organism, and what most characterizes our life is a disjunction and incoherence aggravated by an intolerable rate of change. It is easy to prophesy against us. Our center of political power, Washington, is a literary and intellectual vacuum, or nearly so; the church, in our country, is broken into hundreds of sorry and provincial sects; colleges of Christian foundation hold classes as usual on Good Friday; our cities bristle like quartz clusters with faceless new buildings of aluminum and glass, bare of symbolic ornament because they have nothing to say; our painters and sculptors despair of achieving any human significance, and descend into the world of fashion to market their Coke bottles and optical toys; in the name of the public interest, highways are rammed through old townships and wildlife sanctuaries; all other public expenditure is begrudged, while the bulk of the people withdraw from community into an affluent privacy.

I could go on with such sweeping assertions, and soon, no doubt, would go too far, and would have to admit that anarchy is not confined to America, and that here or there we have the promise of cultural coherence. But I would reluct at making too much of the present boom in education, or the growth of regional theaters and symphony orchestras. Such things may be good in themselves, but they are not the kind of culture I am talking about. Houston has an admirable symphony orchestra, but the nexus of human relations in that city is the credit card, and where art does not arise from and nourish a vital sense of community, it is little more than an incitement to schizophrenia.

The main fact about the American artist, as a good poet said to me the other day, is his feeling of isolation. To Dante, at the other extreme, the world appeared as one vast society, or as a number of intelligibly related societies, actual and spiritual; his *Commedia* was the embodiment and criticism of a comprehensive notion of things that he shared with his age. Or think, if you will, of the sure sense of social relevance with which Milton embarked on the writing of an epic poem which was to be "exemplary to a nation." Or think of that certainty of the moral consensus that lies behind the satires of Alexander Pope, and makes possible a wealth of assured nuance. How often, I wonder, has any American poet spoken so confidently from within the culture?

I began by distinguishing two ways of understanding the word "poetry": first, as verse compositions written by individuals, and second, as ensemble of articulate values by means of which a society shapes and affirms itself. It is the natural business of the first kind of poetry to contribute to the second, clarifying, enriching, and refreshing it; and where the poet is unable to realize himself as the spokesman and loyal critic of an adequate culture, I think that his art and life are in some measure deprived of satisfaction and meaning.

To be sure, every poet is a citizen of the Republic of Letters, that imaginary society whose members come from every age and literature, and it is part of his happiness to converse, as it were, with the whole of tradition; but it is also his desire to put his gift at the service of the people of his own time and place. And that, as I have been saying, is a happiness not easily come by in contemporary America. It is possible, however isolated one may feel, to write out of one's private experiences of nature or God or love; but one's poetry will reflect, in one way or another, the frustration of one's desire to participate in a corporate myth. In some of our poets, the atomism of American life has led to a poetry without people, or an art of nostalgia for childhood. Elsewhere, we find a confessional poetry in which the disorder and distress of the poet's life mirrors that cultural disunity to which he, because of his calling, is peculiarly sensitive. When the poet addresses himself directly to our society, these days, it is commonly in a spirit of reproach or even secession, and seldom indeed in a spirit of celebration. I do not hold the poet responsible for that fact.

At the close of one of his eloquent poems, Archibald MacLeish exhorts the modern poet to "Invent the age! Invent the metaphor!" But it is simply not the business of poets to invent ages, and to fashion cultures singlehanded. It may be that Yeats's Ireland was in good part Yeats's own invention, and he may have made some of it stick; but America is too huge a muddle to be arbitrarily envisioned. The two modern poets who tried to put a high-sounding interpretation on our country–Lindsay, whose Michigan Avenue was a street in heaven, and Crane, whose Brooklyn Bridge leapt toward our spiritual destiny–ended by taking their own lives.

Now, all I wanted to say was that the poet hankers to write in and for a culture, countering its centrifugal development by continually fabricating a common and inclusive language in which all things are connected. But I got carried away by the present difficulty of attaining that happy utility.

Of course I have overstated the matter, and of course there are fortunate exceptions to be pointed out. Robert Frost was strongly aware of the danger that accelerating change might sweep our country bare of all custom and traditional continuity; some of his best poems, like "The Mountain," are about that threat, and it is significant that he defined the poem as "a momentary stay against confusion." Frost staved off confusion by taking his stand inside a New England rural culture which, during the height of his career, still possessed a certain vitality, and remains intelligible (if less vital) today. In general I should say that Frost assumed, rather than expounded, the governing ideas and ideals of that culture; but that, after all, is the way of poetry with ideas. It does not think them up; it does not argue them abstractly; what it does is to realize them within that model of felt experience which is a poem, and so reveal their emotional resonance and their capacity for convincing embodiments.

I was looking the other day at what is doubtless the best-loved American poem of this century, Robert Frost's "Birches," and it occurred to me that it might be both pertinent and a little unexpected if I finished by quoting it and saying one or two things about it.

> When I see birches bend to left and right
> Across the lines of straighter darker trees,
> I like to think some boy's been swinging them.
> But swinging doesn't bend them down to stay

As ice storms do. Often you must have seen them
Loaded with ice a sunny winter morning
After a rain. They click upon themselves
As the breeze rises, and turn many-colored
As the stir cracks and crazes their enamel.
Soon the sun's warmth makes them shed crystal shells
Shattering and avalanching on the snow crust–
Such heaps of broken glass to sweep away
You'd think the inner dome of heaven had fallen.
They are dragged to the withered bracken by the load,
And they seem not to break; though once they are bowed
So low for long, they never right themselves:
You may see their trunks arching in the woods
Years afterwards, trailing their leaves on the ground
Like girls on hands and knees that throw their hair
Before them over their heads to dry in the sun.
But I was going to say when Truth broke in
With all her matter of fact about the ice storm,
I should prefer to have some boy bend them
As he went out and in to fetch the cows–
Some boy too far from town to learn baseball,
Whose only play was what he found himself,
Summer or winter, and could play alone.
One by one he subdued his father's trees
By riding them down over and over again
Until he took the stiffness out of them,
And not one but hung limp, not one was left
For him to conquer. He learned all there was
To learn about not launching out too soon
And so not carrying the tree away
Clear to the ground. He always kept his poise
To the top branches, climbing carefully
With the same pains you use to fill a cup
Up to the brim, and even above the brim.
Then he flung outward, feet first, with a swish,
Kicking his way down through the air to the ground.
So was I once myself a swinger of birches.
And so I dream of going back to be.

It's when I'm weary of considerations,
And life is too much like a pathless wood
Where your face burns and tickles with the cobwebs
Broken across it, and one eye is weeping
From a twig's having lashed across it open.
I'd like to get away from earth awhile.
And then come back to it and begin over.
May no fate willfully misunderstand me
And half grant what I wish and snatch me away
Not to return. Earth's the right place for love:
I don't know where it's likely to go better.
I'd like to go by climbing a birch tree,
And climb black branches up a snow-white trunk
Toward heaven, till the tree could bear no more,
But dipped its top and set me down again.
That would be good both going and coming back.
One could do worse than be a swinger of birches.

To begin with, this poem comes out of the farm and woodland country of northern New England, and everything in it is named in the right language. Moreover, there are moments of brilliant physical realization, as when the breeze "cracks and crazes" the "enamel" of ice-laden birches, or the birch-swinging boy flings out and falls in a perfect kinetic line, "Kicking his way down through the air to the ground." The poem presents a vivid regional milieu, and then subtly expands its range; naturally, and almost insensibly, the ground and sky of New England are magnified into Heaven and Earth.

Considered as self-projection, "Birches" is an example of how the pentameter can be so counterpointed as to force the reader to hear a sectional and personal accent. Frost's talking voice is in the poem, and so, too, is his manner: the drift of the argument is ostensibly casual or even whimsical, but

144

behind the apparent rambling is a strict intelligence; the language lifts into rhetoric or a diffident lyricism, but promptly returns to the colloquial, sometimes by way of humor. The humor of Frost's poem is part of its meaning, because humor arises from a sense of human limitations, and that is what Frost is talking about. His poem is a recommendation of limited aspiration, or high-minded earthliness, and the birch incarnates the idea perfectly, being a tree that lets you climb a while toward heaven but then "dips its top and sets you down again." This is a case in which thought and thing, inside and outside, self and world, admirably correspond.

Because of his colloquialism and his rustic settings, Frost has often been thought of as a nonliterary poet. That is a serious error. Frost was lovingly acquainted with poetic literature all the way back to Theocritus, and he was a conscious continuator and modifier of the tradition. Formally, he adapted the traditional meters and conventions to the natural cadence and tenor of New England speech. Then as for content, while he did not echo the poetry of the past so promiscuously as T. S. Eliot, he was always aware of what else had been written on any subject, and often implied as much. In "Hyla Brook," Frost makes a parenthetical acknowledgment that other poets–Tennyson, Milton, Theocritus perhaps–have dealt more flatteringly with brooks or streams than he feels the need to do.

In "Birches," Frost's reference is more specific, and I am going to reread a few lines now, in which I ask you to listen for the voice of Shelley:

> Often you must have seen them
> Loaded with ice a sunny winter morning
> After a rain. They click uponthemselves

As the breeze rises, and turn many-colored
As the stirs cracks and crazes their enamel.
Soon the sun's warmth makes them shed crystal shells
Shattering and avalanching on the snow crust–
Such heaps of broken glass to sweep away
You'd think the inner dome of heaven had fallen.

"Many-colored." "Glass." "The inner dome of heaven." It would not have been possible for Frost to pack so many echoes of Shelly into six lines and not be aware of it. He is slyly recalling the two most celebrated lines of Shelley's "Adonais":

Life, like a dome of many-colored glass,
Stains the white radiance of eternity.

Such a reminiscence is at the very least a courtesy, a tribute to the beauty of Shelley's lines. But there is more to it than that. Anyone who lets himself be guided by Frost's reference, and reads over the latter stanzas of Shelley's lament for Keats, will find that "Birches," taken as a whole, is in fact an answer to Shelley's kind of boundless neo-Platonic aspiration. It would be laborious, here and now, to point out all the pertinent lines in "Adonais"; suffice it to say that by the close of the poem Keats's soul has been translated to Eternity, to the eternal fountain of beauty, light, and love, and that Shelley, spurning the Earth, is embarking on a one-way upward voyage to the Absolute. The closing stanza goes like this:

The breath whose might I have invoked in song
Descends on me; my spirit's bark is driven
Far from the shore, far from the trembling throng
Whose sails were never to the tempest given;

146

The massy earth and spherèd skies are riven!
I am borne darkly, fearfully, afar;
Whilst, burning through the inmost veil of Heaven,
The soul of Adonais, like a star,
Beacons from the abode where the Eternal are.

Frost's answer to that is "Earth's the right place for love." In his dealings with Shelley's poem, Frost is doing a number of things. He is, for one thing, conversing timelessly with a great poem out of the English tradition; he is, for another thing, contending with that poem in favor of another version of spirituality. And in his quarrel with Shelley, Frost is speaking not only for his own temper but for the practical idealism of the New England spirit. Frost's poem does justice to world, to self, to literary tradition, and to a culture; it is happy in all the ways in which a poem can be happy; and I leave it with you as the best possible kind of answer to the question I have been addressing.

During his tenure as Consultant in Poetry to the Library of Congress, Howard Nemerov persuaded nineteen American poets, myself among them, to discuss their own writing and the current condition of poetry in a manner suitable for broadcast by the Voice of America. The resultant essays or scripts were later gathered into a book called Poets on Poetry (1966). A sense that my remarks were going to be beamed God knows where made me try for perspicuity, and doubtless also inclined me to touch upon the relations of art to culture, ideology, and the state.

ON MY OWN WORK

Since the Second World War, the American people have come to accept the poetry reading as a legitimate and frequently satisfying kind of artistic performance. Prior to the 1940's there were, to be sure, a few vivid or beloved figures to whom our audiences were glad to listen: Robert Frost, with his New England wit and accent; Carl Sandburg, with his guitar; Edna Millay in her white dress; Vachel Lindsay, with his camp-meeting style and his tambourines. But the public attitude toward the verse recital has now so matured that any poet, whether or not he qualifies as a platform personality, is likely to find himself on a platform several times a year. Sometimes it will be in a university auditorium, sometimes in an art gallery or community center, sometimes in a night club or coffee house. The audience may be ten or twenty; or it may be hundreds, even thousands; what matters is that it is now there.

The presence of all these listening faces has already, I think, affected the social posture of the American

148

poet. He shows somewhat less of the conventional romantic defiance, somewhat less of the bitterness of the wallflower; he is increasingly disposed to think of himself as a citizen, who may have a certain critical and expressive office to perform in the community. It goes without saying that this new attitude–or shall I say this revival of an old attitude–has been encouraged by the late President Kennedy's readiness to acknowledge and affirm the dignity of the arts.

I may misinterpret these phenomena, or make too much of them; but let us suppose that I am right and that there really is an increased responsiveness to poetry in America. Our poets will run certain risks, of course, in responding to that responsiveness. It would be too bad if large audiences in the Middle West, and occasional courtesies from Washington, inclined any poet to adjust his work to fancied demands–to become a defender of conventional pieties, or an apologist for official policy, or an entertainer, or (worst of all) a stingless gadfly, one of those public performers who shock their audience in just the way it wants to be shocked.

There are risks of corruption, then, in becoming a poet-citizen rather than an alienated artist, but I myself would consider them risks well taken, because it seems to me that poetry is sterile unless it arises from a sense of community or, at least, from the hope of community. I think this is true even in America, where beneath so much surface homogeneity there lies a radical commitment to diversity and to the toleration of dissent. We are not a settled and monolithic nation; we are not really one culture, and we offer our artists no Byzantine advantages. Yet the incoherence of America need not enforce a stance of alienation in the poet; rather, it may be seen as placing on him a peculiar imaginative burden, and committing him perhaps to something like Yeats's long and loyal quarrel with his native Ireland.

But let me turn back from these large assertions to the subject with which I began: the poetry reading. Very often, at these affairs, the actual reading of poems will be preceded or followed by a question period, during which the audience is invited to interrogate the poet about his art. This is not unusual, of course, in other countries; I have seen Yevgeny Yevtushenko, at a poetry reading in Moscow, cheerfully and patiently replying to the questions of his hearers. But the idea of the poet's accountability to his audience is axiomatic in Russia, as it is not here; and I must confess that question periods are sometimes a strain on my good citizenship. For one thing, I feel (as most poets do) that what I have to say has best been said in my poems, and that in discussing or expounding them I necessarily dilute and falsify. For another thing, I feel a certain mistrust of the desire to be well informed; it strikes me that far too many people are anxious to substitute ideas about poetry for the experience of possessing some poem in itself.

And yet I do try to answer people's questions, and with good will, reminding myself that no true poem can die of being talked about, that the lover of poetry may also be critically informed, and that after all one should be gratified by any show of interest.

For me, the hardest questions to answer are always those which bear broadly, rather than specifically, on my own work. I am sometimes asked, for example, whether I feel that my poems have greatly changed in style or attitude—whether I see myself as having passed through distinct periods of development. At such times I always feel envious of poets more willful and deliberate than I can manage to be. I envy Ezra Pound, whose whole literary performance may be seen as a series of conscious prescriptions for the health of the arts or of society. I envy Dr. Williams, with his explicit and developing aesthetic theories and his dogged metrical experiments. I envy Yeats, whose every collection of verse had a forceful, and I suspect forcible, unity of idea.

Such poets are always able to say what their intentions have been, and when and how their productions have changed in character. That I can make few such statements makes me seem irresponsible, no doubt, and passive; though a kinder word might be "spontaneous." The unit of my poetry, as I experience it, is not the Collected Poems which I may some day publish; nor is it the individual volume, or the sequence or group within the volume; it is the single poem. Every poem of mine is autonomous, or feels so to me in the writing, and consists of an effort to exhaust my present sense of the subject. It is for this reason that a poem sometimes takes me years to finish. No poem of mine is ever undertaken as a technical experiment; the form which it takes, whether conventional or innovating, develops naturally as the poem develops, as a part of the utterance. Nor does my poem ever begin as the statement of a fully grasped idea; I think inside my lines and the thought must get where it can amongst the moods and sounds and gravitating particulars which are appearing there. Robert Frost once said that a poem's beginning is like falling in love, and I feel about the matter as he did: when we fall in love, we are powerfully drawn by something, but we do not yet know what it means.

I am not, in short, a programmatic poet; I have never set about to write in this way or that. The best I can do, therefore, in answer to the question I have quoted, is to back off and play the critic to myself. If I do that, I find myself in slight disagreement with the friendly British reviewer who declared that my later poems do not much differ from the early ones. I think they do. My first poems were written in answer to the inner and outer disorders of the Second World War and they helped me, as poems should, to take ahold of raw events and convert them, provisionally, into experience. At the same time I think that they may at moments have taken refuge from events in language itself–in wordplay, in the coinage of new words, in a certain precocity. At any rate, my writing is now plainer and more straightforward than it used to be. An adverse critic, considering the same evidence, might say that my language has simply grown dull; I can only hope that he would not be right.

Another change in my work has been a partial shift from the ironic meditative lyric toward the dramatic poem. Most American poets of my generation were taught to admire the English Metaphysical poets of the seventeenth century and such contemporary masters of irony as John Crowe Ransom. We were led by our teachers and by the critics whom we read to feel that the most adequate and convincing poetry is that which accommodates mixed feelings, clashing ideas, and incongruous images. Poetry could not be honest, we thought, unless it began by acknowledging the full discordancy of modern life and consciousness.

I still believe that to be a true view of poetry, and

therefore I can still stand behind the poem I am about to read you, the title of which is "A Baroque Wall-Fountain in the Villa Sciarra." It is, in the first place, a minutely descriptive poem, in which I portray a wall-fountain in one of the public gardens of Rome, and then proceed across town to describe the celebrated fountains in St. Peter's Square. At the same time the poem presents, by way of its contrasting fountains, a clash between the ideas of pleasure and joy, of acceptance and transcendence.

A Baroque Wall-Fountain in the Villa Sciarra

Under the bronze crown
Too big for the head of the stone cherub whose feet
    A serpent has begun to eat,
Sweet water brims a cockle and braids down

    Past spattered mosses, breaks
On the tipped edge of a second shell, and fills
    The massive third below. It spills
In threads then from the scalloped rim, and makes

    A scrim or summery tent
For a faun-ménage and their familiar goose.
    Happy in all that ragged, loose
Collapse of water, its effortless descent

    And flatteries of spray,
The stocky god upholds the shell with ease,
    Watching, about his shaggy knees,
The goatish innocence of his babes at play;

    His fauness of the while
Leans forward, slightly, into a clambering mesh
    Of water-lights, her sparkling flesh
In a saecular ecstasy, her blinded smile

Bent on the sand floor
Of the trefoil pool, where ripple-shadows come
And go in swift reticulum,
More addling to the eye than wine, and more

Interminable to thought
Than pleasure's calculus. Yet since this all
Is pleasure, flash, and waterfall,
Must it not be too simple? Are we not

More intricately expressed
In the plain fountains that Maderna set
Before St. Peter's–the main jet
Struggling aloft until it seems at rest

In the act of rising, until
The very wish of water is reversed,
That heaviness borne up to burst
In a clear, high, cavorting head, to fill

With blaze, and then in gauze
Delays, in a gnatlike shimmering, in a fine
Illumined version of itself, decline,
And patter on the stones its own applause?

If that is what men are
Or should be, if those water-saints display
The pattern of our areté,
What of these showered fauns in their bizarre,

Spangled, and plunging house?
They are at rest in fullness of desire
For what is given, they do not tire
Of the smart of the sun, the pleasant water-douse

And riddled pool below,
Reproving our disgust and our ennui

With humble insatiety.
Francis, perhaps, who lay in sister snow

Before the wealthy gate
Freezing and praising, might have seen in this
No trifle, but a shade of bliss–
That land of intolerable flowers, that state

As near and far as grass
Where eyes become the sunlight, and the hand
Is worthy of water: the dreamt land
Toward which all hungers leap, all pleasures pass.

It may be that the poem I have just read arrives at some sort of reconciliation between the claims of pleasure and joy, acceptance and transcendence; but what one hears in most of it is a single meditative voice balancing argument and counterargument, feeling and counterfeeling. I now want to read you a somewhat later poem on very much the same subject, in which there are two distinct voices speaking, both of them dramatic. The title of the poem is "Two Voices in a Meadow," and the speakers are a milkweed and a stone. The milkweed speaks first:

Anonymous as cherubs
Over the crib of God,
White seeds are floating
Out of my burst pod.
What power had I
Before I learned to yield?
Shatter me, great wind:
I shall possess the field.

And now the stone speaks:

As casual as cow-dung

Under the crib of God,
I lie where chance would have me,
Up to the ears in sod.
Why should I move? To move
Befits a light desire.
The sill of Heaven would founder,
Did such as I aspire.

The virtue of the ironic meditative poem is that the poet speaks out of his whole nature, acknowledging the contradictions that inhere in life. The limitation of such a poem is that the atmosphere of contradiction can stifle passion and conduce to a bland evasiveness. The virtue of the dramatic poem is that, while it may not represent the whole self of the poet, it can (like the love song, hymn, or curse) give free expression to some one compelling mood or attitude. The fact is that we are not always divided in spirit and that we sometimes yield utterly to a feeling or idea. Each of these kinds of poem, then, has its own truth to life and without abandoning the first, I have lately been writing more and more of the second.

Another question often asked of the poets of my generation is where they stand in relation to the revolution in American poetry which is said to have begun in the second decade of this century. I think that there truly was a revolution then, in poetry as in the other arts, and if one looks at poetry anthologies of the year 1900 one can see that a revolution was called for–a revolution against trivial formalism, dead rhetoric, and genteel subject matter. The revolution was not a concerted one and there was little agreement on objectives; nor is there now any universal agreement as to what, in that revolution, was most constructive. But certainly it has been of lasting importance that Robinson and Frost chose to enliven traditional meters with the rhythms of colloquial speech; that Sandburg and others insisted on slang and on the brute facts of the urban and industrial scene; and that Pound and Eliot sophisticated American verse by introducing techniques from other literatures, and by reviving and revising our sense of literary tradition.

All of these contributions were inclusive and enlarging in character; but there were also, of course, experiments and movements of a reductive nature, in which one aspect of poetry was stressed at the expense of others. I think of Gertrude Stein's apparent efforts to reduce words to pure sound; I think of the typographical poems of Cummings, which–however engaging–sacrificed the ear to the eye; I think of the free-verse movement, which sought to purify poetry of all but organic rhythms; of the Imagist insistence that ideas be implicit in description, rather than abstractly stated; of the efforts of some poets to abandon logical progression and to write in quasimusical form.

We have seen, in this century, a number of the arts entrapped in reductive theories: music, some have said, is merely sound in time; architecture is nothing but the provision of areas for living or working; painting is only the arrangement of line and color on a plane surface. All these definitions are true enough, except for those words "merely" and "only" and "nothing but," which imply that to go beyond the bare fundamentals of any art is to risk impurity. There have been, as I have said, a number of reductive approaches to poetry in this century, but somehow American poetry has never fallen into such a condition as we now find in American painting, where for the most part one must choose between the solipsism of abstract expressionism and the empty objectivity of so-called pop art.

My own position on poetry, if I have to have one, is that it should include every resource which can be made to work. Aristotle, as you may remember, argued that drama is the highest of the arts because it contains more means and elements than any other. I am not sure that Aristotle is right about the pre-eminence of drama, but I do share his feeling that an art should contain as much as it can and still be itself. As a poet, my relationship to the revolution in question is that I am the grateful inheritor of all that my talent can employ, but that I will not accept any limitations or prohibitions or exclude anything in the name of purity. So far as possible, I try to play the whole instrument.

Let me illustrate, if I may, by presenting another poem of mine. If I understand this poem rightly, it has free and organic rhythm: that is to say, its movement arises naturally from the emotion and from the objects and actions depicted. At the same time, the lines are metrical and disposed in stanzas. The subject matter is both exalted and vulgar. There is, I should think, sufficient description to satisfy the Imagist, but there is also a certain amount of statement; my hope is that the statement seems to grow inevitably out of the situation described. The language of the poem is at one moment elevated and at the next colloquial or slangy: for example, the imposing word "omnipresence" occurs not far from the undignified word "hunks." A critic would find in this poem certain patterns of sound, but those patterns of sound do not constitute an abstract music; they are meant, at any rate, to be inseparable from what is being said, a subordinate aspect of the poem's meaning.

The title of the poem is a quotation from Saint Augustine: "Love Calls Us to the Things of This World." You must imagine the poem as occurring at perhaps seven-thirty in the morning; the scene is a bedroom high up in a city apartment building; outside the bedroom window, the first laundry of the day is being yanked across the sky and one has been awakened by the squeaking pulleys of the laundry line:

LOVE CALLS US TO THE THINGS OF THIS WORLD

The eyes open to a cry of pulleys,
And spirited from sleep, the astounded soul
Hangs for a moment bodiless and simple
As false dawn.
               Outside the open window
The morning air is all awash with angels.

Some are in bed-sheets, some are in blouses,
Some are in smocks: but truly there they are.
Now they are rising together in calm swells
Of halcyon feeling, filling whatever they wear
With the deep joy of their impersonal breathing;

Now they are flying in place, conveying
The terrible speed of their omnipresence, moving
And staying like white water; and now of a sudden
They swoon down into so rapt a quiet
That nobody seems to be there.
                  The soul shrinks

From all that it is about to remember
From the punctual rape of every blessèd day,
And cries,
       "Oh, let there be nothing on earth but laundry,
Nothing but rosy hands in the rising steam
And clear dances done in the sight of heaven."

Yet, as the sun acknowledges
With a warm look the world's hunks and colors,
The soul descends once more in bitter love
To accept the waking body, saying now
In a changed voice as the man yawns and rises,

"Bring them down from their ruddy gallows;
Let there be clean linen for the backs of thieves;
Let lovers go fresh and sweet to be undone,
And the heaviest nuns walk in a pure floating
Of dark habits,
keeping their difficult balance."

I have already stated that each of my poems, as I write it, seems to me unique; complete; quite unrelated to anything else I have done. But when I play the critic to my work, as I am doing now, it is not hard to see that the poems have a number of persistent concerns. The three poems I have included here all have to do (a critic might say) with the proper relation between the tangible world and the intuitions of the spirit. The poems assume that such intuitions are, or may be, true; they incline, however, to favor a spirituality that is not abstracted, not dissociated and world-renouncing. A good part of my work could, I suppose, be understood as a public quarrel with the aesthetics of Edgar Allan Poe.

But enough of that: the ideas of any poet, when reduced to prose statements, sound banal, and mine are no exception. Let me close by making a few observations on the poet's relationship to ideas. Madame Furtseva, the Soviet Minister of Culture, said recently that in her country the leaders of the state are thought to understand the world better than the artists do, and that Soviet artists therefore look to their political leaders for the ideas that they are to

160

express and the goals toward which their art is to inspire the people. How rigorously that theory is applied in the Soviet Union I do not know, but I am sure that I would find it oppressive if it were applied to me. I should not care to limit my poetic thought to politics and economics, which are not, after all, the whole of reality; I should not like to be forbidden that honesty which comes of the admission of doubts, contradictions, and reservations; and if the leaders of my state behaved viciously, as leaders sometimes do, I should like to feel entitled to protest rather than justify.

I do not think poetry can be healthy if it derives its attitudes from any authority. On the other hand, I do not think that society should look to poetry for new philosophies, new religions, and synoptic intellectual structures. That demand has been made repeatedly during the past century, ever since Matthew Arnold, and when poets have taken it seriously the result has been, at best, something like Hart Crane's magnificent botch of a poem, *The Bridge*. Poets are often intelligent men and they are entitled to their thoughts; but intellectual pioneering and the construction of new thought systems are not their special function. Aeschylus's *Oresteia* was not a contribution to Athenian legal theory; Dante's *Commedia* gave us no new theology; and Shakespeare's history plays added no fresh concepts to the political thought of his age.

What poetry does with ideas is to redeem them from abstraction and submerge them in sensibility; it embodies them in persons and things and surrounds them with a weather of feeling; it thereby tests the ability of any ideas to consort with human nature in its contemporary condition. Is it possible, for example, to speak intelligibly of angels in the modern world? Will the psyche of the modern reader consent to be called a soul? The poem I have just presented was a test of those questions.

I include this book review, from the New York
Review of Books, *July 13, 1967, because it is
more encompassing than reviews generally are,
covering–however cursorily–the whole ground of
Poe criticism; also because it presumes by the way
to expose one of Poe's deepest-laid plots.*

THE POE MYSTERY CASE

Poe's is the shakiest of all large American reputa-
tions, and yet, if I remember rightly a statement of
Malcolm Cowley's, there have been more studies of
him than of any other native writer. There is, as
Whitman said, an "indescribable magnetism" about
Poe's much romanticized life, and that would be part
of the explanation. It is also true that Poe is an important point in any brief for Southern letters, that
his supposed morbidity has attracted many diagnos-
ticians of psychic and cultural sickness, and that
some critics have been annoyed into writing about
Poe by a desire to comprehend or explain away his
high standing abroad. Finally, on the whole recently,
a number of people have attempted direct literary
analysis of Poe, moved by a sense that there is more
to him than obsession, mystification, and–as Yeats
put it of "The Pit and the Pendulum"–"an appeal to
the nerves by tawdry physical affrightments."

In any event, the books keep coming. Floyd Stovall,
a veteran critic and scholar of Poe, has recently edited a handsomely made edition of the complete poems. Dwight Macdonald's *Poems of Edgar Allan Poe*
is a selection of thirty-four poems, augmented by a
number of pieces (such as "Silence," "Shadow," and
"Eleonora") which may reasonably be considered
prose poems; to this Macdonald appends certain of
Poe's critical essays and *pensées*. Eric W. Carlson's

The Recognition of Edgar Allan Poe: A Collection of Critical Essays offers a fascinating variety of reactions to Poe–critical, epistolary, biographical, and poetic–extending from 1829 to the present. Some of the material included, such as Griswold's nasty memoir, D. H. Lawrence's essay on Poe's "vampirism," and Mallarmé's great sonnet, will be familiar to many; less known are G. B. Shaw's centenary rave of 1909, and Dostoevsky's notice of 1861, in which he praises Poe's "marvelous acumen and amazing realism" in the depiction of "inner states." (It is interesting that this last piece, published in Dostoevsky's magazine *Wremia* five years before *Crime and Punishment*, stood as introduction to three stories by Poe, two of which– "The Tell-Tale Heart," "The Black Cat"–are accounts of murder, conscience, and confession.) Robert Regan's *Poe: A Collection of Critical Essays* begins with one of the less inferential chapters of Joseph Wood Krutch's Freudian study (1926) and contains eleven other essays, largely from the fifties and sixties. These are well chosen and varied in attack. There is some overlapping between the Regan and Carlson volumes, but both are worth having.

Nineteenth-century writing about Poe, as represented in Carlson's collection, is on many grounds intriguing. But in relation to Poe's substance it is vexingly general, as compared both with today's more precise criticism and with Poe's own practice in such analytic essays as his review of Drake and Halleck. Since Margaret Fuller is who she is, we are attentive when she credits Poe's tales with "penetration into the causes of things," and asserts that "where the effects are fantastic they are not unmeaningly so." Since James is James, we harken respectfully to his dictum that "enthusiasm for Poe is the mark of a decidedly primitive stage of reflection." But since Miss Fuller does not clarify the nature of Poe's depth, and James is equally off-hand about his shallowness, the reader cannot get a dialogue out of their difference. Two broad observations by James Russell Lowell, in a *Graham's Magazine* article in 1845, reverberate through all the last century's criticism of Poe. The first is that Poe combines "a faculty of vigorous yet minute analysis, and a wonderful fecundity of imagination" (resembling in this Poe's hero Dupin, whose genius is both "creative and resolvent"). The second is that the tales present "impalpable shadows of mystery" and at the same time an authenticating "minuteness of detail."

Those two ideas are true, and have deserved reiteration; the big repeated falsehood about Poe was, of course, that he and his works were "worthless and wicked." Though Poe did have personal weaknesses, the notion of his wickedness derived mainly from the calumnies of Griswold, from Poe's critical attacks on moralizing in poetry, from the supra-emotional character of his poems, from the unsettling grisliness of certain of his tales, and from the insistence of Poe's readers on confounding him with his mad and depraved narrators. The view that Poe was a monster, and deservedly an outcast (a view which Baudelaire turned inside out), was held with varying degrees of intensity by almost everyone, here and in England, until the biographical clarifications of the twenties. Bryant refused to chip in for the Poe memorial in Baltimore, because he felt there ought to be "some decided element of goodness" in any person so publicly remembered. Whitman was the only well-known poet to attend the reburial in 1875, and even he hedged the gesture by stating then and there that, while Poe had had genius, he himself preferred a poetry of "health" to one of "delirium." Elsewhere, Whitman said of Poe's verses that they were "almost without the first sign of moral principle." T. W. Higginson, in a characteristic essay of 1879, began by calling Poe a genius and then compulsively proceeded to blackball him as a bounder, a frequently "besotted" person of "low moral tone." And Robert Louis Stevenson, in an 1899 article not collected by Carlson, had this to say: "He who could write 'King Pest' had ceased to be a human being. For his own sake, and out of an infinite compassion for so lost a spirit, one is glad to think of him as dead. . . ."

It is not until 1907 that we come upon a sustained and concrete examination of Poe's work, Brander Matthews's "Poe and the Detective Story." Matthews distinguishes between the Gothic tale of mystery, in which the reader is tantalized by a secret withheld until the close, and the Poe tale of detection, the interest of which lies "in the successive steps whereby [an] analytic observer is enabled to solve a problem that might well be dismissed as beyond human elucidation." Matthews is good also on the anonymous narrator of Poe's detective stories, who mediates between us and the staggering genius of Dupin or Legrand, assuring us of its human possibility and, as Greek chorus or cheerleader, inciting us to astonishment. One thing that Matthews does not see, although he comes near to seeing it, is that "The Murders in the Rue Morgue," for example, is not merely a detective story. As I shall try in a moment to show, there is also a story beneath the story, which we are challenged to detect.

Allen Tate says in his fine essay "The Angelic Imagination" that "readers of Poe . . . are peculiarly liable to the vanity of discovery." That is true, but it is also true, as Stephen Mooney notes, that Poe "believed in a technique that would require the reader to discover for himself where the meaning lies." Again and again in his criticism, Poe says that truly imaginative literature always situates its deepest meaning in an "under current," and that this submerged significance must not be too readily sounded. If we take that contention seriously, and apply it anywhere to the fiction of its author, we will run into various signs of ulterior motives. Let me mention a few of these signs.

Explicit symbolism: We must go to Poe's letters for his admission that the "Haunted Palace" represents "a mind haunted by phantoms," but scattered through his published work are equations quite as plain. "Berenice"'s narrator speaks of "the raven-winged hours," "the gray ruins of memory," "the disordered chamber of my brain." The dead speaker of "For Annie" rejoices that "the fever called 'Living' / Is conquered at last." These are not hit-and-run conjunctions: dark and voracious birds are continually associated with time in Poe; palaces and chambers everywhere imply minds or states of mind; and the idea that earthly life itself is a feverish sickness, if applied to "The Masque of the Red Death," clears the way for such a persuasive interpretation of that tale as Joseph Roppolo achieves in Regan's collection. An attentive reader can, in short, compile a small dictionary of symbolic constants which will give some access to Poe's "under current."

Hints and nudges: The names "Montresor" and "Fortunato," in "The Cask of Amontillado," are nine-letter names both of which connote wealth and good fortune. In "King Pest," a character named Hugh

Tarpaulin encounters and bests Tim Hurleygurly, whose initials are the reverse of his own. In "A Tale of the Ragged Mountains," a man named Bedloe or Bedlo dreams of the death of a man named Oldeb, and dies in his turn. Name-play of that sort, together with Poe's insistence on close kinship, old acquaintance, opposites and doubles, hints at an allegorical dimension in which his characters are not distinct individuals but components of one personality.

Allusions: As Harry Levin has observed, the final sentence of "The Masque of the Red Death" recalls the mock-Miltonic close of Pope's *Dunciad* ("And universal darkness buries All") and so gives the story an appropriate cosmic extension: a tale of the fallen soul's bondage to time and flesh concludes in an implicit vision of the world's end. The first phrase of "The Pit and the Pendulum" ("I was sick–sick unto death") echoes Hezekiah's thanks to Jehovah, in Isaiah 38, for his preservation from "the pit of corruption," thus firmly indicating an allegory of near-damnation and divine mercy. There are also cross-referent allusions, of the same quiet and important kind, within the body of Poe's writings. The "Sonnet–To Science" (1827) begins as follows:

> Science! true daughter of Old Time thou art!
> Who alterest all things with thy peering eyes.
> Why preyest thou thus upon the poet's heart,
> Vulture, whose wings are dull realities?

The poem proceeds to list, among the victims of Science, Diana, the Hamadryad, the Naiad, the Elfin, and (in an early version of the last line) "the summer dream beneath the shrubbery." Turning from that sonnet to "Berenice" (1835), we find the heroine apostrophized as "O sylph amid the shrubberies of Arnheim! O naiad among its fountains!" and are told by the narrator, Egaeus, in his next sentence that "even while I gazed upon her, the spirit of change swept over her." This should make it plain that Egaeus's "disease" is a hypertrophy of the intellect whereby the sense of beauty is destroyed, and should enable us to understand Egaeus's "abstraction" of Berenice's teeth (which he regards as *"des idées"*) without recourse to clinical palaver about the *vagina dentata*. As late as 1843, in "The Tell-Tale Heart," Poe was still darkly clarifying matters by reference to the "Sonnet–To Science": The mad narrator's victim in that story is an "old man" whose heart beats like a timepiece, and who has "the eye of a vulture."

Repeated plot structures: Dwight Macdonald rightly esteems Poe for "the persistence and ingenuity with which he transformed hack writing into his own personal expression." Much of Poe's fiction is partial burlesque, parody, or imitation of fashionable styles or authors, and there is no question that he seasonably exploited popular excitement about such diverse matters as Mesmerism, polar exploration, landscape gardening, the gold fever, and the Mormon thesis concerning the Lost Tribes. There are grounds for Yvor Winters's view of Poe as a "victim of contemporaneity." Beneath the takeoffs and topicalities, however, Poe's fiction is a continual rehearsal and variation of certain plots which convey some part of his vision of things–that vision being a Neo-Platonic one of the souls' conflicts, trials, and cosmic destiny.

One story pattern, about which I have written a good deal elsewhere, is that of the wavering and confused journey which concludes in a vertiginous plunge. What is symbolized by that pattern is the dreaming soul's escape from this temporal and material prison into "the spirit's outer world." The pattern is obvious in such tales as "Ms. Found in a Bottle," less obvious in "The Fall of the House of Usher," and comparatively unobtrusive in "King Pest" and "Landor's Cottage," but it is unmistakably to be found in a large number of ostensibly dissimilar works. Another recurrent plot in Poe is a triangle situation in which a woman's love or honor is the ground of contention between two men, one of them lofty-minded and the other base or brutish. The woman, in such cases, symbolizes Psyche, or redemptive Beauty, while–as the forestalled seduction at the close of "William Wilson" makes plain–the rivals stand for the spiritual and corrupt principles of a single nature. We encounter this plot under all sorts of generic guises. The "Duc de l'Omelette," in what pretends to be a satire on Disraeli, symbolically rescues a "queen" from the power of the Devil. The visionary hero of "The Assignation" escapes with the Marchesa Aphrodite, by double suicide, to the "land of real dreams"; she is thus freed from bondage to the old and "satyr-like" Mentoni. The detective Dupin, in "The Purloined Letter," releases a royal lady from the power of his "unprincipled" double, the Minister D–. The court fool "Hop-Frog," avenging his master's coarse insult to Trippetta, attires the king as an orangutan–thus manifesting the king's true nature–and destroys him by fire; Hop-Frog and Trippetta then escape "to their own country."

And so on. Let me get back now to "The Murders in the Rue Morgue." Poe invented the detective story, but our sense of what he might be up to in a "tale of ratiocination" should not be limited by what the form has become in other hands. Those other hands have narrowed the form; so far as I know, G. K. Chesterton is Poe's only continuator in the writing of detective fiction having an allegorical stratum. In any case, straightforward whodunit writers like Agatha Christie do not define Poe, any more than chemistry defines alchemy.

Marshall McLuhan lately made this observation on television: "Edgar Allan Poe discovered that if you take the story line off the detective story, the audience has to participate and make the story as it goes." The meaning of that sentence is probably to be found somewhere in McLuhan's writings, but as it stands I find it cryptic. How can a story that has been imagined backward be "made as it goes" by the readers? Surely the detective story consists, as Poe said, in the unraveling of a web which the author has woven, and surely the reader must consent to follow the right thread toward the one solution. But perhaps McLuhan means this: that so long as the "story" of the crime (the solution, that is) is withheld, and there is uninterpreted evidence before us, we participate, by reasoning and guessing, in the "story" of the detective's progress toward the truth.

That would be right enough, but I wish that McLuhan meant something else as well. Maybe he does. "The Murders in the Rue Morgue" has pleased millions of readers as a description–to quote one of Poe's letters–of "the exercise of ingenuity in detecting a murderer." Yet anyone who reads it in a chair, rather than a hammock, is likely to feel teased into "participating," into trying to account for a sense that he is reading more than a tale of detection. In the first place, Dupin is far more than a hero of "ingenuity"–a term which, within the story, is treated with scorn. Though sometimes depicted as a reasoner, he is the embodiment of an idea, strongly urged in Eureka and elsewhere, that poetic intuition is a supralogical faculty, infallible in nature, which includes and obviates analytical genius. As Kepler guessed his laws, the dreamer Dupin guesses his solutions, making especial use of a mind-reading power so sure that it can divine the thought sequences of persons he has never met. Dupin's divinations are instantaneous, as some say the Creation was instantaneous, and his recital to the narrator of his "chain of reasoning" is, like Genesis, a sequential shadowing-forth of something otherwise inexpressible.

Denis Marion and others have noted that Dupin's logic, as reported in "The Murders in the Rue Morgue," is not inevitable, either when he "reads" a long concatenation of the narrator's thoughts, or when he reconstructs the "reasoning" that led to his solution of the crime. The ear-witnesses of the murder have heard two voices within Mme. L'Espanaye's chambers, one exclaiming in French and the other in a tongue conjectured to be this or that, but in all cases unintelligible to the particular witness. Because an Italian, an Englishman, a Spaniard, a Hollander, and a Frenchman have all declared the second voice to be foreign to them, Dupin makes the "sole proper deduction" that the voice is that of a beast. This is to brush aside, as Marion says, several possibilities: that the speaker was Turkish or Bantu, that he had a speech defect, or that some or all of the witnesses were mistaken. Again, Dupin draws from the fact that the killer did not take Mme. L'Espanaye's gold the conclusion that the crime was without motive; but theft is not the only possible motive for murder.

The fact is that Dupin's logic, proceeding with a charmed arbitrariness toward the solution that seems to justify it, has what Poe called an "air of method," but is really intuition in disguise.

There is a decided duplicity, then, in Poe's presentation of Dupin; he is in one aspect a master detective who, as A. H. Quinn was persuaded, "proceeds not by guessing but by analysis," and in another aspect he is a seer who infallibly knows. This ambiguity of Dupin, together with various unlikelihoods in the narrative (why should two women be "arranging some papers" in an iron chest at three in the morning?), should make the reader receptive to suggestions that an allegorical "under current" flows beneath the detective tale.

Like Roderick Usher and the divided William Wilson, Dupin has two distinct speaking voices, one high and one low. The narrator makes much of this phenomenon, and toys with the thought that these voices express "a double Dupin." The narrator thus introduces, early on, the crucial idea that one person may contain several natures. When we arrive, soon after, at a report of the crime in the Rue Morgue, a major emphasis is laid on the two voices—one low and one high—which have issued from the murder room, and which later will be found to belong to a sailor and his escaped orangutan. It is hard not to suspect some kind of connection between these contrasting voices and Dupin's two registers, and Dupin himself (speaking in his vaticinal treble) shortly offers a hint as to how we are to solve the relationship. "Murder," he says, "has been committed by some third party; and the voices of this third party were those heard in contention." It appears that while Dupin may be regarded as "double" or multiple, other figures in the story–the sailor and the orangutan–may be combined and considered as a single "party." The implication is that the mastermind Dupin, who can intuitively "fathom" all the other characters of the narrative, is to be seen as including them all–that the other "persons" of the tale are to be taken allegorically as elements of one person, whereof Dupin is the presiding faculty.

This impression strengthens when the police arrest a young clerk, Adolphe Le Bon, on suspicion of the murders. Dupin at once involves himself in the case, with the intention of exonerating Le Bon, who, he says, "once rendered me a service for which I am not ungrateful." A similar surprising revelation of old acquaintance occurs in "The Purloined Letter," where Dupin belatedly tells how the Minister D– "at Vienna once, did me an evil turn, which I told him, quite good-humoredly, that I should remember." If the Minister D– is "evil," it is evident from Le Bon's name that he is good, and it is not hard to see in "Adolphe Le Bon" a variation on the name "Auguste Dupin." Le Bon is, allegorically, a humbly virtuous aspect of Dupin's character, which he must vindicate by making a proper assignment of the blame.

The sliest hint in the story comes at the point near the close, where Dupin shows the narrator the newspaper notice which, he hopes, will bring the owner of the orangutan to their quarters. The owner is invited to present himself at a certain address in the Faubourg St. Germain, *"au troisiéme."* We have already been told that Dupin and the narrator live quite alone in a retired mansion, the shutters of which are closed against the daylight; now, with the aid of our first-year French, we discover that their quarters are on the fourth floor, and the discovery is electrifying.

For Mme. L'Espanaye and her daughter also live, as we have been told in English, on the fourth floor of a building otherwise untenanted, in a "very lonely" part of Paris, and see no company, and keep their shutters closed. Once the similarity of the tale's two major households has been felt, we think of a third couple in another building–of the sailor who, "at his own residence in Paris," has sought to keep his captured orangutan "carefully secluded." The imaginative consequence of this is that–as when the scattered stars of the universe rush together in *Eureka*– the three secluded ménages of the story are telescoped into one, the three buildings becoming a single structure which signifies the reintegrated and harmonized consciousness of Dupin. Allegorically, the action of the story has been a soul's fathoming and ordering of itself, its "apprehension" of that base or evil force within it (the orangutan) which would destroy the redemptive principle embodied in Mme. L'Espanaye and her daughter. A Scots clergyman once described Poe as "a combination, in almost equal proportions, of the field, the brute, and the genius": Dupin, in "The Murders in the Rue Morgue," uses his genius to detect and restrain the brute in himself, thus exorcising the fiend.

"However true it is that the final task in literary criticism is the task of evaluation, it is certainly true also that the initial work that must be done is to determine as exactly as possible *what is there*." So says Patrick Quinn in his good essay on "The French Response to Poe." If the sort of thing I have been pointing at is really there, it should be easy to see what kinds of Poe criticism are going to be of the greatest present use to us. Marie Bonaparte's Freudian study of the works, though absurd in all the expected ways, does them the honor of close study, and comes up with many constants of imagery and narrative pattern. Jean-Paul Weber, another psychological critic, subscribes to the dreary idea that all authors, as children, accidentally witness the love-making of their parents, misunderstand it as violence, and grow up to write obsessively of nothing else; nevertheless, his study of "The Theme of the Clock" in Poe is valuable in the same way that the Bonaparte study is valuable. Gaston Bachelard's profound observations on Poe's elemental imagery, Georges Poulet's piece on Poe's "dialectic of time," Maurice Beebe's application of *Eureka* to "The Fall of the House of Usher," Sidney Kaplan's linguistic investigation into the last chapter of *Pym*–such highly attentive criticism, done in the faith that Poe's least details as well as his general structures may repay examination, will in time let us know something of "what is there."

Those who dismiss Poe often do so on the basis of style; Eliot called Poe's prose "slipshod," Lawrence called it "meretricious." But the fact is, as Allen Tate remarks, that Poe has many styles, including a "lucid and dispassionate" critical voice. The prose varies widely from work to work, and one gradual realization of current criticism has been that this variation may be deliberate and strategic. W. H. Auden once quoted a passage from "William Wilson" describing it as "terrible, vague, verbose" writing, but then went on to note "how well it reveals the William Wilson who narrates the story in his real colors, as the fantastic self who refuses contact with reality." James Gargano's recent essay "The Question of Poe's Narrators" justly develops that idea, contending that the language of Poe's fiction belongs not to Poe, but to his narrators, and that it often serves to damn them out of their own mouths. Gargano's question is one that needs to be pursued and broadened, until the whole range of Poe's voices has been assessed, not by some fixed standard of "good writing," but as organic expressions of this or that faculty or *état d'âme*. And then there are other questions to be attacked. How far, for instance, is it useful to regard the figures in Poe's fiction as people, and how far are they to be understood as states or principles of the psyche? Is Poe's symbolism personal, traditional, or both? Was he a highly conscious writer, as I think, or was he not? Was he an obscurantist, whose "under currents" are too often at the bottom of the sea? If, as Regan thinks, Poe's stories contain a "stratification of meanings," and if the superficial narratives vary greatly in sufficiency, can we say that the stratum in which Poe rehearses his fundamental drama of the soul's struggle is always the essential one? When these questions have been further worried by careful readers, we will be better able to say what reputation Poe deserves.

The first paragraph of this small essay, which appeared in the New York Times Book Review *of March 17, 1968, explains how it came to be undertaken. I have dared to assume that Burns was the author or shaper of "A Red, Red Rose," despite his description of it, in a letter of 1794, as "a simple old Scots song" which he had "pickt up." But the question of authorship is not crucial; my essay is simply an enquiry into how the song operates.*

EXPLAINING THE OBVIOUS

O My Luve's like a red, red rose,
  That's newly sprung in June;
O My Luve's like the melodie
  That's sweetly played in tune.

As fair art thou, my bonnie lass,
  So deep in luve am I;
And I will luve thee still, my dear,
  Till a' the seas gang dry.

Till a' the seas gang dry, my dear,
  And the rocks melt wi' the sun:
O I will luve thee still, my dear,
  While the sands o' life shall run.

And fare thee weel, my only luve,
  And fare thee weel awhile!
And I will come again, my luve,
  Though it were ten thousand mile.

Some months ago a professor friend, who was putting together a textbook on explication, invited me to take a poem of my own choosing and attempt to model commentary on it. I began, of course, by trying to think of something knotty about which to be clever, but the lines from Burns which I have quoted, and which are often in my mind, kept proposing themselves. I am fond of "A Red, Red Rose," and what we like, we like to talk about. Was there, however, anything much to be said about a poem so admirably simple? My curiosity obliged me to write what follows.

The first four lines of Burns's poem are often quoted as examples of simile, and the remaining quatrains could reasonably be searched, in a beginners' English class, for such other rhetorical devices as hyperbole. Except for these illustrative uses, however, the poem does not seem to invite analysis. What is being asserted is very plain; a man is declaring his deep and lasting love for a woman; and one would not listen straight-faced to any interpretation which sought, for example, to discover religious allegory in the poem's "rose symbolism" or "end-of-the-world motif."

The individual words of the poem present no difficulties or ambiguities, and there is no actual need of footnotes to tell us that "gang" and "weel" are Scots dialect words for "go" and "well." I suppose that some reader might waver between two understandings of lines 5 and 6–do they mean "My love is proportional to your beauty" or "You are as fair, and I as enamored, as the foregoing would suggest"?– but the uncertainty would not derail his reading of the whole.

There is really no end to what need not be said about this poem, and, of course, it is one mark of the good critic that he abstains from busywork. If we encountered the phrase "all Hell broke loose" in a poem by T. S. Eliot, we would be well advised to trace it back as far as "Paradise Lost," with a view to applying Milton's adjacent lines and general thought to the Eliot passage. But if we found the same phrase in a doggerel poem by Robert W. Service, we would presumably have the sense to forget about Milton, and to remember that the expression in question is well established in offhand, everyday speech.

A similar discrimination is called for in deciding how much to make of the supposed echoes and borrowings in this little Burns poem. The words "Till a' the seas gang dry" might legitimately put us in mind of Isaiah's Jehovah, who thunders, "Behold, at my rebuke I dry up the sea," or of this sort of thing from Revelation: "And I saw a new heaven and a new earth: for the first heaven and the first earth are passed away; and the sea is no more."

But the good likelihood that such passages underlie Burns's line need not be dwelt upon. The poem has precious little to do with Isaiah or John, and it would be foolishly pedantic to leave the amorous preserve of Burns's little song for the domain of prophecy. The most we should say of "Till a' the seas gang dry" is that, in a Bible-quoting age and a Calvinist culture, it was a ready and vivid way of saying "Indefinitely," and that in any age it is intelligible without recourse to Scripture.

Burns's editors tell us that "A Red, Red Rose" also contains borrowings, of a more provable kind, from Scottish folk songs. This is not surprising, since at the time of the poem's composition Burns was engaged in gathering and editing the traditional songs of his countrymen. Do we need to know the folk sources on which Burns drew? Probably not. It might somewhat improve our feeling for the convention in which Burns was writing if we saw a few of his words in their original settings; but those settings, those contexts, would be unlikely to add anything specific to our understanding of his straightforward utterance here. Self-evidently, "A Red, Red Rose" is an autonomous work, the articulate gesture of one imagination, and its echoes enforce no excursions.

Or that is how it strikes me and most people. But supposing there were some reader unable to prove the unity of the poem on his pulses, someone who saw it instead as a loose sheaf or anthology of pretty lines–could one hope to change his mind for him? The attempt would best begin, I should think, with an apparent concession: the implicit dramatic situation of the poem *can* seem inconsistent or uncertain. In the first four lines, Burns's lover is praising his love in the third person, and to nobody in particular; she does not seem in any sense to be "there." In the second and third quatrains, however, repeated assurances of fidelity are directed to the beloved, who now turns up in the second person. Should one imagine her as present, or merely as present to mind? Is she being addressed, or evoked? The question can be difficult to decide, and the "fare thee weel" of the last stanza can leave one still in doubts. If this is a good-bye poem, spoken to a woman, is not the fact of parting unconscionably delayed? Or if the poem is not to be read as arising from an implicit "scene," may one not condemn the thirteenth line as abrupt and opportunistic, a way of getting a little more hyperbolic mileage out of the material?

Such questions and charges cannot be answered with that air of scientific demonstration to which explication so often aspires; but a reasonable argument for the poem's coherent shape can be made on two grounds, the rhetorical and the psychological. George Gascoigne once said that when praising a

181

lady the poet should "neither praise her chrystal eye nor her cherry lip, etc.," these notions being trite and obvious; he should, rather, find some means whereby his pen might "walk in the superlative degree." Burns's first quatrain consists of comparisons that are essentially stale poetic compliments, *trita et obvia*, but which are freshened and rendered "sincere" by colloquial simplicity and the implications of dialect. The effect is of a pastoral eloquence, and this eloquence, warming to itself, proceeds in the remainder to speak of love not in roses and melodies but in brave hyperboles which stop just short of eternity and infinity. The peak of excitement comes in lines 8 and 9, where the poet's first bold figure is raptly or vauntingly repeated, with one stanza sailing on into the next; lines 12 and 16 then continue and exhaust the hyperbolic attack. What we seem to have, then, is a poem that moves from one rhetoric to another, a flight of words that begins on the ground of conventional simile and soars into excessive affirmations which, though not without literary precedent, here seem spontaneous. The shape of the poem can be described as the escape of a fervent imagination into its own language, and anyone may prove this in a moment by reading the poem aloud, con amore.

There is also another and congruent development in the poem as I read it, and that is the movement of the thought away from the nominal subject. Burns's first stanza may be conventional compliment, but it has to do with the young lady, and argues a concentration of the poet's thought upon the definition of her beauty. From line 6 onward, however, that subject has been left behind; "my dear" becomes almost perfunctory, and in the most striking and exultant passages of the poem what the poet celebrates is the stamina of his own feeling. All of the magnitudes of the poem belong, not to the lady, but to the lover's devotion. It may be argued that love-songs, if they are to be fresh, cannot forever be dealing foursquare with the addressee, but must come at her with some inventive obliquity. But whereas such a song as Byron's "There Be None of Beauty's Daughters" (which I recommend for general comparison) withdraws from its lady into the elaboration of a simile, and then converts all into praise of her at the close, Burns's poem forsakes the lady to glory in Love itself, and does not really return. We are dealing, in other words, with romantic love, in which the beloved is a means to high emotion, and physical separation can serve as a stimulant to ideal passion. Once this is recognized, once we see that the emotion of the poem is self-enchanted and entails a spiritual remove, the presence or absence of the lady becomes unimportant, and the idea of parting seems less the occasion of feeling than an expression of it.

It is oddly difficult to write about romantic love without inclining to denounce or ridicule it; we have our reservations about the emotional economy even in the present age, when a version of romantic love is celebrated by all media, high or low, and the speeches of Friar Laurence are impatiently cut in every production of *Romeo*. We still understand when La Rochefoucauld says, "There are some people so full of themselves, that when they are in love, they find means to be occupied with their passion, without being so with the person they love." Molière's Alceste still amuses us by telling Célimène that he could wish her wretched, friendless, and obscure, so that he then might raise her from the dust and

> proudly prove
> The purity and vastness of my love.

We join Célimène in laughing at a lover who can so separate "his love" from its presumptive object as to imagine exalting the one at the cost of the other's suffering. We can also be persuaded by W. H. Auden's criticism of romantic love in his poem "As I Walked Out One Evening." The "I" of Auden's poem overhears a lover making large promises which are surely reminiscent of Burns:

> I'll love you, dear, I'll love you
> Till China and Africa meet,
> And the river jumps over the mountain
> And the salmon sing in the street.
>
> I'll love you till the ocean
> Is folded and hung up to dry,
> And the seven stars go squawking
> Like geese about the sky . . .

The poem then proceeds to rebut these lines, saying that the human heart is too selfish and perverse to make such promises in good faith, and that the one real hope lies in striving, despite all weakness, to

> love your crooked neighbor
> With your crooked heart.

How far does Burns's poem expose itself to that kind of correction? Not at all. His poem is not a play, within which the consequences of romantic feeling can be tested in action; it is an effusion *in vacuo*. Nor is Burns's poem an argument or medication, as Auden's essentially is. It is a song. Like all true songs, it is simple and relaxed in its language, allowing only so much point or verbal brilliance per line; it is full of repetitions of word and idea; its grammatical divisions coincide with the line endings; it is perfectly suited to being set and sung, and though beautiful in itself could profit by the complement; finally, it has one thought or mood, which is developed to full intensity. While some poems–the Auden poem just cited, for one–make artful use of song techniques for the projection of complex and contradictory matter, the song in pure form is an unqualified cry. A cry does not argue with itself or with us; nor we with it. We do not question the resentment of the still-charmed lover in Champion's "When Thou Must Home," or the right of D'Urfey's "Roaring Boy" to roar; "A Red, Red Rose" is one state of soul handsomely vented, and that is all we ask. The emotions of song are privileged.

In the spring of 1969, the Friends of the Wesleyan Library held a meeting in honor of the one hundred and fiftieth anniversary of Whitman's birth. These few remarks were prefaced to a reading, with connective commentary, of various sections of "Song of Myself."

THE PRESENT STATE OF WHITMAN

I suppose that my early notions of Whitman were much like those of any other bookish child of my generation. In grade school, I was told that Whitman was the poet of American democracy, and that he was buried over in Camden. We students were briefly exposed to "I Hear America Singing" and that uncharacteristic poem "O Captain! My Captain!" That was it; we read no more of Whitman in grade school, and I do not remember encountering him again at any later stage of my schooling, even in college. Once, during the turmoil of puberty, I overheard a friend of my mother's saying that Whitman was grossly specific about physical things, and I went hopefully to the Untermeyer anthology on my parents' bookshelves. It did not seem to contain the pertinent poems, and so I did not find what I was after; however, it may have been at that time that my youthful morbidity took possession of the beautiful song of the bird in "When Lilacs Last in the Dooryard Bloom'd":

Come lovely and soothing death,
Undulate round the world, serenely arriving, ariving,
In the day, in the night, to all, to each,
Sooner or later delicate death.

When I turned sixteen, my grandparents gave me

Hart Crane's poems, which I consumed in toto without in the least understanding why, in *The Bridge,* Crane kept invoking the spirit of Whitman. And when my twelfth-grade English teacher told us that Carl Sandburg, in his free verse and in his celebrations of the common people, was Whitman's continuator, I was too ignorant to criticize that judgment by recalling the important ways in which Sandburg was not like Whitman at all. A final youthful impression of Whitman derived from my reading of left-wing magazines, from which I vaguely gathered that Whitman had been a prophet of popular-front radicalism, and that the "comrades" of which he spoke, had they lasted into the 1930s, would have been Earl Browder's sort of comrade.

I tell you of this not because I am proud of a history of incomprehension, but because I think my case is typical of my generation, and perhaps of other generations. Back in 1888, four years before his death, Whitman wrote: "From a worldly and business point of view 'Leaves of Grass' has been worse than a failure . . . public criticism of the book . . . yet shows anger and contempt more than anything else." The contempt is gone, the sales have gone up, Whitman scholarship is vast, and there is a thick slab of the poems in every anthology; nevertheless, I suspect that now, as formerly, Whitman is little explored by the general reader, and little understood. He exists chiefly as a great, garbled rumor, a name with continental and cosmic reverberations, an American something of monumental size; but the "great audiences" that he addressed seem never to have been there.

For my own generation, I think I can offer some explanations. In the first place, bulk. Despite Crane's

Bridge and Williams's *Paterson*, despite the book-club successes of Benét and E. A. Robinson, it must be said that the long poem has gone more and more out of use since the nineteenth century. For a good part of the present century, and especially during the ascendancy of Eliot, the norm of American poetry has been a short-winded, dense, and highly charged lyric. Readers accustomed to the imaginative economy of that norm could not readily adapt to Whitman's lengthiness, his oratorical profuseness, his prosiness, his drifting illogic, the elusiveness of his structures. It is also possible, I think, that readers have been put off Whitman by false expectations as to his main subjects–some of them fostered by Whitman himself in his latter years. If you go looking for paeans to America, and find them, you will probably have found Whitman at his weakest. If you look for laudations of political democracy in that great poem "The Sleepers," it will seem to be well off the point. And approached as a poem about President Lincoln, "When Lilacs Last in the Dooryard Bloom'd" could seem very unsteady in focus. There are, moreover, certain of Whitman's ideas which cannot have appealed to the last several decades: his literary nationalism, for instance, his hope for a spontaneous and cut-off American culture, surely went against the grain in a period of eclectic traditionalism. But above all I should guess that Whitman has lost many readers in this century through his poetic posture and its artistic consequences. Whitman called Emerson his master, and indeed Whitman is just what Emerson asked for in his essay on "The Poet." He was not an impersonal wordsmith contriving artifacts; he was a seer or prophet, and a highly personal one, harkening to the divine in himself and shouting across his poems to someone called "you," in whom he sought to provoke a visionary state of mind. The Whitmanian idea of poetry places the emphasis on the poet and the reader, not the poem; the inspired conception and the inspired response are what matter most, and the mere words–what Hollywood calls the "paperwork"–may be expected to be uneven. Emerson thought little of what he called "industry and skill in meter," and Whitman once said, "No one will get at my verses who insists upon viewing them as a literary performance." I suppose that no great poet is so damnably uneven as Whitman is: there are passages in his best work where the rhythms have an exact expressiveness, and the language is prodigal with permanent surprises; yet, without warning, he can fall for pages on end into a slack journalese, or lapse into a repellently pretentious phrase like "promulging the grand ideas of American ensemble." There is a rhetorical strain in Whitman which reminds me of nothing so much as the old Loew's State Theatre lobby. Many readers trained to expect of the poet a craftsman's self-effacement, and a craftsman's consistency and taste, have doubtless opened Whitman at the wrong page and given up on him for good.

I shall be surprised, however, if Whitman is not now in process of acquiring a larger audience than ever before. The late Randall Jarrell, back in the 1950s, wrote a spirited and influential essay in which he urged that Whitman be read for a change, and not as a specimen in American Studies but simply for the delight that is in his poems. Hyatt Waggoner, in his new survey of American poetry, proposes a revised view of our poetic tradition in which Emerson marks the main channel and Whitman is the high-water mark. And there are developments in recent poetry, not all of them salutary in themselves, which will make it easier for readers to go back and look at Whitman. Confessional poetry, so called, has accustomed us to verse of a highly personal and sometimes exhibitionistic character. There is a concern, in and around poetry, with Zen Buddhism and the oriental religions, and that has its pertinence to a grasp of Whitman. Meter and rhyme and traditional artifice have once again been proclaimed dead, for the traditional reasons. Nondiscursive, nonlogical structure, for which there is precedent in Eliot and Pound, now flourishes in the field poetry of the Black Mountain poets, as well as in the irrationalism of the Sixties group and the New York School. Particular poets now address themselves in their work to Whitman's ghost: Louis Simpson does so in his book *At the End of the Open Road,* and Allen Ginsberg not only invokes Whitman but comes near to reincarnating him. Ginsberg's disheveled guru stance, his declamatory free verse, his orientalisms, his attitude toward sex, his whole kit of ideas, are authentic derivations from Whitman. Finally, certain critics, and in particular Malcolm Cowley, have lately helped us to see what kind of a poet Whitman really is, so that we may approach him again without fumbling.

I mean to end, shortly, by reading you one or two selections from Whitman, and I see that I have left too little time for a proper account of his present aspect. But let me try to say it in a few words. Whitman now emerges for us as a religious poet; his political and social attitudes are not primary, but are based on a mystic sense of the divinity of the individual soul. His best poem, and his central text, is "Song of Myself." If we shake that poem down for ideas, what we discover is Emersonian transcendentalism plus an acceptance of the body. The soul, we learn, is a parcel of God; when we see with the eye of the soul, we see that all things and persons are divine and deathless, and that every creature contains and implies the occult unity of things. Since each thing is an index of the infinite, since every mouse is a miracle, it follows that all things are equal, that all things are beautiful, that all things are good. Emerson, in his poems and essays, expounds such thoughts as these; but the tissue of Whitman's poetry is not argumentative. Ideas, in Whitman, are seen struggling for clarity and truth within the flux of the whole psyche, moving with or against the tides of reverie, musing, and nightmare, and the drift of association. The ideas that "Song of Myself" asserts are conferred at first, in section 5 of the poem, as mystic intuitions, and then the soul sets out, in the poem's vast catalogues, to accept all creatures as equal, all experience as good; this affirmative movement is continually troubled or obstructed by evocations of evil, of sexual shame, or pain and death; there are moments of near-despair at which the poet cries "Enough! Enough! Enough!"; yet counter-moments of euphoric insight enable the soul to win through to its final affirmations. Whitman is, in short, a poet of psychic battle, and his great strength as a poet of ideas is that his conceptions are tested, contradicted, endangered, and so seem fairly earned. And of course there are other reasons for Whitman's power as a religious poet: for one thing, he is the most inclusive of mystics, and he will not scorn the material, the physical, the urban, the vernacular, the particular and everyday. He leaves nothing out. How astonishing it is that a poetry aimed at the infinite should catch so unforgettably "the sluff of boot-soles" on the pavement, or should give us, for the first and only time in literature, a bird's-eye view of a sharp-peaked farmhouse roof, "with its scallop'd scum and slender shoots from the gutters."

But that will do. As Randall Jarrell once said, the best way to advocate Whitman is to quote him, as I now mean to do at length.

It was a privilege to write an introduction for A Sense of Place (1972), the handsome collection of paintings and texts by American landscape artists, which my friend Alan Gussow edited for The Friends of the Earth.

REGARDING PLACES

The Irish poet Patrick Kavanagh speaks scornfully in one of his poems of bustling, abstract men who sit on committees and cannot perceive "the undying difference in the corner of a field." I have found that phrase a good means of guessing anyone's origins: those who were city bred hear it blankly, but those who grew up on farms often know what it means. Even in fast-changing America, a man can come back after fifty years and find the expression of some angle of land much the same: it may have been plowed, dumped on, bulldozed, or otherwise altered, and there will have been changes in wall, fence, or hedge; yet in some relationship of rocks, perhaps, some degree of slope, some presence of water which makes for greenness, the stubborn peculiarity of the place will be there. It is hard to say why this should matter so much to some people.

A feeling for the lay and character of the land must have been near universal in the ancient Mediterranean world; for the Greeks, places had their genii, and all the gods, however eclectically fused and generalized by the poets, were local. Japan, to this day, is attentive and imaginatively responsive to every natural scene. But my friend from New York, an excellent abstract artist, walks through our Berkshire woods smoking Gauloises and talking of Berlin. It is too bad that he cannot be where he is, enjoying the glades and closures, the climbs, the descents, the flat stretches strewn with Canada Mayflower and wintergreen; I should like to see him catch the first rumor of a stream up ahead, or notice how we leave the beech grove behind and enter a stand of hemlock and laurel. These woods have a delectable variety, because there is some overlapping of forests here: the black oak is not found much farther north, and the larch thins out to the south of us. The elaborate arrangement of the hop hornbeam's leaves would engage my friend's exquisite sense of line and pattern, if only he would see it, but he will not. "Forgive me," he says. "To me, this is all a smear of green." And so he walks along in an envelope of smoke and talk.

Cardinal Newman comes to mind, because I happen to have been reading him. *The Apologia* is not an inclusive biography, but an effort on Newman's part to describe the development of his religious opinions and to defend the honesty of his progress toward conversion. Nevertheless, Newman's defense does take the form of a biographical account, and it consists not merely of the drily doctrinal but also the powerful figures of speech and dramatic effects of tone and timing. In a life story with so many emotive elements, the reader might expect to encounter evocations of place, but they are not forthcoming. Newman goes on walks, but will not say what he sees; abroad, he tells us that he "went to various coasts of the Mediterranean" and "found pleasure in historical sites and beautiful scenes"; back home again, he finds himself "amid familiar scenes and faces." One could scarcely be less vivid than that. Newman does, in fact, prepare us throughout his first chapter for the starvation of our mind's eye: he tells us that he has had since boyhood a "feeling of separation from the visible world," and a conviction as to "the unreality of material phenomena." *The Apologia* makes frequent use of metaphors (of light and dark, for example), in which things are instantly converted into spiritual meanings, but I can remember only one sustained passage in which Newman's surroundings are acknowledged as such, and thought and feeling attach to specific "material phenomena." It comes when Newman has gone over to Roman Catholicism, and is leaving Oxford after thirty years:

> . . . I called on Dr. Ogle, one of my oldest friends, for he was my private Tutor, when I was an Undergraduate. In him I took leave of my first college, Trinity, which was so dear to me. . . . Trinity had never been unkind to me. There used to be much snapdragon growing on the walls opposite my freshman's rooms there, and I had for years taken it as the emblem of my own perpetual residence even unto death in my University.
> on the morning of the 23rd I left the Observatory. I have never seen Oxford since, excepting its spires, as they are seen from the railway.

The snapdragon and the spires are emblems, as for Newman's sensibility they would have to be; but three decades of Oxford have also impressed them on his mind as beloved objects. The passage is deeply affecting, while at the same time it makes us aware of the rarity of such consciousness in *The Apologia*, and points to something missing or avoided in a great and fiery spirit.

For Yeats, the task of the soul was to encompass all the varied or opposing states or stances of which souls are capable; yet first and last his poetry is that of an "antithetical" or subjective man who asserts, as in "Blood and the Moon," that the mind creates the world. For such a poet there can be only a limited sense of place, and even the rocks and moorhens of the later verse are symbols which seldom threaten to assert a life of their own. The celebrated "Lake Isle of Innisfree" is not an island at all, but a projection in natural images of the state of reverie. We feel this most strongly when Yeats somewhat endangers his tone:

> Nine bean-rows will I have there, a hive for the honeybee,
> And live alone in the bee-loud glade.

Those beans, and the implication of manual exertion, are incongruous, and we are put in mind, by contrasft, of Henry David Thoreau, whose beans, whatever else he made of them, were in the first place actual. Reading Yeats's poems, magnificent though they are, I often recall with relief that opposed extremist Robinson Jeffers, for whom

> The beauty of things was born before eyes and
> sufficient to itself; the heart-breaking beauty
> Will remain when there is no heart to break for it . . .

or remember Jorge Guillén's infinitely bracing line,

> The landscape imagines me.

Pétrus Borel denounced the trees for producing, year after year, the same tiresome green. There have always been, I suppose, and especially in the last two centuries, natures unresponsive or even hostile to their surroundings; and no doubt it is the most original natures who are most susceptible of deformity and detachment. What bothers me more than Pétrus Borel is my memory of a motel in South Carolina, which my wife and I settled for at the end of a long day's drive on a fast highway. Its rectangular asphalt parking lot had been hacked out of a stand of trees far from any town, and in the dim light one could not see what trees they were. The usual shoe-box-like structure was surrounded by cars from all over America; between the motel and the road was the usual fenced swimming pool. Within were an office, a restaurant that did not offer grits on the breakfast menu, and, for the rest, long corridors lined with identical rooms in which hung pictures of the Pont Neuf and the Arc de Triomphe. Walking down my corridor, cardboard bucket in hand, to visit the niche where stood an ice machine, I heard television voices coming through the doors, talking from everywhere else. In bed that night, I imagined that I heard a field crying out from beneath the asphalt, asking to be a place again, a place in Carolina. And I had the bad fancy that we Americans might be becoming a race which, for all its restless motion, moves by preference through a repetitive labyrinth of highway, ramp, lobby, snack bar, escalator, and concourse—an anaesthetic modular world in which we are at home only because things are everywhere the same.

The Englishwoman, looking up at my lofty and ragged mock orange, said, "You Americans like your nature rather . . . wild, do you not?" I suspect that she was making a conventional observation, yet it is still one truth about us that many Americans have a liking for the rough and unpruned–a liking for the wild which goes far beyond that "picturesque" aesthetic still visible in so much English parkland. It is a taste with political overtones, having to do with freedom and self-realization, and it also entails an atavistic gesture toward the frontier.

We have often comfortably balanced that taste with the advantages of civilized community. So William Cullen Bryant seems to have done. It is interesting that when Bryant, the poet of wild nature and the advocate of the Hudson River painters, was growing up in Cummington, the population was twice its present number and the land mostly cleared and worked. It was a rural place, but scarcely savage. Fortunately, there were thirty acres of virgin timber just down hill from the Bryant homestead, in which a doctor's son with a literary bent could nourish a sense of wilderness.

Asher Durand's painting of Bryant and Thomas Cole, in which the two are dwarfed by the sublime scenery of a Catskill gorge, amuses us because of the formality of the small, gazing figures: Mr. Bryant is dressed as what he was, not the Deerslayer but the editor of the New York Post. We are amused by a frock coat in the wilds; but would Bryant truly look more "natural" in buckskin? It is natural for men to live and work in society, and to reflect in their dress and manner whatever fashions and customs are in force. I daresay that Durand's picture does, after all, represent a harmony.

It is not merely gorges and virgin forests in which the feeling of place awakens, and we find ourselves in surroundings that answer to the spirit. A Vermont town sitting well in its valley, or an Italian town on its hill, looks no more artificial than a bee-hive. Seen from a rocky slope by Constance Richardson, the city of Duluth is in key with earth and water. And a great city like Rome, which honors its river and its topography, which is full of parks, fountains, and an endless variety of architecture, could almost suffice us forever. If the Campidoglio is not a place, what is? Cities and suburbs estrange us from the world only when they rape and obliterate their sites (as El Paso is now ingesting its mountains) and spread about so widely and drearily as to lose all focus, character, and congruence with extra-human nature. From such "material phenomena" the senses pull back, to the spirit's cost.

Several years ago, I took part in a panel discussion at a Southern university. The topic was, as so often, the relationship of art to society, and it chanced that the panelist who opened the discussion dealt so elegantly with the matter in ten minutes as to leave us with nothing to say. I then begged leave to change the subject, and to ask a question that I thought might be well answered at the seat of the Agrarian movement. What was the value to us, I asked, of unspoiled nature, and why should we not exterminate the whooping crane? It had not been my intention to cast a pall on the occasion, but that is what happened: a shyness came over panel and audience, and our symposium did not recover its verve. Undoubtedly there was something like unanimity of feeling about the issue, but we lacked the terms in which to recommend our feelings, or to come to an articulate agreement.

I mentioned my disruptive questions, a few days later, to a clever man who had been a writer of presidential speeches. "As for the whooping crane," he said, "I wouldn't have it vanish because that would deprive me of a possible experience." Not the loftiest of answers, perhaps, but a hard, honest one, and better than silence.

In part, at least, all men approach the landscape self-centeredly or self-expressively, looking for what agrees with their temperaments, what seems to embody their emotions, what suits them as decor or theater of action. Some have the luck to be born, and to remain, in country that is continuous with their personalities; others ramble about until they can say at last, like Brigham Young, "This is the place." Certain affinities are understandable, or can be made so: there is the man of daring philosophic mind, whose chief happiness lies in mountaineering; and there is W. H. Auden's poem "In Praise of Limestone," which brilliantly shows the correspondence between one kind of scenery and one human disposition. Other affinities are more obscure, though doubtless as profound: a painter writes simply, "I don't like New England. . . I like desert, I like rocks. . . ."

In the introduction to a recent anthology of nature poetry, William Cole reports his inability to find any suitable poems about the desert. Painters appear to have done more and better with the subject, and I remember one who told me how long it had taken him to adjust his eye and brush and palette to New Mexico. At first the dunes, mesas, mountains, and sky had impressed him as vast, empty, and paralyzing, and he had made out only four or five colors. It was a whole half-year before he apprehended great motions in the landscape, and a granular subtlety of color which called, so he judged, for a species of pointillist attack. Observation, the adaptation of his technique, and the discovery of what in himself the scenery might declare had at last made it possible for him to paint. He had invented New Mexico: what I like about his account, however, is that it implies no easy affinity, no facile personalization or imposition of mood, but a struggle with something powerfully other. Could one not just as well say that the desert, in requiring of the painter a fresh self, had in its own good time imagined him?

Certain ways and means of perceiving nature are fast being lost to us. The small farm is vanishing, and the experience of great solitudes is harder to come by. The common language of rural topography–that vocabulary of dell, swale, coppice, and coomb which Hardy used so well–has fallen into disuse, so that we are relatively speechless before the landscape. In New England, the precise word "intervale" begins to sound consciously old-Yankee, there being less and less practical reason to specify "a low tract of land between hills, especially along a river." Bryant's homiletic woods, Emerson's or Whitman's symbolic streams or grasses, all latter versions and warpings of the old notion that nature is a book of revelations, have lost much credit in this century; the book has grown difficult to read, and when one hears it read in poem or pulpit, it is commonly done with small fidelity or conviction. This is unfortunate for the imagination, which when in best health neither slights the world of fact nor stops with it, but seeks the invisible through the visible.

But shall we not soon be forced to recoup, and to recover a view of nature that is not purely exploitative? Between the last paragraph and this, I sat in our kitchen eating lunch and heard Lord Ritchie-

Calder speak on the radio of things which no one can now ignore–the crisis in population growth and food supply, the pollution of Earth's water systems and atmosphere, the finding of DDT in antarctic fauna, our perilous storing of radioactive wastes in the state of Washington. . . . Unless we elect to despair, we are now obliged to make choices that will reconcile us with a natural system of which we are only a part, and I do not doubt that the process will bring not only a fresh sense of how nature may be used, but also of what it is. Scripture asserts that we are worth many sparrows, and that may well be so; we may soon better remember what else scripture says of the sparrow–that it possesses infinite value and meaning in itself. There are many signs that, impelled by the present emergency, people are groping toward a reconciliation with this planet: to mention but one, new editions of Thoreau are appearing, and people of all ages are reading him again. I hope they may reject in him the neurotic opposition of nature and society, while prizing his power of vision and communion.

It is not necessary that everything be major: there are pleasant scenic poems, quite free of grand institutions, which one would be poorer without, and I see no reason why painters should not enrich us with nostalgic dooryards, optical studies, and blithe cuneiform sketches of gulls and waves. But for landscape painting to attempt its fullest possibilities in any period, there must be some painters who embody the attitude of V. D. Perrine, who said of rocks, trees, and rivers that they were "symbols of a great Universal Power . . . which makes and shapes tree and rock and river equally with myself." Provided the holder of such a view can also paint, he may help

to redeem us from indifference or subjective deformity by his achievements of place–a place being a
fusion of human and natural order, and a peculiar
window on the whole.

This essay was given as the Joseph Warren Beach Memorial Lecture, at the University of Minnesota, on April 27, 1972. It later appeared in The Hudson Review.

POETRY'S DEBT TO POETRY

I remember a dinner party at a house in Cambridge, years ago. Almost everyone at the table that evening could be considered some sort of an artist, and it occurred to our host to suggest that we all testify, in turn, as to how we had first felt the call to practice one art or another. To tell the truth, I have forgotten most of the testimony, but I do recall what kind of thing was said. The novelist, let's suppose, had come across a set of Trollope in a summerhouse; the composer had heard Caruso on the gramophone, or an organist practicing Bach in an empty church; the portrait painter, perhaps, had gone with his mother to call on Mr. Sargent in his studio. It was all like that. Not one of the deponents had anything to say about the turmoil of first love, the song of the thrush, or the Bay of Naples. What had started them off as artists, they said, were no such approved stimuli, but the encounter with art itself. Astonished by a poem, a painting, a fugue, they had wanted to make something like that.

The fact that art is provoked by art should not surprise us; it is, after all, in a general view of nature, a very peculiar and acquired thing to sing an aria or weave a tapestry. An old Kansas farmer, who disagreed with Darwin, once said to me, "Son, you go get yourself a monkey, and put him in a cage, and sit there and watch him; and when he turns into a man, you come tell me." I didn't make the proposed experiment, but if I had, and if the monkey had turned into a man, I wouldn't then have sat and waited for the man to compose a sestina. Some poetry of great power was once written by a man in a cage–by Ezra Pound, at Pisa; but he was a cultured man of this late century, with a specific poetic calling, who wrote in communion with the long-developed art of many ages, aiming to make it new. It does not suffice, of course, to speak of art exclusively as inherited matter and traditional artifice. Such a view would take too little note of our everpresent adaptive need to reshape the past; and it would slight the fact of individual genius. Sir Kenneth Clark tells us that art history knows no influence which could account for the dramatic expressiveness of Giotto; it appears that Giotto was in that respect simply original, and we are glad to hear it. Furthermore, we know that a work of art is not merely a finished conventional object, but also an instrument–a means of articulating the spirit of a time or a people, a means of transforming crude life, as it comes, into experience, and of embodying personal passion and wisdom. Out of such a sense of his function, Wordsworth denounced artifice and rule, and held that a poem should grow organically, like the Meadow-flower or Forest-tree; the apparent joke is that he said all this in a perfectly constructed sonnet. Emerson wrote scornfully of mere technical felicity, and called for poetry of prophetic inspiration; accordingly, though he could write so finished a poem as the "Concord Hymn," he roughened his verse to make it seem spontaneous, and fell at times into a spasmodic doggerel. Blake, if I am not mistaken, was another prophet who cultivated an expressive raggedness. The fact is, I think, that all good poets are also antipoets–or, as John Peale Bishop said, all poets are both conservative and radical. Any healthy imagination will rebel against art in some sense and in some degree, because it is laborious and solitary, and cheats the artist of common things, because it tends toward escapism, because it pretends to fill the place of politics and religion and does not, or because it so often takes the artist's freshest inspirations and suffocates them with conventional language and technique. All such objections are true, or may be; but as for the last it is also true, as Yeats said, that the soul which would sing must study "monuments of its own magnificence," must go to school to the masters. When Blake wished to shake off the smooth manner which he had so beautifully exemplified in his poem "To the Muses," he did not merely snatch a new style out of the air, but turned back also to Elizabethan models. Some relationship to some tradition, and the devising of an excellent style appropriate to one's vision, are not to be avoided; I was pleased when Richard Howard, not long ago, criticized Allen Ginsberg's cult of artless genius by quoting William Blake as follows: "Invention depends Altogether upon Execution or Organisation; as that is right or wrong, so is the Invention perfect or imperfect. Whoever is set to undermine the Execution of Art is set to destroy Art." Effective "artlessness," then, is just another style; and all revolutions in art are palace revolutions.

What I want to talk about, here, are a few examples of the indebtedness of art to art, and the fascinating difficulty of finding words for describing such indebtedness. Let us begin with the phenomenon at its most trivial, as it may appear in the so-called art of conversation. A host asks his guest what he will have to drink, and the guest replies, "What I want is a Martini; but it would be a far, far better thing for me to have a gin-and-tonic." Certainly the guest is not seriously referring to Dicken's Sydney Carton ascending the scaffold; he is merely being playful in a mild and perfunctory way. An hour later, when the host's memories of Shakespeare have been blurred by drink, he ushers his guest into the dining room, saying, "Lead on, Macduff." It would be wrong of the guest to read into that familiar misquotation any allusion to the murderous hospitality of Macbeth.

Conversation is full of the sort of reminiscence I have just illustrated. There is a higher plane, the plane of learning and wit, on which references are deliberately and pertinently made, and styles are knowledgeably taken on or off; but we do most of our talking well below that level, on a plane where echoes of literary phrase or manner mean very little, and seem intended chiefly to relieve banality of thought, as carbonation is felt to add gaiety to a poor wine.

In written art, it is certainly amongst the titles of novels that we find the most meaningless cases of borrowing. Consider these lines from Ernest Dowson's most celebrated poem:

> I have forgot much, Cynara! gone with the wind,
> Flung roses, roses, riotously with the throng,
> Dancing, to put thy pale, lost lilies out of mind. . . .

It seems a safe bet that Margaret Mitchell's *Gone With the Wind* lifted its title from that passage, but the borrowed words, as they apply to Miss Mitchell's Civil war novel, have nothing whatever to do with Dowson's lurid poem, whether in theme or in tone, and they are even different in grammar.* (*A hearer of this lecture kindly pointed out to me the following two sentences in Joyce's *Ulysses* (Modern Library edition, page 141): "Gone with the Wind. Hosts at Mullaghmast and Tara of the Kings." A correspondent of the *Atlantic,* in the April 1973 issue, cites the same passage in the same connection. It appears that Joyce adapted Dowson's words to his own purposes, associating them with Tara, and that Miss Mitchell's novel, for its purposes, then borrowed from Joyce.) Similarly, there is little but confusion to be gained by turning from Thomas Wolfe's *Look Homeward, Angel* to that passage of "Lycidas" which furnished him the title. I am not attacking Margaret Mitchell or Thomas Wolfe: I am simply observing that what publishers of novels call a "good title" is often a resonant phrase full of thematic largeness, which, though it has a vague air of previous success, is now quite divorced from its first context.

But let me talk now of artistic debts that mean something, and that might profitably be noticed by critic or scholar. I shall speak largely of poetry from here on, because that's presumably my province. When one poet has been prompted by another, he will sometimes say so flatly in capital letters, as when Wallace Stevens entitles a poem, "Variations on a Theme by Williams." Similarly, the dedication of a poem to another poet will often amount to a public I.O.U., and the light-verse writer who adapts another's idea to a fresh occasion may subtitle his poem "With Apologies to So-and-So." The uses of the epigraph in poetry and prose are varied; epigraphs are often subtle, oblique in their operation, and hard to describe; yet it stands to reason that most epigraphs are, in part, acknowledgments. To take a famous instance, Eliot prefaced his poem "The Hollow Men" with two quotations, one of which goes "Mistah Kurtz–he dead." What the quotation asks is that we call to mind the whole drift of Conrad's *Heart of Darkness*, and in particular the horror of Kurtz's moral emptiness at the close, and that we then use our memory of the noel as a pitch pipe whereby to key our reading of the Eliot poem that follows. An additional effect of that epigraph, I think, is to declare that the art and thought of Eliot were beholden to the art and thought of Conrad. Acknowledgment may also take the form of homage or invocation, and here I helplessly think of Whitman: what poet has been more saluted and summoned in this century than he? Ezra Pound, overcoming an early resistance, hails him filially as the poet who "broke the new wood"; Hart Crane, in the Hatteras section of *The Bridge*, gropes explicitly for Walt's hand and vision; and Theodore Roethke, in his poem "The Abyss," cries out, "Be with me, Whitman, maker of catalogues."

And then there is quotation within the body of a text: the poems of Marianne Moore are full of scrupulous inverted commas, and Elizabeth Bishop, seeing the glittering water at Wellfleet, is reminded of a phrase of Herbert's and writes, "the sea is 'all a case of knives,'" putting the last five words into quotes. There are some words that we may dare to quote without quotation marks–"incarnadine," for example; we know who the only begetter of that word was, and when it appears in any verse or sentence it brings the thought of Shakespeare with it. Nor did Thoreau have to use quotes in his description of the swamps to which he sometimes rambled:

where the swamp-pink and
dogwood grow, the red alder-
berry glows like eyes of imps, the
waxwork grooves and crushes the
hardest wood in its folds, and the
wild-holly berries make the
beholder forget his home with
their beauty, and he is dazzled and
tempted by nameless other wild
forbidden fruits, too fair for
mortal taste.

There is a glancing reminiscence of *Comus* in that
passage, but what we most hear are the opening lines
of *Paradise Lost*–"Of man's first disobedience, and the
fruit / Of that forbidden tree, whose mortal taste /
Brought death into the world. . . ." In speaking of
"wild forbidden fruits, too fair for mortal taste,"
Thoreau is playfully shifting Milton's words about,
and modifying their senses: it reminds me of the way
jazz musicians of the 1930s used to toss a phrase from
one tune into their rendition of another. But in evok-
ing Milton, and Milton's thought, Thoreau is also
saying, with majesty and economy, that the ponds
and woods of the Concord region are paradisal, holy,
and too ambrosial for the senses of degraded man.

All of these open admissions of poetic indebtedness are attractive and useful; they remind us that
art is ultimately a loose collective enterprise, and they
tell something of the particular writer by exposing
his affinities. Still, they must not be taken too simple-
mindedly: it is not of much interest to assign Ezra
Pound to something called the "Whitman Tradition,"
and let it go at that. Pound's poem of capitulating
praise should move its commentator to discern what
in Whitman Pound could actually use, what was not

to his purpose, and what he still could not stand. Literary historians, in their taxonomic fury, often talk as if the process of influence were like decalcomania, as if writers simply copied each other's productions, as Macy's might match Gimbel's in item and price; but such is not the case, and that character in Borgès who was so influenced by Cervantes as to write Don Quixote is fictitious. To be sure, there are people other than scribes, plagiarists, and forgers who copy art or try to; they are not in the full sense artists, and they cannot help it. Think of those who have aped the spare and addictive Hemingway sentence, without having the peculiarly resigned sense of life that required it; or those who, with no apparent sense of its function, have copied that long Faulkner sentence which is so suitable for conveying simultaneities of awareness and action. And what of all those instant Welshmen of twenty years ago, who dropped everything and wrote in the distinctive rhapsodic manner of Dylan Thomas? We cannot remember their names, and the reason we cannot is that Wordsworth was right: art must grow naturally, like a plant, from its own roots and in its own soil and climate. A plant may be pruned or trained or grafted to advantage, but only within the limits of its own nature. The saddest epitaph I have ever heard was spoken by Robert Frost; he said of another writer, "He wanted to be me." It is fatal for a writer to have one hero only; submitting to a single model, admiring but one syntax and lexicon, means that you will say what you do not mean, and that you will never find the right words for what you do mean. A commanding imagination, as many have said before me, steals not from one writer, but selectively from all writers, taking whatever will help in the articulation of its own sense of things.

In this connection, the most precarious of the fine poets of our century was Theodore Roethke. The poems of his first book, *Open House,* are noticeably affected by certain women poets whose work he loved–Louise Bogan, Elinor Wylie, Léonie Adams. Roethke was well aware of the fact, and in his essay "How to Write Like Somebody Else," he accounted for the fact in a remarkable way, saying that his early work had been touched by a compulsion to praise; out of his admiration for Léonie Adams, he said, he felt driven "to create something that would honor her in her own terms." In the shorter poems of Roethke's next period, especially the wonderful greenhouse pieces, I find no moments of celebratory imitation, and the voice seems entirely the poet's own; the long poems of that time, such as "The Shape of the Fire," have, as Roethke put it, certain "ancestors"–among them Mother Goose, the songs and ranges in Elizabethan and Jacobean plays, Thomas Traherne, and (I should think) James Joyce and the psychology of Jung. But whatever means he may have borrowed for these poems of psychic struggle, of regression and rebirth, everything had been mastered and turned to his own fresh purposes. If the poems sometimes fail through a too unmediated subjectivity, they are nevertheless powerfully original. And therefore it is a shock to find Roethke, in the next phase of his work, succumbing frequently and totally to the style of William Butler Yeats, so much so that in one poem he must declare with a certain bravado,

I take this cadence from a man named Yeats;
I take it, and I give it back again. . . .

The candor is disarming, but still one feels like answering, "Why?" When Roethke writes in the voice of Yeats, the results are often felicitous, as in the stunning poem from which I have just quoted, and yet one is disquieted, as by those free translations in which Robert Lowell makes Rilke sound like Lowell, and provides him with additional stanzas. One thinks, "This is good, but what is it?" In cases of this kind it is impossible not to be nagged by the question of authenticity, the question of who, after all, is talking.

Delmore Schwartz, writing in 1959, asked himself why an exceptional poet, at the height of his powers, should take to imitating Yeats, and concluded that Roethke's chief reason was probably "to guard against the deadly habit of self-imitation." I think that may have been part of the story. I also think– indeed, I know–that his marriage in the early 1950's gave Roethke a new entrée to life, calling for a new poetic vein, a vein that he could not at once invent. There are poets for whom the discovery of style is easy, because their purchase on the world is rational and social, and therefore readily expressed in some version of urbane discourse. But Roethke was not a rational, social poet; the great spur of his poetry was a romantic longing to escape the bounds of self, to escape the rational mind and its estranging formulations, and to become at one with the whole of life through communion and vision. A poetry of the subverbal and the supraverbal, which pursues the wordless through the wordless, does not find its true voice, or modify that voice, without some floundering and casting-about.

One thing that moves a poet to translate from other tongues, as I know from my own experience, is the urge to broaden his utterance through imposture, to say things he is not yet able to say in his own person. That sounds disgraceful, but it need not be. You can't translate, after all, without having an affinity for the original. If you bring over the ghazals of Saadi into English, as one of my students is doing, then you have done three things: you have improved the English reader's access to the genius of Persia, you have provided English poetry with some new Persian tricks, and you have rendered more articulate that part of you which resembles Saadi. It was something like this last result, I think, that came of Roethke's impersonation of Yeats. What was it that Yeats could offer Roethke? Technically, he offered a muscular and often end-stopped pentameter line which Roethke was equipped to exploit–for Roethke was, above all, a poet of the striking line. Yeats offered also a ruggedly vatic style in which such words as "soul" could sound convincing and modern, in which one could get away with talking of visions, of "Heaven blazing into the head," and of that beatitude called "unity of being," wherein self and world miraculously agree. Furthermore, and much to Roethke's purpose, Yeats offered a physical mysticism of the dancing body and of the marriage bed. Many of Roethke's Yeatsian poems succeed; some fail, as Yeats himself could fail, through the blustering rhetorical question, the willful transport, the mantic resolution which does not ring true. In any case, Roethke's impersonation of Yeats seems to me to have kept him talking, to have limbered, emboldened, and extended him, so that he became capable of those last poems which are better than ever and so much more his own.

Am I right about all that? Heaven knows. Let us agree that such a case is infinitely interesting and problematical, and proceed to other business.

Every now and then one is astonished by stumbling upon the unfamiliar antecedent of some familiar style. That happened to me recently when I read for the first time Winthrop Macworth Praed's poem "The Vicar." Praed was a witty English poet of the early nineteenth century, but he reminds me, and will surely remind you, if he has not already, of an American poet of the early twentieth. Here is a sample stanza of "The Vicar":

> His talk was like a stream, which runs
> With rapid change from rocks to roses:
> It slipped from politics to puns,
> It passed from Mahomet to Moses;
> Beginning with the laws which keep
> The planets in their radiant courses,
> And ending with some precept deep
> For dressing eels, or shoeing horses.

We think first, perhaps, of particular lines of Edwin Arlington Robinson, such as:

> The beauty, shattered by the laws
> Which have creation in their keeping,
> No longer trembles at applause,
> Or over children who are sleeping. . .

And then, perhaps, we recall that the eight-line stanza in which Praed describes his village vicar is very like the stanza that Robinson so frequently favored for the description of the citizens of his fictitious Tilbury Town. The eight-line tetrameter stanza, as used by him and by Praed, tends to have a jaunty rocking or balancing movement within the line, often stressed by alliteration, as well as balancings between line and line, between pairs of lines, and between the first four lines and the second. Through all these rockings, great and small, there flows a supple, sustained, and rather virtuoso grammar, which somehow produces all the necessary rhymes at the right junctures, and completes its thought precisely at the stanza's close: it is like a long, undulant line of deft skaters, who crack the whip and swing round to end in a circle. Here is one more of Praed's stanzas about the Vicar:

> His sermon never said or showed
>> That Earth is foul, that Heaven is gracious,
> Without refreshment on the road
>> From Jerome, or from Athanasius:
> And sure a righteous zeal inspired
>> The hand and head that penned and planned them,
> For all who understood admired,
>> And some who did not understand them.

We all know Robinson, and there is no need to hammer the point home with parallel passages. Robinson plainly owes a debt to Praed's piece of village portraiture, in respect of technique and tone and details of language, and I find that I am not the first to notice it. A trip to the library revealed that someone else had noticed these things thirty years ago, and I was glad to have his support of my quite independent discovery. When we suddenly come upon such an indebtedness as this, it is likely to shake up our tidy conceptions of classification and magnitude. Praed, after all, was a fine light-verse poet, or a writer of what is called vers de société; if Robinson derives in some part from him, may it not be that Robinson is less serious and less major than we have imagined? Well, what is it to be major? In a recent *New Yorker*, Auden praises Housman warmly, yet considers him a minor poet because he did not develop– because the late work is scarcely distinguishable from the early. I should not know how to apply that criterion to George Herbert, because he did so much of his work within a period of three years; and I hesitate also to apply it to Robinson: his work did change, but since by and large it changed for the worse, the fact of change does not seem to enhance his case. I wonder if an alternative measure of stature might not be the extent to which any poet has given sustained, forceful, and original treatment to a theme of some consequence? If that will do as a criterion, I will say with Roy Harvey Pearce that Robinson does have a large theme–that he is the poet of the breakdown of community in American society, and points again and again to that ignorance of the hearts of others, and consequent ignorance of self, which result from the substitution of the ash nexus for other and more humane forms of relationship. There are poems like "Miniver Cheevy" which, taken by themselves, seem dexterous, amusing, but not inexhaustible; taken in quantity, however, Robinson adds up at the very least to a consistent and serious view of things. Therefore whatever he took from Praed should work one way in Praed and another way in Robinson, as lemon has one character in lemonade and another in hollandaise. I think that is just what happens. At his best, Robinson takes forms whose rhymes and rhythms would in other hands be tricky, and converts them to the music of obsession, of fatality, and of that wryness and irony which his out-

217

look entailed.

I draw two morals from this matter of Robinson and Praed, and one is that poets do not always go about being influenced in the way in which critics and scholars would have them do. Critics and scholars, if I may be flippant about them for a moment, like literature to be organized sensibly in schools and streams–on the one hand, the Sons of Ben, on the other the Spenserians; they think it convenient for writers to be explainable by reference to immediate forerunners and major contemporaries. How wistfully scholars speak of the possibility that the paths of Milton and Donne may have crossed, when Milton was an adolescent student at St. Paul's, and Donne was dead of the Cathedral; but if it happened, it brought nothing about, and Milton went stubbornly on to elect such outlandish influences as Cardinal Bembo. It is always that way with the best poets– they do not travel in gangs, and they make surprising decisions as to who shall teach them. Not all our hindsight can make it seem predictable that Ezra Pound, in such and such a year, should have turned to Gautier for inspiration. In America today, there are critics of poetry prepared to tell us whither we are tending and just who the dominant influences are; and there is truth and interest in what they say; nevertheless, if you were to creep up behind some really good young poet on the street, you might well hear him muttering something unauthorized like Catullus, Whittier, or Coventry Patmore.

My second point may be quickly made. We have gradually put behind us, during the last two centuries, that notion of form and diction. In late generations poets have made more and more use, for serious purposes, of light, popular, slangy, or otherwise

218

nonelevated means: obvious examples would be Louis MacNeice's use of jazz language and movement, the indebtedness of Eliot's "Sweeney Agonistes" to the music hall, and the amazing rhetorical inclusiveness of John Berryman's Dream Songs. It is because Robinson's relationship to Praed is such a subtle and threshold instance of this tendency that I find it so intriguing.

Now I should like to give you a ballad written in 1803 by the English poet and lyricist Thomas Moore. It is called "The Lake of the Dismal Swamp," and it is based on the story of a young man of Norfolk, Virginia, who went mad with grief because of the death of his beloved. He developed the delusion that the girl was not dead, but had gone into the nearby Dismal Swamp, and when he vanished one day and never came back, it was assumed that the boggy wilderness had claimed him. You must imagine that the first two stanzas of Moore's ballad are spoken by the distraught young man.

"They made her a grave, too cold and damp
    For a soul so warm and true;
And she's gone to the Lake of the Dismal Swamp,
Where, all night long, by a fire-fly lamp,
    She paddles her white canoe.

"And her fire-fly lamp I soon shall see,
    And her paddle I soon shall hear;
Long and loving our life shall be,
And I'll hide the maid in a cypress tree,
    When the footstep of death is near."

Away to the Dismal Swamp he speeds–

His path was rugged and sore,
Through tangled juniper, beds of reeds,
Through many a fen, where the serpent feeds,
And man never trod before.

And, when on earth he sunk to sleep,
    If slumber his eyelids knew,
He lay, where the deadly vine doth weep
Its venomous tear and nightly steep
The flesh with blistering dew!

And near him the she-wolf stirr'd the brake,
    And the copper-snake breathed in his ear,
Till he starting cried, from his dream awake,
"Oh! when shall I see the dusky Lake,
    And the white canoe of my dear?"

He saw the Lake, and a meteor bright
    Quick over its surface play'd–
"Welcome," he said, "my dear one's light!"
And the dim shore echoed, for many a night,
    The name of the death-cold maid.

Till he hollow'd a boat of the birchen bark,
    Which carried him off from shore;
Far, far he follow'd the meteor spark,
The wind was high and the clouds were dark,
    And the boat return'd no more.

But oft, from the Indian hunter's camp,
    This lover and maid so true
Are seen at the hour of midnight damp
To cross the Lake by a fire-fly lamp
    And paddle their white canoe!

If we ask ourselves why that ballad sounds like a
parody, it soon occurs to us that Edward Lear, who
parodied such forgotten poems as this, has inter-

vened between us and Moore, with the odd and anachronistic result that Moore's ballad, when we happen on it, sounds to us like a muted and less outrageous version of Lear. Listen to these lines from the last stanza of Edward Lear's "The Jumbles":

> And in twenty years they all came back,
>   In twenty years or more,
> And everyone said, "How tall they've grown!
> For they've been to the Lakes, and the Torrible Zone,
>   And the hills of the Chankly Bore. . . ."

We could stick that into Moore's poem at any point and, though it might confuse the narrative, it would be almost perfectly in agreement with the stanza form of the ballad, its tripping sonority, and its spooky tone. Then as for vocabulary and phrasing, one feels that Lear's *Nonsense Songs* could easily yield a dozen close approximations of such a line as Moore's "Far, far he follow'd the meteor spark"–not to mention that other mournful line "And the boat return'd no more." Lear mimics and exaggerates Moore's poem, or poems of its kind, in mood and movement, in language and technique; and once one has registered these things, one then reflects on something still more striking–the degree to which Lear's customary plots resemble this plot of Thomas Moore's. I think particularly of "The Dong with a Luminous Nose." The scenery of that poem is also exotic, wild, and nocturnal, with strange flora and fauna. The Dong, we are told, was once happily in love with a beautiful Jumbly girl, but she sailed away and left him on the shore. Whereupon, Lear tells us, the Dong went mad with grief and loneliness:

But when the sun was low in the West,
  The Dong arose and said,–
"What little sense I once possessed
  Has quite gone out of my head!"
And since that day he wanders still
By lake and forest, marsh and hill,
Singing–"O somewhere, in valley or plain,
Might I find my Jumbly Girl again!
Forever I'll seek by lake and shore
Till I find my Jumbly Girl once more!"

Then, as you will remember, he constructs a long artificial nose containing a lamp, to light his steps during his nightlong wanders: it is not much more improbable than the firefly lamp imagined by a mad youth of Moore's poem, and it, too, by the way, is likened to a meteor. But let me not press too hard for detailed resemblances: it is enough to notice how similar the two stories are, even in their final tableaux, and to remember also, if you will, how characteristic the Dong is of the figures we find in Lear's poems. When they are not animals, like the Owl and the Pussycat, or inanimate objects like the Table and the Chair, they are grotesque persons like the blue-and-green Jumblies or the Quangle Wangle Quee. There are moments of happiness in the lives of these characters, but in general such happiness is fugitive in both senses of the word; for the most part, their experiences are sad. They are deprived, as the Pobble of his toes or the Yonghy-Bonghy-Bò of his beloved; they are often lonely, deserted, and weary; others have gone away and not returned, and they themselves are moved, like the Nutcrackers and the Sugar-Tongs, to fade away and never come back.

T. S. Eliot once observed that he could think of no poet, other than Lear, who appeared to have based his style on a study of Edgar Allan Poe. It is certainly easy to catch Lear writing with Poe in mind: if we turn to "Incidents in the Life of My Uncle Arly," we find Lear telling how once, when Uncle Arly stooped down to pick up a railway ticket, a pea-green cricket settled on his nose. The next three lines read as follows:

> Never–never more–oh! never,
> Did that Cricket leave him ever,–
> Dawn or evening, day or night. . . .

Needless to say Lear's adhesive cricket is a joke about Poe's raven, who croaked "Nevermore" and likewise never left. It could similarly be shown that, both in form and in tenor, Lear imitated and parodied Tennyson. Let me now ask what these three chosen influences have in common–Poe, Tennyson, and the Moore who wrote "The Lake of the Dismal Swamp." In respect to technique, all three are alike in that they could write balladic poems of a strongly musical and haunting character, and it was such verse that Lear felt drawn to imitate and distort. But furthermore, and quite as important, all three wrote on occasion weird, exotic, and morbid poems on those painful themes that underlie so much of Lear's nonsense–isolation, unbearable loss, abandonment, weariness, the wish to fade out of the world. Moore's mad young man, Tennyson's Mariana, Poe's lost Lenore and her lover, all have their queer relatives on the Coast of Coromandel and the great Gromboolian plain. I am aware that I am now inviting the rage of those who would have all humor jolly and shallow, and who interrupt one to say, "You seem to forget that nonsense is funny." But such people lack the discernment of children, who always know that Lear's poems are a very rich mix indeed. He is, for one thing, a parodist, which a literate child can at least partly perceive; secondly, he is a fine and catchy versifier, whom children very quickly get by heart; thirdly, he is a violent and fantastic humorist, and all children laugh with him; finally, he is a poet of heartbreak, and I have known him to move my children to tears. When I think of Edward Lear, I am sometimes put in mind of those characters in Russian novels who express their pain and humiliation through buffoonery. Or maybe a better comparison would be to that grotesque and lovely man Jimmy Durante, who ends his performances by saying, with a Thespian sweep of his arm, "Good night, Mrs. Calabash, wherever you are!" If I'm not mistaken, that is at once parodistic, ludicrous, and touching.

Assuming that I have not talked nonsense about Edward Lear, it would plainly be insufficient merely to call him a parodist, because he differs so from other kinds of parodist. It is true that he pokes fun at certain poets, but it is also true that in so doing he expresses, in the only manner possible to his shy and quirky nature, a sympathy for their painful themes. With Louis Untermeyer, for example, the case is far simpler: when he shows us how "Little Boy Blue" might have sounded if written by Edna Millay, the mannerisms of Millay are amusingly magnified through their bestowal on a small subject, but the parodist does not express himself otherwise than by exhibiting his wit. Edmund Wilson's famous parody, "The Omelet of A. MacLeish," differs from the Untermeyer sort of thing in that it is vicious, and in that its material is the career of MacLeish adversely described in a travesty of MacLeish's style: ironically, such an attack cannot avoid being in some part flattering, since it concedes that its victim has a distinct and memorable way of writing. It seems likely that parody works more simply and accountably in Wilson and Untermeyer than it does in Lear; and yet we must always be alert, in reading parodic poetry, for some ambiguities of motive and effect. Here, for example, is a little note which Randall Jarrell prefaced, in 1942, to his poem "The Country Was": "This," he said, "is supposed to be a parody of Miss Marianne Moore's poetry. I hope that it is accurate, admiring, and a little critical."

There is a rare kind of imitative poetry for which I know no name. It is not parody, because it involves no mockery or broad caricature, no subversion by means of bathos. The Jarrell piece just mentioned comes close, in fact, to being the sort of thing I mean, but Auden's poem "Their Lonely Betters" is a pure specimen. In subject, "Their Lonely Betters" is a casual rumination about the difference between man and the other creatures, and about how language is suitably restricted to man. The first stanza goes like this:

> As I listened from a beach-chair in the shade
> To all the noises that my garden made,
> It seemed to me only proper that words
> Should be withheld from vegetables and birds.

That is colloquial and playful, but it is not exactly Auden's kind of colloquial play, and the voice grows stranger as we read into the second stanza and are told how

. . . rustling flowers for some third party waited
To say which pairs, if any, should get mated.

There is a clear reminiscence, in that, of a poem by
Frost called "A Winter Eden," and it begins to dawn
on the reader that Auden's poem, in title, theme, attitude, and style, is far more Frost than it is Auden.
In the fourth and last stanza Auden gracefully lets
us know what he has been up to, when he says of
birds and flowers,

> Let them leave language to their lonely betters
> Who count some days and long for certain letters;
> We, too, make noises when we laugh or weep;
> Words are for those with promises to keep.

The poem closes with a frank echo of "Stopping
by Woods on a Snowy Evening," and thus declares
its purpose: out of his admiration for Robert Frost,
Auden has done his best to write a Frost poem on a
Frost subject. John Malcolm Brinnin has produced
several poems of a similar generosity; for example,
his poem "A Thin Façade for Edith Sitwell" does not
exaggerate Dame Edith's already flamboyant early
style, but honors her by a strict emulation of it. Such
performances are never weighty and major, but they
are very hard to bring off, requiring as they do a
lack of malice, a gift for self-effacement, and a mi-
metic faculty more exquisite perhaps than the
parodist's. Small wonder that productions of the kind
are rare, and that very able hands have sometimes
failed in the effort to write them. Louise Bogan once
published a poem called "Evening in the Sani-
tarium," with a subtitle reading "Imitated from

Auden"; alas, Miss Bogan proved to be helplessly herself, and without the subtitle one would scarcely have guessed that she had had Auden in mind. Fortunately, the piece was a superlative Bogan poem, and in later printings the subtitle was dispensed with, or relegated to a footnote.

We are now speaking of the kind of poetic response that arises from affection and professional respect, and I am reminded of two good poems the relationship of which has long intrigued me. One is by Delmore Schwartz, and goes like this:

> Tired and unhappy, you think of houses
> Soft-carpeted and warm in the December evening,
> While snow's white pieces fall past the window,
> And the orange firelight leaps.
> 				A young girl sings
> That song of Gluck where Orpheus pleads with Death;
> Her elders watch, nodding their happiness
> To see time fresh again in her self-conscious eyes:
> The servants bring the coffee, the children retire,
> Elder and younger yawn and go to bed,
> The coals fade and glow, rose and ashen,
> It is time to shake yourself! and break this
> Banal dream, and turn your head
> Where the underground is charged, where the weight
> Of the lean buildings is seen,
> Where close in the subway rush, anonymous
> In the audience, well-dressed or mean,
> So many surround you, ringing your fate,
> Caught in an anger exact as a machine!

Beginning with fatigue and sadness, Schwartz's poem moves off into a fantasy of comfort and familial happiness, from which at the close the "you" of the poem is brusquely awakened to face his real condition, as an anonymous person in a violent city. John Berryman's poem "Desires of Men and Women" is a deliberate variation on this poem of Schwartz's. It is exactly one line longer; it, too, moves from unhappiness into fantasies of a gracious house and ordered life; and it, too, ends with a brutal awakening. Here is the poem:

Exasperated, worn, you conjure a mansion,
The absolute butlers in the spacious hall,
Old silver, lace, and privacy, a house
Where nothing has for years been out of place,
Neither shoehorn nor affection been out of place,
Breakfast in summer on the eastern terrace,
All justice and all grace.
                              At the reception
Most beautifully you conduct yourselves–
Expensive and accustomed, bow, speak French,
That Cinquecento miniature recall
The Duke presented to your great-grandmother–

And none of us, my dears, would dream of you
The half-lit and lascivious apartments
That are in fact your goal, forwhich you'd do
Murder if you had not your cowardice
To prop the law; or dream of you the rooms,
Glaring and inconceivably vulgar,
Where now you are, where now you wish for life,
Whence you project your naked fantasies.

I once asked Berryman in what spirit he had written a poem so strictly parallel to Schwartz's, and he told me that what he had intended was "both a tribute and a criticism." Of Berryman's deep admiration for Schwartz, and for the poem in question, there can be no doubt; it is also clear, given such admiration, that in criticizing Schwartz's poem Berryman was not trying to outdo him publicly, but simply to speak to him as poet to poet. Well, in what differences between the two poems might Berryman's criticism inhere? Metrically, Schwartz's poem is loose and varied; Berryman's stays close to the pentameter and is more vigorous in movement. The "you" addressed in Schwartz's poem may be less universal than the "you" of Berryman's, but of that I am not sure. In Schwartz's poem, the fantasy is full of sentimental warmth, while in Berryman the dream is of elegance. Schwartz's language is less rhetorical than Berryman's, which has many clever appositions of abstract and concrete. All these differences are there to be noted, yet none seems to me to constitute Berryman's criticism of Schwartz: I find that criticism in the contrast between the awakenings with which the two poems terminate. When Schwartz's poem returns us to bitter reality, it is to a condition of loneliness in a dehumanized urban world. The corresponding statement in Berryman is that our condition is vulgar and sordid, and our wishes also: we do not truly long for order and grace, but rather for "half-lit and lascivious apartments." In short, what Berryman's poem says to Schwartz is this: our unhappiness, from which we sometimes flee into pathetic daydreams, derives not from our oppressive circumstances but from the corruption of our hearts.

The courteous conversing of one poem with another is artistic response at its best. When we think of Dante welcomed by the great pagan poets in Limbo, or of Yeats saying "I shall dine at end of day / With Landor and with Donne," it is not literary chitchat which we imagine, but conversation of this perfected kind. I. A. Richards, in a brilliant talk, once showed Coleridge conversing with Wordsworth

229

about inspiration in the metaphor of light, and Longfellow conversing with them both in the same figure. We have the thing at its most magnificent in Lycidas, where Milton addresses the whole pastoral tradition, both honoring and transcending it. Let me offer as my last exhibit a singular instance of conversing.

Thomas Lovell Beddoes, that strange death-obsessed poet whom Ezra Pound rightly called the "prince of morticians," wrote at some time in the 1840's a poem called "The Phantom-Wooer." It is an uneven work which at times is mere Gothic grisliness, but the first lines of the second verse are exceptionally beautiful. This is a ghost who loves a lady fair, and who is asking her to join him in death:

> Young soul, put off your flesh, and come
> With me into the quiet tomb;
> Our bed is lovely, dark, and sweet;
> The earth will swing us, as she goes,
> Beneath our coverlid of snows,
> And the warm leaden sheet.

Hearing those lines, and especially the line "Our bed is lovely, dark, and sweet," it is impossible not to be reminded of the latter portion of Robert Frost's "Stopping by Woods," in which a winter traveler is somehow tempted by the roadside woods to forsake his journey. The horse, as you will remember, is all for moving on:

> He gives his harness bells a shake
> To ask if there is some mistake.
> The only other sound's the sweep
> Of easy wind and downy flake.

The woods are lovely, dark and deep.
But I have promises to keep,
And miles to go before I sleep,
And miles to go before I sleep.

In this portion of the poem, which depicts the snowy woods, there is no mention of cold. The characterizing words are "easy," "downy," "lovely," "dark," and "deep," words that evoke just such a snowy coverlet and featherbed as were offered in Beddoes' poem, and which oblige Frost twice over to put away the thought of "sleep." One evening in the late 1940's I asked Frost whether he was fond of Beddoes, and he said he was; but he said so with what seemed to me a warning glitter in his eye, and I did not pursue the subject. But I was right then, and am right now, in believing that Frost's "Stopping by Woods" converses with a poem by Beddoes, declines its invitation, and pays its beauty the tribute of resistance. This is not to say that Frost's poem is about death; that would be a little crude; better to say that the poem is about impulses which we sometimes associate with the deep sleep of death–the luxurious thought of giving up the struggle, the temptation not to go on.

I have scarcely begun to count the ways in which poetry may be indebted or reactive to other poetry. There are poets, for instance, who treat certain predecessors as the priests of a secret doctrine, and I think I could show at fearful length that Yeats's volume *The Tower* is permeated with a profound understanding of Milton's companion poems "L'Allegro" and "Il Penseroso." And I should love to try to say exactly what happens when the French poet Baudelaire takes the most celebrated quatrain of

231

Gray's "Elegy" and turns it into the sestet of his sonnet "Le Guignon." But it seems about time to sum up and be still. I have said that art is prompted, in the first place, by other art, and that artists, however original, respond to other artists in various manners: by borrowing, theft, adaptation, translation, impersonation, parody, and so on. In discussing any particular case, I have found that such terms as these were seldom wholly adequate to the description of apparent motive and effect; we lack a handy vocabulary for describing what goes on in Edward Lear, for example, and it may be that in any challenging instance one must use an ad hoc and groping terminology. That does not, however, excuse the too cautious critic who tells us merely, "In this passage, Miss Brontë would seem to owe something to Byron." Any writer on literature who is afraid to use inference and a trained intuition is in the wrong racket. To attempt to define the nature of any literary debt is a chancy business, but it is one of infinite interest, and the truth of such matters is not beyond all conjecture. If you have found some of my conjectures interestingly wrong, I shall not mind; and if you feel that I have sometimes only scratched the surface—that much more might have been said—I shall feel that my point has been made.

When asked by Greg Kuzma, in 1974, to do some-
thing for a special Frost issue of his magazine
Pebble, I reflected that I had never read or heard
any comment on "The Gum-Gatherer," and so was
led to make these notes upon it.

ON ROBERT FROST'S "THE GUM-GATHERER"

THE GUM-GATHERER

There overtook me and drew me in
To his downhill, early-morning stride,
And set me five miles on my road
Better than if he had had me ride,
A man with a swinging bag for load
And half the bag wound round his hand.
We talked like barking above the din
Of water we walked along beside.
And for my telling him where I'd been
And where I lived in mountain land
To be coming home the way I was,
He told me a little about himself.
He came from higher up in the pass
Where the grist of the new-beginning brooks
Is blocks split off the mountain mass–
And hopeless grist enough it looks
Ever to grind to soil for grass.
(The way it is will do for moss.)
There he had built his stolen shack.
It had to be a stolen shack
Because of the fears of fire and loss
That trouble the sleep of lumber folk:
Visions of half the world burned black
And the sun shrunken yellow in smoke.
We know who when they come to own
Bring berries under the wagon seat,
Or a basket of eggs between their feet;
What this man brought in a cotton sack

Was gum, the gum of the mountain spruce.
He showed me lumps of the scented stuff
Like uncut jewels, dull and rough.
It comes to market golden brown;
But turns to pink between the teeth.

I told him this is a pleasant life
To set your breast to the bark of trees
That all your days are dim beneath,
And reaching up with a little knife,
To loose the resin and take it down
And bring it to market when you please.

In Frost's *Selected Poems*, "The Gum-Gatherer" is preceded by "After Apple Picking" and "Birches," and followed by "The Mountain." I think that the poem, so placed by its author, gains a good deal in resonance and weight. Putting it roughly, as one must, let us say that all the poems in question are concerned with spiritual activity (religion, the bestowal of love, the writing of poems), and with balancing the claims of earth and heaven. In all cases, the central imagery is of altitude, of trees or mountains, of climbing and descending. "After Apple Picking," the monologue of a farmer dizzy with fatigue, is at its most general a poem about the strain and imbalance that attend an obsessed perfectionism in any high undertaking. The apple-picker is not to be judged a fool, I think: he has climbed not to heaven but toward it, seeking perfection in a finite task, and he has come down from his ladder with real apples. Furthermore, as the poem says, he is superior to such creatures as the woodchuck, who are never troubled by the aftereffects of aspiration. It is "human" to do (or overdo) as he has done, and the poem is only incidentally cautionary.

"Birches," for all its whimsy, is more assertive, and, as I have said elsewhere, it may be read as a rejection of the sort of soaring idealism we find in Shelley, whose famous lines about Life and Eternity lie shattered in Frost's description of the ice storm. The poem "asks of us a certain height," but counsels also a fidelity to "earth"–to the actual, the familiar, the mundane. A similar recommendation of down-to-earth high-mindedness may be derived from "The Mountain," which brings together two characters–a farmer who has never climbed the mountain at the foot of which he lives, and a visitor who has half a mind to make the climb. Opposing impulses toward "earth" and "heaven" are thus embodied, and the friendly give-and-take between the two characters implies the balance that Frost urges. The fact that the mountain is named Hor, or Horeb perhaps, gives a historical dimension to the poem's latent argument. Thinking of the Biblical Hor, one thinks of Moses and Aaron, of prophecy, or priesthood, and of talking with God on mountaintops. What "The Mountain" finally implies (and what "Sitting by a Busy in Broad Sunlight" flatly asserts, in contradiction to Emerson) is that our diminished age should not aspire to high visions and revelations; the thing to do is to keep faith with what has been revealed, and dwell in the shelter of it.

"The Gum-Gatherer" is slighter, perhaps, than the other poems in the constellation I have been considering. Like the others, it treats such fundamental ideas as altitude with its own specific mood and emphasis. It is the least concerned with balance, the most positive about aspiration, the most obviously a metaphor for the poetic experience. Whereas Frost's apple-picker spoke for himself, the gum-gatherer is encountered by another character, who portrays and interviews him. But there are no real differences in personality between the two men. The speaker of the poem describes the other as if he were describing the best, happiest, and most energetic part of his own nature. The gum-gatherer is a climber indeed: he lives in the mountains, "higher up in the pass" than the speaker, and what he does up there is to climb spruce trees, "reaching up" to gather resin from the hollows in the bark. As the poem begins, we find him striding downhill, bringing a sack of spruce gum to market, where presumably it will be bought by makers of varnish, turpentine, or medicaments. The gum-gatherer's descent from mountain to market is like the birch-swinger's return to earth, yet in this poem descent is at best a necessary comedown. The stress is on the joy of working at a pure and lonely altitude.

The gum-gatherer is lofty and original; he is associated with early morning and with "new-beginning brooks"–those high springs that in Frost's topography ("The Mountain," "West-Running Brook," "Directive") symbolize the divine source of things. It may not be irrelevant to recall Genesis 2:11-12, where the first river of Eden, Pison, waters a land rich in the gum resin called bdellium. In any case, the gum-gatherer's crop is more spiritual, more leisurely taken, less profitable, and less geared to the market than products raised or owned by valley dwellers or city dwellers. Far below, where ground rock has been turned into "soil for grass," are dairy farms, berry patches, and barnyards, all serving the economy, and anxiously sleeping owners of timberland for whom a commercial loss would seem the fiery end of the world. It is clear that the gum-gatherer's "visions" are of a better kind, and that his resinous goods, as they take on more and more symbolic meaning, have that relative inutility which has sometimes been claimed for art.

The last line of the poem sends one to passages of "New Hampshire" or "Build Soil," in which Frost is speaking of poetry as a product that must come to market like any other, but that should be slowly and inwardly made, not hurried to the consumer "in commercial quantities." Tityrus, in the latter poem, advises making "a late start to market." These lumps the gum-gatherer carries in a sack–these "scented... jewels," these pieces of myrrh or frankincense or amber– are poems on their way to publication, but they have been harvested in uplifted isolation and with no forethought of reward or use.

One of the seemingly offhand beauties of "The Gum-Gatherer" is a sequence of visual images, images of rounded and colored forms, which begins in the thirty-third line. From a half-blackened globe Frost moves to a dwindled yellow sun, and thence by way of berries and eggs to golden-brown lumps which, if chewed, turn pink. The final picture of gum-chewing is a deflationary return to literal fact, but the sequence as a whole uses similarity to underline the difference between low visions and high. The charred world and shrunken sun are nightmares of destruction and loss arising from greed; the eggs and berries (though Frost could elsewhere turn blueberries into jewels) are here mere commercial goods; the resin lumps, however, are depicted both realistically ("dull and rough") and in terms suggestive of rarity, beauty, preciousness, creation, and, I think, preservation. The vaguest line in the poem is "That all your days are dim beneath"; it has always impressed me as abruptly "poetic," grammatically hazy, and a probable incitement to imaginative daring. Undoubtedly it means that, day after day, the gum-gatherer may look down from whatever perch and see a forest floor bedimmed by the shade of spruces. Yet I cannot help thinking also of the Upper Earth of the Phaedo, with its pure philosophic jewels and of the Attendant Spirit in Comus, who dwells there "Above the smoke and stir of this dim spot, / Which men call Earth." While to claim any such Platonic transcendence would be uncharacteristic of Frost, I nevertheless see his gum-gatherer as a poet who has ascended some distance above the daily flux so as to distill it into something of the first water. The jewel he gathers may literally be the resin of the spruce, but I am further put in mind of that fossil resin amber, in which poems have so often seen a symbol of their own power to salvage things from time.

Two last remarks. Frost once said to an interviewer, when asked whether poets must misbehave like Rimbaud, that he had not the flexibility "to live in filth and write in the treetops." And finally, since poetry is nothing if not the choosing of right words, how quietly brilliant was the poet's decision, in the final paragraph of his poem, to say, not "chest," but "breast."

The Boston publisher David Godine brought out a beautiful new edition of Pym *in 1973, illustrated by Gerry Hoover and containing this introduction. Illustrations and introduction were complementary in their interpretations, the former stressing the tale's literal gruesomeness, the latter its allegorical dimension.*

"THE NARRATIVE OF ARTHUR GORDON PYM"

We pretty well know what practical considerations moved Poe to write this, his only finished novel. Through J. K. Paulding, whose defense of Negro slavery he would soon favorably review for the *Southern Literary Messenger,* Poe had sought in early 1836 to place a volume of short stories with the New York firm of Harper & Brothers. The publishers respectfully declined the collection, one of their reasons being that "Readers in this country have a decided and strong preference for works (especially fiction) in which a single and connected story occupies the whole volume." Paulding, in shipping the manuscript back to Poe, expressed a similar sense of the market: "I think it would be worth your while," he wrote, "if other engagements permit, to undertake a Tale in a couple of volumes." Poe evidently let himself be guided by such counsel and, in the *Messenger* for January-February of the next year, was able to publish a first portion of *The Narrative of Arthur Gordon Pym.* The novel as a whole was finished in 1837 and brought out by Harper–alas, with little profit or éclat–in 1838.

If the length of *Arthur Gordon Pym* may somewhat be explained by the author's poverty and the public taste for long-winded fiction, Poe's choice of subject may in part be ascribed to his journalist's sense of the fashionable and sensational. Phrenology, California gold, balloon flights, galvanism, prophecies of Judgment Day–Poe's fiction took prompt advantage, superficially at least, of popular fascination with any topic whatever. In deciding to write a sustained tale of nautical adventure, full of stowing-away, mutiny, shipwreck, and cannibalism, Poe hoped to capitalize on a seemingly inexhaustible demand for sea stories; but *Pym* was also aimed–like "Ms. Found in a Bottle," which preceded it by five years–at exploiting a widespread and intense interest in polar exploration. In 1818 Captain John Cleves Symmes had advanced his theory that the earth is "hollow, habitable, and widely open about the poles"; the idea was taken-off, in the 1820 novel *Symzonia*, by the pseudonymous "Adam Seaborn," and more seriously taken by Poe both in "Ms." (1833) and in "Hans Phaall" (1835), where the hero descries from his moon-bound balloon an Arctic polar gulf "of the most absolute and impenetrable blackness." A longtime defender of the Symmes theory, Jeremiah N. Reynolds, addressed the House of Representatives in 1836, recommending that the government sponsor an expedition to the South Pole, and Poe supported Reynolds in the pages of the *Messenger*. In 1838, as a result of Reynolds's efforts, the government-financed Wilkes expedition, which was destined to make important discoveries, left Norfolk for the South Pacific and the Antarctic. Poe's novel, which in its terminal note makes reference to "the governmental expedition now preparing for the Southern Ocean," could scarcely have been more topical.

Poe had little experience of the sea (he had sailed to England and back as a child, and made one or two coastwise voyages); it was thus inevitable that

Pym should draw upon other texts. There are straight-forward quotations, in the novel, from Reynolds's congressional address, and from Benjamin Morrell's *Narrative of Four Voyages to the South Sea and the Pacific.* There are in addition, as scholars have discovered, a slew of unacknowledged borrowings from Morrell and from other nautical books–borrowings calculated to produce that salty authenticity which Conrad praised in Poe, and also perhaps to pad the narrative. In "Ms. Found in a Bottle," Poe had sent a skeptical narrator on a voyage which began prosaically in Batavia and ended wonderfully with the plunge of a phantom ship into a South Polar whirl-pool. The story–which was au fond an allegory of the dreaming soul's departure from this world, and its glimpsing of the Beyond–anchored itself initially in mundane fact with such aggressively "accurate" sentences as these:

> Our vessel was a beautiful ship of about four hundred tons, copper-fastened, and built at Bombay of Malabar teak. She was freighted with cotton-wool and oil, from the Lachadive Islands. We had also on board *coir, jaggeree, ghee,* coconuts, and a few cases of opium. The stowage was clumsily done, and the vessel consequently *crank.*

Are comparable effects achieved in *Pym*? Unquestionably so. As *Pym*, like "Ms.," modulates toward the uncanny, an exact terminology and a spirit of concrete observation serve to sustain the reader's assent, and to keep any "mystic" meaning implicit, as Poe said it should be. The following, taken at random from chapter 1 of *Pym*, has an air of objective accuracy which persists throughout the novel:

> The boat was going through the water at a terrible rate–full before the wind–no reef in either jib or mainsail–running her bows completely under the foam. It was a thousand wonders she did not broach to. . . . I summoned up the resolution of despair, and rushing to the mainsail, let it go by the run. As might have been expected, it flew over the bows, and, getting drenched with water, carried away the mast short off by the board.

Is a similar effect gained, however, by *Pym's* long parenthetical essays on stowage, the art of lying-to in a gale, petrels, and the like? It may be that Poe intended these passages, too, to supply a tension between matter-of-fact chronicling and our growing intimations of the "mystic"; yet to me they seem obvious cullings, employed in some part as filler, and far less functional than the informative digressions of that later novel of whiteness and the sea, *Moby Dick*.

Not only did Poe's novel borrow from nautical literature; it adapted ideas from his other reading as well. From Irving's account of the Northwest fur trade, *Astoria*, which Poe reviewed in early 1837, he appropriated the explosion of the ship *Tonquin*, the Black Hills, with their "broken and predatory tribes," and the "desolate sterility" of the Great American Desert. In Stephens's *Travels in Arabia Petraea*, which with the help of the eminent classicist Charles Anthon he discussed for the *New York Review,* he found the city of Petra, the tortuous defile that approaches it, the cave-inscriptions at Sinai, and turned all these into aspects of his imaginary Tsalal: Klock-Klock and its gorge, the chasms and their hieroglyphs. If the reader of this introduction is interested in literary indebtedness, let him proceed from *Pym* to Stephens, Morrell, Irving, and other texts to which scholarship will direct him; he will find continual occasion to cry "Aha!," since all of Poe's works (unless we consider that forgotten hack job entitled *The Conchologist's First Book) Pym* most frequently filches or reprocesses the materials of other writers.

Detractors of the novel may then say, with some justice, that *Pym* was undertaken as a potboiler by a writer whose real gift was for short fiction, that it proposed to exploit a current sensation, and that it borrowed right and left. Let us also concede to the prosecution that the novel lacks the structural whole-ness of Poe's finest short stories: its plot does not steadily build as "Ligeia"'s does, and it has not the fine continuous webwork of significant language that we find in "The Fall of the House of Usher." *Pym's* experience in the hold of the *Grampus,* as supple-mented by his friend Augustus, is perhaps dispro-portionately long; certainly chapters 14-16 consist too largely of informational collage; and there are other faults to find. In his "Philosophy of Composition," Poe remarked that such a work as *Robinson Crusoe* "demands no unity," and it must be granted that Poe's own sea story has its architectural deficiencies. There are also clear indications of hasty writing here and there: for example, Pym speaks in the first chap-ter, and more specifically in the fifth, of having dis-cussed his adventures with Augustus after a lapse of "many years"–forgetting that Augustus will die in chapter 13. But having admitted all these things, let me counter by saying that not only his public, but Poe himself, was genuinely fascinated by polar exploration; that Poe's concern with it was both literal and imaginative; that *Pym* is a coherent allegory throughout; and that what Poe took from his many sources–forgetting, for the moment, his borrowings for mere authenticity's sake–is made to coalesce, especially at the close, into a powerful vision which is Poe's and nobody else's.

The background of Poe's allegorical fiction is cosmic. We must imagine a "big bang" cosmos which was created by God's self-radiation into space, which has now begun to fall into disharmony, and which will soon regather toward the original divine unity. Earth, as we learn in "The Conqueror Worm," now hears but "fitfully" the music of the spheres; it has lost that sense of beauty and proportion through which souls and planets are attuned to divinity, and has succumbed to a low-thoughted rationalism and materialism whereby the spirit of man has been darkened and the face of the globe defiled. Since the cosmos is deity diffused, and God now exists only in "infinite individualizations of Himself," it follows that every man, tree, or pebble on earth is a portion of God–but of God corrupted and obscured. From the point of view of earth, then, there is a black-and-white gnostic contrast between the world as it is and the once-and-future unity of God. The task of the soul in this situation is to reject the world utterly and–as Poe once claimed to do–"live continually in a reverie of the future," remembering the lost harmony of things and re-creating God through the combinative power of visionary thought. In Poe's essential myth, as in gnostic belief, the soul in restoring itself restores God.

An English critic has described *Pym* as a "spiritual autobiography." That could be close to the truth, I think, if understood in terms of the vision I have just presented in condensed and synthetic form, and to which I shall recur. But the novel also contains autobiographical elements of a more literal kind, as might be expected from an author who gave William Wilson his own birth date and his own English schoolmaster, Dr. Bransby, and who sprinkled his other tales with similar personal references of a cryptic sort. One's sense of this kind of content in *Pym* begins with the hero's name: "Arthur Gordon Pym" has the same number and disposition of syllables as "Edgar Allan Poe," the same terminal r and n, the same initial P. The fourth sentence of the story proper refers to Pym's grandfather's holdings in "the Edgarton New Bank," and soon thereafter we are told that Pym, as a boy, studied at New Bedford under "old Mr. Ricketts, a gentleman with only one arm." According to J. H. Whitty, there was in fact a one-armed schoolmaster of that name in Poe's home city of Richmond. There is no report—to proceed with the names in *Pym's* first paragraph—of a Richmond schoolmaster named "E. Ronald," yet the reader may be forgiven, after so much name-play, if he notes that "Ronald" is an anagram of "Arnold," the family name of Poe's mother, Elizabeth. The name of Pym's school friend, Augustus Barnard, is less obviously suggestive, since recent biography has made little mention of Poe's boyhood companion, Ebenezer Burling. But it will readily be seen that "Augustus" and "Ebenezer" have eight letters each, while "Barnard" and "Burling" have seven each and an initial B in common; furthermore, there is a certain symmetry in the transformation of "Edgar" and "Ebenezer" into "Arthur" and "Augustus." If a modicum of what biographers say of Burling is true, then Poe assuredly had him in mind when composing the first chapter of *Pym*. Edgar and his friend, we are told, often sailed on the James in the latter's boat; they read *Robinson Crusoe* together; Ebenezer was a precocious drinker, and was drunk when he accompanied Edgar on his flight to Norfolk in 1827, turning back to Richmond when he sobered up, and leaving Edgar to embark for Boston. It is likely that, in conceiving the character of Augustus, Poe combined Burling with William Henry Poe, his elder brother by two years, who had gone to sea and returned with a good repertoire of yarns. Sarah Elmira Royster, Poe's boyhood sweetheart, left record of Edgar's calling at her Richmond house in the summer of 1825, accompanied by Ebenezer and by William Henry, the latter in "nautical uniform."

The sort of critic who flatly identifies the figures of Poe's fiction as John Allan or Virginia Poe, often on the scantiest evidence, should be pleased with the opening of *Pym*, since the author unquestionably begins his novel with a quantity of personal references, both conspicuous and veiled, pertaining for the most part to his Richmond boyhood and to his chancy embarkation on life following the breach with his stepfather. There is no reason not to go along with Hervey Allen and see John Allan in the choleric grandfather whose heir Pym expected to be; and perhaps there is some message in the fact that two men named Allen who appear in the narrative are provided with violent deaths. Yet it must be granted that, once the story gets under way, the autobiographical touches grow rare, and that it is vain to look for parallels between *Pym's* adventures and the literal career of Edgar Poe. What may be said about all this sly self-reference, I think, is that Poe, like many another author, drew upon memory; that his sense of things derived not merely from Gothic, Hermetic, or other literature, but from his own experience; and that the vision of *Pym,* though not reducible to his personal history, was something at which he had personally arrived.

It is a waste of time to try to understand the characters of Poe's major fiction as so many real people with real-life originals and ordinary motives. They are, in the dimension that matters, figures of dream allegory, representing the principles or awarenesses of a single consciousness which is the envelope of the tale. In "William Wilson," Poe openly presents the two Wilsons as tragically divided portions of a once harmonious soul; in such a story as "The Purloined Letter," where the allegory is more subaqueous, the reader must catch certain hints if he is to divine that Dupin and the Minister D–are antagonistic elements of one nature; in *Pym,* which pretends to be the credible memoir of a fairly average young man, one is less overtly incited to make such discoveries, and yet few commentators have failed to react to such sentences as these regarding Augustus:

> I used frequently to go home with
> him, and remain all day, and
> sometimes all night. We occupied
> the same bed, and he would be
> sure to keep me awake until
> almost light, telling me stories. . . .

> Augustus thoroughly entered into
> my state of mind. It is probable,
> indeed, that our intimate commun-
> ion had resulted in a partial
> interchange of character.

Augustus and Arthur are complements or alter egos, as Arthur and Dirk Peters will later plainly be, and to see this is to gain an initial purchase on the ulterior plot. But in a chronicle so long and loosely eventful as this, with so many supernumeraries and spear carriers, it is only at the close, and in a generalizing retrospect, that one can interpret the story as the act of a single consciousness.

"The Pit and the Pendulum" is short enough to take its structure, quite perceptibly, from a normal chain of psychic conditions: somnolence, falling asleep, a sequence of nightmares, and a welcome return to waking life. Similarly, the voyage portion of "The Domain of Arnheim" embodies a carefully demarcated passage through reverie and the hypnagogic state to a final plunge into the land of dreams. *Pym*, as I have said, is far harder to experience as one dream process, or as a logical concatenation of mental status: it is broken and episodic. Nevertheless, readers familiar with Poe will find the novel full of Poe's preoccupation with irrational consciousness (swoons, hallucinations, intoxications, fevers, stupors, transitional states in which "the reasoning or imaginative faculties flicker, alternately, one above the other") and of the symbols by which Poe elsewhere renders oneiric experience concrete. The "narrow and intricate windings" of Pym's path through the hold of the *Grampus* (like the sinuous gorge that leads to Klock-Klock) resemble all those winding streets, paths, and streams of Poe's shorter fiction which express the drowsing mind's confused sense of place, and anticipate a vertiginous descent into unconsciousness. The box that Augustus has prepared for Arthur to hide in, and that the latter describes as a "little apartment," provides that quality of enclosure which accompanies dreaming in Poe, while the darkness and airlessness of its situation accord as always with the dreamer's separation from the external world. (In the more comfortable "apartments" of other tales, Poe's visionaries may enjoy their own dazzling illumination, and rich draperies may be swayed by mysterious artificial currents of air: here the equivalents are privative, but the condition of dream is no less implied.) It is also symbolic that Pym's watch (lent him by Augustus) repeatedly runs down during his incarceration: the imagination or dreaming mind, in Poe, is always at odds with the temporal–with clocks, with watches, with heartbeats–and Dream-Land is said to be "out of SPACE–out of TIME." As for the "dull humming sound" which Pym hears in chapter 2, it is ascribed to a gale without, but it is also one of Poe's habitual signals for the blurring of auditory sensation at the onset of dream: what duly ensues is "a profound sleep, or rather stupor" in which Pym dreams of strange trees and black water and desolation.

It would be tedious to trace the occurrence of such signals throughout the whole work; they are, in any case, most patent and concentrated during Pym's Jonah-like voyage in the belly of the *Grampus*. There is, however, one device of dream representation of which a few instances should be given. It is characteristic of dream, and of Poe's dream narratives, that significance should be subtly hinted at and gradually unfolded–that the dreamer should, as it were, be darkly beckoned onward. Thus, in the third paragraph of "Ms." the narrator sees "spiral exhalations" in the heated air, which foreshadow the gigantic vortex into which he will descend at the close. Similarly, in chapter 1 of *Pym*, Arthur and Augustus are run down off Nantucket by a ship called the *Penguin*–a bird with which Pym will be very familiar by chapter 14. At which point in the story, by the way, there is a premonitory increase in the frequency of the crucial words "white" and "black," and events begin to stress a symbolism of hue and color. As the *Jane Guy* sails unwittingly toward Tsalal, a white-pelted and red-eyed Arctic bear is encountered; later, the sailors pick up a bush full of red berries, and the carcass of an unknown white beast with scarlet claws. Approaching Bennet's Islet at the end of chapter 17, Pym's ship observes "a singular ledge of rock" resembling "corded bales of cotton"; this, as Harry Levin has remarked, evokes the American South, and prepares us for Poe's implicit comparisons (incidental, I think, but unmistakable and vicious) of the black Tsalalians to the slaves of his homeland. Going ashore on the island, their last landfall before Tsalal, the voyagers find

> near the shore, half buried in a pile
> of loose stones, a piece of wood,
> which seemed to have formed the
> prow of a canoe. There had
> evidently been some attempt at
> carving upon it, and Captain Guy
> fancied that he made out the
> figure of a tortoise.

This is the sort of token or invitation that Legrand, in "The Gold Bug," finds on the coast of the mainland near Sullivan's Island. It foreglimpses the tortoises and native canoes of Tsalal, and the lone canoe that is to be the story's final vessel. And Pym's description of it, in its extreme uncertainty ("seemed," "evidently," "fancied"), contributes to the tale's mounting sense of strangeness.

Tsalal, to which I seem to have drifted, has been much discussed. Early reactions to the island, from readers who took the forepart of the narrative for fact, and then found themselves confronted with preposterous streams of purplish water, were often indignant. Today's reader, with his quite different expectations, will no doubt find his interest growing as the improbable draws near. As the savage Nu-Nu informs Pym, Tsalal is one of a group of eight islands governed by a king named Tsalemon or Psalemoun. It is a place of blackness: the inshore waters about it are dark, the terrain is dark, the birds and animals are dark; there are, in fact (except for some unexplained white arrowheads), "no light-coloured substances of any kind upon the island." The blackness of the natives themselves extends even to their teeth, and they react to any white thing with terrified cries of "Tekeli-li!" Nine miles deep in the interior lies their sole settlement, a fortress village called Klock-Klock, which is surrounded by a "precipitous ledge" and may be approached from the south only, by way of a deep, meandering ravine. The village dwellings consist of mutilated trees, dead-branch lean-tos, holes in the ground, and "shallow caverns" scratched out of the rock face: of these, Pym observes that they are "miserable," and "unlike those of even the lowest of the savage races with which mankind are acquainted." The Tsalalians appear, indeed, to represent an extreme of nondevelopment or of degradation: they lack most of the basic arts of civilization; a meal of "palpitating entrails" is to them a delicacy, and the four canoes they possess are not of their own construction, but have been obtained "by merest accident" from another island. They are also extreme in a moral sense, Pym finding them for good reason "the most wicked, hypocritical, vindictive, bloodthirsty and altogether fiendish race of men upon the face of the globe."

The detailed resemblance of Klock-Klock to Stephens's description of Petra, the likeness of Tsalemon to "Salmono," and the reminiscence in "Tekeli-li!" of Daniel 5:25 inevitably start the reader thinking of the Old Testament, of Israel and her neighbors. This theme becomes explicit in the supposed editor's note which concludes the book, where it is asserted that the shapes of the chasms that *Pym* and Peters explore in chapter 23, and the seeming inscription observed in one of them, are Ethiopian, Arabic, and Egyptian characters having to do with the darkness of Tsalal and the whiteness of some region to the south. Nor is that all. Sidney Kaplan, in his interesting essay on *Pym*, points out that "Tsalal" is a Hebrew word for "to be black," and that "Tsalemon" may likewise be related to "tsal," the Hebrew word for "shadow." My linguistic counsel (I have no more Hebrew than Poe did) feel that certain other translations of Mr. Kaplan's are dubious or strained: from the Tsalalians' habitual exclamation "Anamoo-moo! Lama-Lama!" they can derive little more Hebrew or other meaning than "Prithee . . . why? why?" whereas Mr. Kaplan Homerically renders it "What ship is this? What evil sent by God upon the water?" My own guess is that the name "Klock-Klock" has more to do with temporality than with dirtiness or blackness. Be all that as it may, the fact remains that we readily recognize "Lama" as one of Jesus' last words upon the cross (Matthew 27:46) and apprehend that Poe's Tsalalians, whose island and king bear Hebrew names, speak in some garbled, hybrid, or debased version of the Hebrew tongue.

Stephens, in musing on the capital city of Edom, declares that one can see "the handwriting of God himself in the desolation and eternal ruin" of Petra. We are surely to see the handwriting of God in the chasms of Poe's Tsalal, whose huge glyphic forms could not be read by any but a heavenly eye. Lest there be any doubt about this, Poe concludes his work with a "Biblical" verse of his own manufacture, in which the Lord proclaims, *I have graven it within the hills, and my vengeance upon the dust within the rock.* Tsalal, then, is an *accursèd* place, like that Edom upon which the prophecies of Isaiah (34) and Ezekiel (35)—quoted by Poe in his review of Stephens—were fulfilled. And indeed the various prophecies against Edom would appear to have guided Poe in depicting Tsalal as a waste country of scant forage, a haunt of the bittern where foliage, when mentioned, is withered and dry. The Lord proclaims through Jeremiah (49) that "Edom shall be a desolation," and so say the prophets in chorus. The dark terrain and water of Tsalal may owe something to the following threat of Isaiah's (34): "And the streams thereof shall be turned into pitch, and the dust thereof into brimstone, and the land thereof shall become burning pitch." And lest there be any doubt of the damnation of the inhabitants, Ezekial (32) says that the Edomites shall be "with them that go down to the pit."

Edom is not the only accursèd land that Poe has in mind. When, in chapter 24, Pym and Peters have managed to descend from their precipitous hill in the vicinity of "the ravine which has proved the tomb of our friends," we are given the following sketch of the landscape:

> The place was one of singular wildness, and its aspect brought to my mind the description given by travellers of those dreary regions marking the site of degraded Babylon. Not to speak of the ruins of the disrupted cliff, which formed a chaotic barrier to the vista to the northward, the surface of the ground in every other direction was strewn with huge tumuli, apparently the wreck of some gigantic structures of art; although, in detail, no semblance of art could be detected. . . . Of vegetation there were no traces whatever throughout the whole of the desolate area within sight.

"Desolation" is promised to the Babylonian captors of Israel in Isaiah (13) and Jeremiah (50, 51), and Psalm 137 sings of the coming destruction of Edom and Babylon alike. What Poe's evocation of the "ruins" of "degraded Babylon" accomplishes here is to fortify one's sense of the Tsalalians not as a primitive people but as a fallen people *reduced* to savagery through their own wickedness and the vengeance of Jehovah. The same idea is furthered by the

Tsalalian cry of "Tekeli-li!" which reminds us of Belshazzar's feast, of his blasphemy in permitting his princes, wives, and concubines to drink from vessels sacred to Israel's God, and of Daniel's interpretation of the handwriting on the wall as a prophecy of Babylon's fall to the Medes and Persians.

In reviewing Stephens, Poe writes at length of the Biblical prophecies against Egypt, and remarks that the country, in its present "base and degraded" state, "is . . . but the *shadow* of the Egypt of the Pharaohs." The italics are Poe's, and, recalling that "Tsalal" is a verbal formation from the Hebrew word for "shadow," we may surmise that we are noting one possible source of the duskiness of Poe's fictional island. Another might be the following etymology, which I find in Malcolm's Bible dictionary of 1830: "The name *Egypt* was given it by the Greeks, and signifies either the land of the Copts . . . or the *land of blackness,* because the soil and water are of a blackish color." In any case, Kaplan is surely right in thinking that Poe, in devising Tsalal, had in mind both Egypt and the Hamitic peoples generally. While Noah's son Japheth was the progenitor of the Indo-European peoples, and Shem of the Semites, Genesis (9-10) tells how Noah cursed the irreverent Ham in his progeny, who were in good part to be the dark-skinned peoples of northeast Africa, hostile to the Lord and destined to servitude. Psalm 105, which celebrates the deliverance of Israel from Pharaoh, contains some verses that may be pertinent:

> He sent Moses his servant; and Aaron whom he had chosen.
> He shewed his signs among them, and wonders in the land of Ham.
> He sent darkness, and made it dark; and they rebelled not

against his word.
He turned their waters into blood, and slew their fish.

Have we here, in what will become a catalogue of the "plagues" sent upon Egypt by Moses' God, yet another way of understanding the darkness of Tsalal, and the peculiarity of its streams, the purplish water which is made up of "distinct veins"? I incline to think so.

Tsalal is a composite place and people, punished for its sins with blackness, ruin, and desolation. Though it may seem sufficiently cursed already, let me mention a final and rather topical source and be done with it. The notion that the American Indians are the descendants of the Lost Tribes of Israel has been with us since colonial days, but it gained a special vitality during Poe's lifetime, with the publication of such books as Ethan Smith's *View of the Hebrews* (1823) and Israel Worsley's *A View of the American Indians* (1828). In 1830 Joseph Smith published his *Book of Mormon*, which he claimed to have found by angelic aid and translated from golden plates with miraculous spectacles. (The charactery of the plates, much to the continuing vexation of Poe's friend Professor Anthon, was said by the Mormons to have been certified by him as "Reformed Egyptian.") What was novel about the *Book of Mormon*, in relation to the Hebraic theory of Indian origin, was that it offered firm scriptural confirmation of it, telling how Lehi and his sons left Jerusalem *circa* 590 B.C., at the bidding of the Lord, and sailed to find a promised land in South America. Of their subsequent history, what is most to our purpose is 2 Nephi 5, in which the Lamanites rebel against their leader, Nephi, and are therefore cursed with dark pigmentation:

256

Wherefore, the word of the Lord
was fulfilled which he spake unto
me. . . . And behold, they were cut
off from his presence.

And he had caused the cursing to
come upon them, yea, even a sore
cursing, because of their iniquity.
For behold, they had hardened
their hearts against him, that they
had become like unto a flint;
wherefore, as they were white, and
exceeding fair and delightsome,
that they might not be enticing
unto my people the Lord God did
cause a skin of blackness to come
upon them.

And thus saith the Lord God: I
will cause that they shall be
loathsome unto thy people, save
they shall repent of their
iniquities. . . .

And because of the cursing
which was upon them they did
become an idle people, full of
mischief and subtlety, and did
seek in the wilderness for beasts of
prey.

Is it necessary to suppose that Joseph Smith, or
the rumor of him, or what Anthon may have said of
the Mormons, contributed to Poe's picture of Tsalal?
Given Edom, Babylon, and all the sons of Ham, must
we have the Lamanites as well? Perhaps not. Still, as
I have said, Poe was ready to make something of
any current sensation; and to evoke the Lamanites
was to evoke a degraded people speaking an "al-

tered" Egyptian and Hebrew (*Mormon*, chapter 9, 32-3), explicitly cursed by the Lord with a "skin of blackness," and dwelling in the southern part of the Western Hemisphere.

If "Ligeia" is not understood as a dream of its narrator's, in which the transformation of Rowena is effected by the hero's imaginative power, then it will be misunderstood as a horror tale in which a dead woman's soul usurps a living body, and the narrator is but a witness. One can readily mistake *Pym* in the same way, and here is W. H. Auden being (if I understand him) partially and rather discerningly mistaken: "The hero [of *Pym*] is as purely passive as the I in dreams; nothing that happens is the result of his personal choice, everything happens to him." Mr. Auden notes that the novel is dreamlike, but does not see Pym as presiding over the dream events. It is largely true, in a literal sense, that Pym *does* less than most of the other characters, good or bad. It is Augustus who interests Arthur in going to sea, who instigates the preliminary escapade on the *Ariel*, and who makes all arrangements for Arthur's secret passage on the *Grampus*, even to bringing aboard the dog Tiger. Later in the tale, the half-breed Peters takes over Augustus's active and managerial role. Pym's transitive moments are precious few: it is he who conceives the notion, in chapter 7, of terrifying the mate through an impersonation of the murdered sailor Rogers; in chapter 11 (subsequent to the efforts of Peters and Parker) he descends into the flooded hold of the *Grampus* and brings up a bottle of wine; in the next chapter he salvages an axe from the forecastle; and in chapters 17 and 18, somewhat to our surprise, he has "acquired much influence" over Captain Guy, repeatedly strengthening the latter's resolve to continue southward. As for the acts of violence that are committed in this bloody story, Pym's hands are all but lily-white. When the *Grampus* is retaken from the mutineers in chapter 8, Pym's masquerade causes the guilty mate to die of fright, but that is scarcely to be accounted murder; for the rest, Pym stuns one opponent with a pump handle, while Peters, Augustus, and the dog Tiger do the killing. When it comes to cannibalism, as it does in chapters 11 and 12, Pym firmly rejects Parker's initial proposal "that one should die to preserve the existence of the others," but then is forced by Peters, Augustus, and Parker to consent to a drawing of lots; when Parker, through poetic justice, draws the fatal splinter, Pym swoons, and it is Peters who slaughters the victim. Though he does not forgo his share of Parker, Pym is clearly the least sullied of the four. If Pym's pistols, in chapter 24, fell two of the five savages who have ambushed Peters, thus enabling Peters to dash out the brains of the remaining three, the deed is done in his comrade's defense; furthermore, one of Pym's victims turns out to be quite unharmed. Pushing off from Tsalal at the end of the chapter, with "an immense crowd of natives" in howling pursuit, Pym and Peters find that they cannot shake off two savages who have got hold of their canoe: "We were forced," Pym says, "to despatch them with our knives," and the reader quickly acquits him of any malice.

On the literal plane, then, Pym initiates very little action and is nearly–perhaps wholly–free of blood guilt. Yet on the plane of dream allegory or vision, Pym's obviously *must* be the imagination that drives and determines the narrative, since he is the one "character" to experience the story from beginning to end. What kind of imagination has he? As we learn in the first paragraph of the second chapter, he is "melancholy," and has a positive desire for privation, desolation, affliction, abandonment, solitude–being in this like Robinson Crusoe, who describes himself from the first as temperamentally fated to pursue misfortune. Pym's "terrific" dreams in the hold of the *Grampus* not only foresee Tsalal–its black water, serpents, leafless trees, and desert character–but require the action to move toward such a place and to create it. Pym, like his successive complements Augustus and Peters (and in some measure Captain Guy), desires always to push southward, and that is what the story is impelled, despite all seeming obstacles, to do. The theme of mutiny begins aboard the *Penguin,* in chapter 1; by means of mutiny, countermutiny, poison, drowning, cannibalism, gangrene, mass inhumation, spear thrust, explosion, knife, club, pistol, and sheer terror, Pym's dream disposes of a cast of thousands, bears him southward from craft to craft, keeps him intact and innocent, provides him with the sufferings he is after, and brings him at last, alone with his alter ego, to the brink of an immaculate mystery.

That *Pym* is latently a spiritual quest is indicated in many ways. "By sleep and its world alone is *Death* imagined," wrote Poe in his "Colloquy of Monos and Una," and Arthur's sleeping quarters in the hold of the *Grampus*–"four feet high, and full six long, but very narrow"–are very like a coffin. This idea is subtly supported by the "putrefaction" of the leg of mutton, and by Arthur's "phosphorus" matches, with their associations of decay. (When Augustus's rotted leg slips into the sea in chapter 13, it is a "mass of putrefaction" surrounded by "a glare of phosphoric light.") At one point Augustus calls softly to Arthur from the trap door, telling him among other things that he has been "buried" for three days and nights; later, when Arthur makes his way to the trap and finds it sealed, he is full of horror at being "thus entombed." So long as he remains in the brig's hold, Arthur is like a dead man; and, needless to say, while he sleeps in his provisioned box (to which a long cord is attached) he resembles an embryo as well. These two ideas together–death and birth–constitute the repeated rhythm of the whole narrative, and what is in question is not physical dissolution or recovery but the death or recovery of the soul. What Pym is up to, as Daniel Hoffman says, is "dying and being reborn." Rescued from his incarceration at the end of chapter 3, Arthur feels like one "redeemed from the jaws of the tomb," and redemption is indeed his concern throughout.

It is not any limitation of Poe's (or Pym's) vocabulary that makes for the dense repetition, everywhere in the novel, of the words "hope" and "despair." The vicissitudes of the narrative are sufficient to motivate strong shifts of emotion, and to prompt the use of those words in their more everyday and secular senses; but hope is also a virtue by which, as Saint Paul says, we are saved, and despair is its contrary. The language of perdition is frequent in *Pym*: persons and feelings are "fiendish" or "diabolical," and when, for example, the *Penguin* is about to run down the *Ariel*, there is "a long scream or yell, as from the throats of a thousand demons." Caught in the cavein of a fissure on Tsalal, Pym speaks not only of the fear of bodily death but of the "utter darkness" of Matthew 25:30 and Milton's Hell, of the thought of being "lost for ever," and of the "blackness of darkness" to which Jude consigns the wicked. Resolving, however, Pym's oscillations between hope and despair, and countering his fears of separation from God, we have continual instances of "deliverance and reanimation," of "mercy," of "preservation," of "new life." The reader who wishes to convince himself that this adventure story is an allegory of regeneration can do no better than to study the third and fourth paragraphs of chapter 24, where Pym is descending a precipice by means of pegs which Peters has driven into the rock face. To a movie camera, the passage would be a simple cliff-hanger; but we are privy to the thoughts of the hero. He begins the descent with "trepidation," and then through a "crisis of fancy" begins to imagine what it would be to fall. A spirit of self-destructive perversity masters him, and forces him to look "far down within the abyss."

> For one moment my fingers clutched convulsively upon their hold, while, with the movement, the faintest possible idea of escape wandered, like a shadow, through my mind–in the next my whole soul was pervaded with a *longing to fall;* a desire, a yearning, a passion utterly uncontrollable. I let go at once my grasp upon the peg, and, turning half round from the precipice, remained tottering for an instant against its naked face. But now there came a spinning of the brain; a shrill-sounding and phantom voice screamed within my ears; a dusky, fiendish, and

> filmy figure stood immediately
> beneath me; and, sighing, I sunk
> down with a bursting heart, and
> plunged within its arms.

It is not, however, a dusky fiend of Hell's abyss who receives him; it is Peters, whose voice he has heard, who breaks his fall, and who is the agent of his "preservation"–as General Lasalle, at the last instant, preserves the tottering hero of "The Pit and the Pendulum." Recovering, Pym is soon wholly free of "trepidation," and feels "a new being."

Does Pym's soul grow progressively stronger, owing to its deaths and rebirths, its trials and deliverances? If we consider Pym as a discrete character, which in the last analysis he is not, the contention can be argued with some success; but more certainly Poe embodies the idea by providing Pym with Dirk Peters as a sidekick. Peters, as introduced, is a phallic figure in name and aspect; he has "prodigious strength when under excitement"; he wears a wig of animal fur and is half Indian; his expression is demonic. When first we hear of him, he is dubiously recommended as one of "the less bloodthirsty" of the mutineers, and is said to be a capricious and unstable mind. Yet despite his poor spiritual credentials, Peters turns out to be kind and protective toward Augustus, repeatedly saving the latter's life. By chapter 7 he is ascribing his participation in the recent mutiny to "insanity," and thereafter he proves as steady-minded as a succession of harrowing circumstances will allow. His deep and bloody groin wound in chapter 9 would appear to be part of a process of purification whereby Peters, though undiminished in strength, sloughs off his animality and ambiguity. It surely means something, in this novel where race and color bear major symbolic values, that Peters, who is referred to in the earlier pages as "the hybrid," has by the end of chapter 21 become a "white man." Let me be blunt about it and assert my opinion that Peters, as Pym's alter ego in the latter portion of the novel, is one gauge of the hero's gradual regeneration and of his acquisition of spiritual force.

I think it has not been noticed that Pym's spiritual journey brings him to Tsalal on January 19, the birthday of Edgar Allan Poe. The meaning of this extraordinary autobiographical insinuation is not hard to divine. Poe's dream voyagers, when they push off from the here and now, travel not merely *away* but *backward in time*, which is why the narrator of "Ms." fitfully experiences, in studying the ghost ship which is bearing him toward the pole, "a sensation of familiar things." What he is remembering in flashes, as he sails into the past and toward "the brink of eternity," is the original and unfallen condition of his soul. The poet of "To Helen" is ferried "home" through reversed time toward the same goal, there symbolized as ancient Greece and Rome in their glory and grandeur. And the same tale is far more darkly told in the opening tableau or dumb show of "The Assignation," where the narrator, borne by a gondola down the Canal San Marco, beholds the rescue of a child from the "abyss" of the waters. Tsalal is not, of course, the goal and salvation of Pym; that lies beyond it to the south. In terms of Pym's backward quest, the island represents an evil epoch or event which must be nullified, a curse which must be lifted before the soul may complete its journey. Poe's typical hero, from his first poems onward, is one who suffers an early "fall" from that condition of spiritual harmony and wholeness which is personified in Ligeia, Helen, Eleonora, and Poe's angelic beloveds generally. While Poe insists at times upon man's free will and responsibility, there is a fatality in the pattern: its hero does not elect to have a divided and degraded nature, but "falls," rather, in proportion as time estranges him from childhood and exposes him to the life of a corrupted Earth. It is the "Condor years" which are at fault, it is Poe's black bird of time–condor, culture, or raven–which blights the hero's spirit. A "dark alloy" falls from time's wing upon his soul, "a shadow gathers over [his] brain." This happens in "Tamerlane" at the end of boyhood, and in "Eleonora" at the fifteenth year, but in some cases–"William Wilson," for one–the spiritual calamity would seem to occur either in "earliest infancy" or at the very moment of earthly incarnation. That, I think, is what Poe means by bringing his fictional self, Arthur Gordon Pym, to Tsalal on the nineteenth of January. If Pym can get past Tsalal, thus undoing the curse of his birth, he can leave his life behind like a cast snakeskin and proceed toward God as a regenerate spirit.

It is clear enough, from what I have just said, that one need not depend solely on Edomites and Lamanites for an understanding of the blackness of Tsalal: the black birds and clouds and shadows of Poe's inveterate symbolism could account for that. And the sonnet "To Zante," published in the same issue of the *Messenger* that carried the opening chapters of *Pym* (and the pieces on Reynolds and *Astoria*), tells of an island that has become "accursèd ground" through the absence of a maiden who signifies, as usual, supernal order and beauty. There is more than one fruitful approach to the definition of Tsalal, but in fact all of these convergent approaches are needed, since Pym is a multiple allegory: it describes the infinite regress of a single visionary soul, but the story is also planetary and cosmic. For Poe, the soul and the cosmos have like histories: each proceeds from unity to diversity and then, by way of purification, returns to unity. Furthermore, the rhythms of soul and cosmos interact: if the soul is incarnated on a planet that has fallen away from divine harmony, it will partake of a "fallen" dissonance; and if that soul, despite its circumstances, can move in vision toward the lost divine wholeness, it will contribute to the redemption of its star or planet and to the restoration of God. Thus Pym, in retracting and annulling his own life, is in some measure purging Earth of its sin (here symbolized by Babylon and the like) and giving impetus to a universal atonement. That is why, at various moments of the novel, events and actions have cosmic overtones. The word "trepidation," which so often appears, may refer to trembling or agitation in a man, but it also may bring to mind—as here, with the greatest pertinence, it does–irregularity of motion in heavenly bodies. The voice of Tiger, heard by Pym in dream, is like "the thunder of the firmament." The great concussion attending the cave-in of Tsalal's gorge gives Pym "a vague conception . . . that the whole foundations of the solid globe were suddenly rent asunder, and that the day of universal dissolution was at hand." And as the hero's canoe drifts southward from Tsalal–where all things, animal, vegetable, and mineral, share in the one darkness–his captive, Nu-Nu, tells of Tsalal and Tsalemon in speech full of the hissing note of the bittern, while white birds fly out of the vapor screaming "*Tekeli-li!*" When men begin to hiss like birds, and birds to scream like men, we know that we are moving away from disjunction of earthly consciousness into a growing sense of connaturalness of all things—a sense that will ultimately repeal all diversity and convoke the stars to their destruction.

The final leg of the trip is many things. Insofar as *Pym* is imaginative propaganda for polar exploration, the southward voyage through the "wide and desolate Antarctic ocean" is a vindication of Symmes and Reynolds; there has been no ice since Bennet's Islet (82Y50' south latitude, 42Y20' west longitude), and the sea grows increasingly warmer as the chasmal pole approaches. For the literal-minded reader of nautical adventures, the last pages are the last straw; despite the fact that Pym declares the thickening precipitation of "fine white powder" not to be ash, such a reader may make allowances for Pym's state of mind and recall Morrell's description of volcanic ash staining the sea; he will also remember, perhaps, that "scoria" or volcanic rocks were noted on Tsalal; but the gigantic and snow-white human figure which rises to meet Pym in the last sentence will, for such a reader, be sheer hoax and pure exasperation. Yet to the reader who understands that the tale is covertly a dream of spiritual return, the figure will be recognizable as Anthropos, or the Primal Man, or the snow-white Ancient of Days (Daniel 7:9), or the "one like unto the Son of man" in Revelation 1:13, whose "head and . . . hairs were white like wool, as white as snow." In other words, the figure stands for the coming reunion of the voyager's soul with God or—what is the same thing—with the divinity in himself.

All is "drowsiness" and "dreaminess" after the canoe's entry, on March 1, into "a region of novelty and wonder," and those familiar with Poe's many treatments of the hypnagogic state will understand why the vapor curtain in the polar distance is full of "wild flickerings," exhibits "all the wild variations of the Aurora Borealis," and parts at times to reveal "a chaos of flitting and indistinct images." Though *Pym* is not, as I have said, tidily geared to the phases of dream experience, Poe suitably invests the tale's final seascape with such abstract, elusive "psychal impressions" as occur "where the confines of the waking world blend with those of the world of dreams." These are said in Poe's "Marginalia" to have an *"absoluteness of novelty,"* and to constitute glimpses "of the spirit's outer world." It is thither, of course, that Pym is bound. And if the "flickerings" ahead also put us in mind of volcanic eruption, it is enhancing to recall Jehovah's association with such phenomena, and the purifying fire in which the world will end.

Israel, delivered from Egypt, set forth for a promised land "flowing with milk and honey"; Pym, delivered from Tsalal, sets forth upon waters which are increasingly "of a milky consistency and hue." Will that possibly do as a symbolic explanation of the milky Antarctic seas? Or should we be satisfied to observe that milky seas are white, and therefore suit the décor of Poe's Antarctic fantasy? A third answer, not exclusive of the others, strikes me as more important. If there is one constant explicit theme in this tale of a hero who yearns for "shipwreck and famine," it is that of eating and drinking, of hunger and thirst. I find an old marginal note in my copy of the book which reads, "'Gold Bug' is a quest for absolute treasure, 'Ms.' for absolute knowledge, *Pym* for absolute nutrition." Is not "absolute nutrition" what

Pym commences to enjoy, once free of Tsalal and of fleshly captivity? Born again for the last and happiest time, he embarks upon a sea of milk, which is the sustenance of the newly born. It is, of course, such milk of the spirit as Isaiah offers in his fifty-fifth chapter. During the novel, Pym has been "tantalized," in the words of Poe's poem "For Annie"—deprived, like Tantalus, of the food and drink he desires; or else he has been forced to imbibe the "accurst" and "naphthalene" waters of this world. But now, or soon, it will be possible for him to say

> I have drank of a water
> That quenches all thirst,

—the water of everlasting life that is proffered in John 4:14.

When, in vision or in death, the gnostic soul seeks to return to the transcendent world, it rises up through the spheres or zones of the cosmos, divesting itself in each sphere of some "gift" which it was given, during its descent, as equipment for the dark business of worldly life. "The ascent," Hans Jonas writes in his *The Gnostic Religion*, "is described as a series of progressive subtractions which leaves the 'naked' true self, an instance of Primal Man as he was before his cosmic fall, free to enter the divine realm and become one again with God." I do not think that Poe's allegorical novel offers the reader an orderly series of "progressive subtractions"; Hermes Trismegistus, by contrast, tells in his *Poimandres* at just what cosmic stations the soul casts off such gifts as evil cunning, ambition, and greed. Yet Poe's dream story does resemble the pattern of gnostic return in its unqualified repudiation of all things earthly, in its series of deaths and rebirths, and in the way in which the divine spark or *pneuma* (Pym) shucks off, in the form of the narrative's myriad characters, its various worldly selves. For that is what they are, despite all the novel's realism: the whole cast of sailors and savages, of islanders north and south, constitutes a lapsed individual being from which a "true self" is at last liberated. Solitary at the end, save for the purified Peters and a dead savage, the hero is drawn at "hideous velocity" toward a mystery which is awesome yet not unhappy. "And now," Pym says, "we rushed into the embraces of the cataract, where a chasm threw itself open to receive us." That is the language of homecoming.

Bard College held a lively conference on poetry in latter 1948, at which there were knock-down discussions of poetic form. This brash article was written, on the invitation of Theodore Weiss, in reaction to addresses by Louise Bogan and William Carlos Williams, and was ultimately published, together with their speeches, in the Quarterly Review of Literature.

THE BOTTLES BECOME NEW, TOO

An object is more and other than what is
implied in the idea of it.

-José Ortega y Gasset

Outside
        outside myself
                there is a world . . .
-W. C. Williams

What I like about Dr. Williams's talk is what I like about the letters which Emile Bernard extorted from Cézanne: both are unsatisfactory in an inspiring way. In each case you hear the voice of a practicing master too deep in his own work to talk like a critic. In Cézanne's most incoherent and contradictory statements, when he is best illustrating his own assertion that "talks on art are almost useless," you hear the ring of authority, you are aware of a stubborn sureness which depends not on his prowess as an elucidator of art, but wholly on his achievement as a painter. Dr. Williams is not incoherent, but he is certainly eccentric. There is authority in what he says, not because what he says makes perfect sense, but because listening to him you are aware that this is the sort of lopsided view of literature a real poet might have to have.

In order to write in earnest it is necessary to choose and to make a way of writing, and this involves rejecting other ways of writing, past and present. In some writers this rejection encompasses almost the entire body of literature, and that is perfectly healthy. Very few good writers can afford to admit the existence of "literature" as critics mean that term. The critic thinks of literature as a stream, an unfinished edifice, a series of significant suppurations, or an inexhaustible banquet. He has the privilege of seeing the good in everything. But in proportion as a poet sees the good in everything, his own work is likely–just likely–to lack focus and character. His attitudes toward other poets, and toward critical notions about writing poems, will probably be extreme, and are bound to be intimately connected with his own projects. There are, of course, Inquisitorial critics, but on the whole the critic has less *need* of violent choice than the writer. The younger French poets of today have made Valéry into a blacker villain than he could be; this is a necessary piece of personal strategy, and has to do with safeguarding the novelty and the integrity of the poem each will write tomorrow. I should say that Dr. Williams's slights on the sonnet, on quatrains, on the British language, on grammatical inversion, Elizabethan rhetoric, and so on, are likewise not judicial but strategic. His strategy is successful, and there is ample proof of that.

But this does not mean that his critical ideas are right. Miss Bogan, on the other hand, is both an excellent poet, and critically right.

The main danger of formalism, as both Dr. Williams and Miss Bogan observe, is that the choice of a much used meter and form is likely to evoke in the poet's mind a swarm of past uses. The sonnet, I suppose, is the riskiest form of all for an English or American poet to try, if he is troubled by good memory. There are so many good sonnets in our language–or languages–that it is particularly easy in writing one to bear "The second burthen of a former child." Poems made out of poetry; utterance without real reference; self-cuckoldry; lines which smell of sanction–there is the risk, and there are few who have not sometime or other failed in this regard.

But the tendency of poems to feed on other poems (we sometimes call this "writing in the Tradition") is only one aspect of the really great and frequent failing of poetry: its weakness for autonomy, its wish to inhabit the world which it creates, its larval self-satisfaction, its pleasure in manufacturing hermetic prisms. How often you see a poet fashion, out of a genuine interaction with the world, a personal system of imagery, and then slowly retire within it, praised by some for having "integrated his vision," but deplored by others for having gone unspeakably stale. It is the province of poems to make some order in the world, but poets can't afford to forget that there is a reality of things which survives all orders great and small. Things *are*. The cow is there. No poetry can have any strength unless it continually bashes itself against the reality of things.

That is why the first act of *Le Misanthrope* is so splendid. The vain and effeminate courtier reads to Alceste a competent, brittle, and conventional cavalier poem, and demands his opinion. Although it is a poem well done of its kind, Alceste can't bear it because it is so neat and chilly, because it is a loveless love poem. Because it is mere autonomous artifice. He strides to the footlights–strides almost out of the play itself–and declaims, with great gusto and with tears in his eyes, a popular song in celebration of love, gay, genuine, and having blood in it. The thirst for the genuine, which elsewhere makes a fool of Alceste, here shows him a hero. This is a damnation of self-existent artifice, spoken within a play– and a play is artifice. This is a gesture toward life from the midst of art, and it takes the art of a Molière to contain such a thing.

The newspaper excerpts of Dr. Williams's *Paterson* aim at the same thing. The chapters on cetology in *Moby Dick* are the same thing, punctuating the development of a vast symbolism with the confrontation of real whales and everyday whaling. Melville has for this reason a greater stretch and a profounder mythic power than a modern symbolist like Kafka, who turns all to symbol and makes all imaginatively disposable.

In a time of bad communications, when any self-transcendence is hard to come by, to perceive the existence of a reality beyond all constructions of the consciousness is to experience a kind of call to prophecy. To insist on the real existence of the four elements, of objects, of animals, taking these things as isolable representatives of the ambient reality, is a kind of minimum devoutness in these days. It is a step toward believing in people.

I see this devoutness expressed in many ways in recent writing. In the vivid and careful descriptions of Marianne Moore, in her extreme fairness, it is present. Also in Dr. Williams's ash cans, wastepaper, and red wheelbarrows. There are several chapters of *Let Us Now Praise Famous Men* in which James Agee makes a heroic effort to apprehend the "real" nature of various household objects. The French poet

Francis Ponge has put his gift of speech at the service of the rain, the blackberry, the shrimp, the pine grove, the fire, in a kind of witty but heartfelt subservience to the external which no American poetry has yet come to. One might also mention the late Antonin Artaud, who proclaimed that "reality is a thing terribly superior to all histories, all fables, all divinities, all surrealities." Of those to whom the praise of the world's alterity became a cause, Lawrence is surely the foremost; Lawrence who discovered that truth and justice are the profoundest sensual experiences, and turned in rage upon the "obscene ego." And then there is Robinson Jeffers, who has gone over utterly to the side of the crags and the hawks.

Plainly there are many degrees of this kind of devoutness, from the humanity of Marianne Moore to the inhumanity of Jeffers. There are some who recognize and confront the unknown reality, and there are others who go and live in it. Or die in it, like Lawrence. To contemn the consciousness, as Lawrence did and Jeffers seems to me to do, is to deprive existence of its dynamism. Likewise the other extreme—a vacuum-packed consciousness—is undynamic. Neither the mysterious world nor the formative mind can be denied. As Cézanne said of painting, "One cannot be too scrupulous or too sincere or too submissive to nature; but one is more or less master of one's model, and above all, of the means of expression." In the best paintings of Cézanne you are aware of the tremendous mass, immediacy, and entity of the world, and at the same time of the mastery of the mind which got that into a frame. Every Cézanne is a moment of tension between a formative mind and a reality which that mind insists on recognizing. It is a dynamic balance, a fierce calm like that in Delacroix's fresco at Saint-Sulpice of the struggle between Jacob and the Angel. Sainte-Victoire is more than any painting of it. But the important thing is to have a relation to the mountain.

What is the rain-dancer doing but trying to establish a *relation* to the rain? It is true that he is trying to get power over the rain for a very vital economic reason. However, since he fails so very often and still goes on dancing, there is obviously something else at stake in the dance. As Susanne Langer says, ". . . the most important virtue of the rite is not so much its practical as its religious success . . . its power to articulate a relation between man and nature. . . ."

The rain-dancer casts down his fingers like rain shafts, or beats with his feet somewhat as the rain tramples the earth. But it isn't really like the rain; it can't begin to substitute for what it refers to. It is not a mere imitation, but a magic borrowing of the powers it wants to approach, and a translation of what is borrowed into the language of the dancing human body. How are fingers to reproduce the concurrent precision and dishevelment of rainfall, or feet to approximate the delicate yet thudding sound of rain striking the earth? Moreover, there is so much in the dance which does not seem to refer directly to the rain at all: patterns, intervals, repetitions. Above all, the *difficulty*.

Rain probably has no difficulty in falling; it ought to be the easiest thing in the world. The difficulty and intricacy in the rain-dance arise not from emulation, and not from virtuosity in the dances, but from the difficulty–the impossibility–of achieving a direct expressive relationship with the rain, or with any other real thing. In each art the difficulty of the form is a substitution for the difficulty of direct apprehension and expression of the object. The first difficulty may be more or less overcome, but the second is insuperable; thus every poem begins, or ought to, by a disorderly retreat to defensible positions. Or, rather, by a perception of the hopelessness of direct combat, and a resort to the warfare of spells, effigies, and prophecies. The relation between an artist and reality is always an oblique one, and indeed there is no good art which is not consciously oblique. If you respect the reality of the world, you know that you can approach that reality only by indirect means. The painter who throws away the frame and rebels at composition is not a painter any more: he thinks the world is himself, and that there is no need of a devious and delimited struggle with it. He lacks that feeling of inadequacy which must precede every genuine act of creation.

So that paradoxically it is respect for reality which makes a necessity of artifice. Poetry's prime weapon is words, used for the naming, comparison, and contrast of things. Its auxiliary weapons are rhythms, formal patterns, and rhymes. It is by means of all these that poets create difficulties for themselves, which they then try to surmount. I cannot see that any of them needs or ought to be dispensed with.

In criticizing Dr. Williams's criticism, I am not out to attack free verse (though personally I have little use for most of it) or anything else. What I wish to do is to say a few words in favor of some of the things he has attacked. In the first place, I would like to assert that any basic rhythm—iambic, for example—is a perfectly artificial and abstract thing. I am aware that any rhythm bears some relation to the heartbeat and the breath cycle, and has in that sense a human "meaning." But no rhythm may reasonably be thought to be inherently linked to a particular age or culture. If the rhythms of *Beowulf*, lately established by Professor Pope, are not much used now, it is not because they were somehow darkly suitable then. All you can say is that they flourished then and do not now, but may again if enough poets get interested. A basic rhythm is as timeless and noncommittal as the triangle. The horses of the nineteenth century did not run in iambs, any more than the Studebakers of the twentieth do. To be sure, Byron went on an anapaestic blind when he described cavalry warfare in *The Destruction of Sennacherib*, and Dos Passos has a sentence somewhere which goes, as I remember, "The little train chugged along in dactyls." But neither of these is a perception of inherent meaning in the rhythm, and though there were a hundred items of supporting evidence, we would obviously be in error if we cried, "Down with the horse-drawn anapaest; the dactyl is the foot of the future!"

There are not so many possible basic rhythms for American or English poets, but the possibilities of varying these rhythms are infinite. One thing modern poets do not write, thank heaven, is virtuoso poems of near perfect conformity to basic rhythms, as Byron, Swinburne, and Browning did in their worst moments. By good poets of any age, rhythm is generally varied cleverly and forcefully to abet the expressive purposes of the whole poem. Modern variations on basic rhythms are likely to suggest the speech patterns, phrasing, and familiar beats of contemporary life, and this is desirable. But the rhythmic variations cannot do this unless the whole expression of the poem reflects a contemporary sensibility: rhythm cannot be modern per se: it may, however, be modern in the ensemble of a poem, in the way it works with the words.

Of sonnets, terza rima, quatrains, and so on, I should say the same thing that I have said of rhythms–that they have no inherent meaning, that they are not at all "dated," and that writing in them does not oblige one to sacrifice novelty. This may be said with even more certainty of stanza forms devised and followed by the individual poet himself. Recurring to my statement that difficulties of form are a substitute for the superable difficulties of direct expression, I would add that the formidably meaningless seems to me the best substitute for the alien, and that therefore strict stanzas are preferable to "free" or "organic" form. Another point in favor of formal structure is that there is no way of noticing certain subtleties and stresses and variations unless there is a norm, an apparent regular structure, from which divergences are made. Owing to the presence of a circular track and a tape, it is possible to judge a mile run as a work of art, to admire the runner's quick start and steady pace, his sprint and sailing at the end–and also to enjoy any variations he may make on the normal pattern of the race. But the same runner dashing limitlessly across open fields, now going full tilt, now decelerating, now hurdling a stump, is beyond one's power to appreciate, because there are no terms in which to evaluate his incomparable behavior. To provide a "norm" in writing a poem it is not obligatory to write in a traditional form: a single line whose basic rhythm and length are to be maintained and varied, or a single stanza, however novel, which is to be adhered to, constitutes a norm.

Rhyme also has the virtue of meaninglessness, and if it is austerely used it has the virtue of difficulty. It is always bad when rhymes write a poem. But rhyme is a device of great formal and magical value, and many writers have demonstrated that it is possible not to let it run away with you. A really rigorous rhyming poet can redeem from banality almost any rhyme in the language, even the perilous *cat / rat.*

As a matter of fact, it is precisely in its power to suggest comparisons and connections–unusual ones–to the poet that one of the incidental merits of rhyme may be said to lie. Say to yourself lake, rake, and then write down all the metaphors and other reconciliations of these terms which occur to you within one or two minutes. It is likely to be a long list, extending from visual images of wind furrowing the water, to punning reminiscences of Lancelot and Guinevere. The presence of potential rhymes sets the imagination working with the same briskness and license with which a patient's mind responds to the psychologist's word-association tests. When a poet is fishing among rhymes, he may and must reject most of the spontaneous reconciliations (and all of the hackneyed ones) produced by trial combinations of rhyming words, and keep in mind the preconceived direction and object of his poem; but the suggestions of rhyme are so nimble and so many that it is an invaluable means to the discovery of poetic raw material which is, in the very best sense, farfetched. I hope it is perfectly clear that I am not advocating automatic writing or any such supinity: one may get full suggestive use out of the contemplation of rhymes without letting them write the poem.

Dr. Williams's excellent poem *The Yachts* starts out to be terza rima, but he gives up the rhymes at line five. I do not think it would have been a better poem if he had sustained the rhymes, but I doubt that it would have been the worse for it–and I am perfectly sure that there would have been no danger of Dante or Shelley creeping in. If a poem arises from a dynamic relation with reality, it will be fresh whatever formal difficulties the poet chooses to overcome in the writing of it. If not, it will be like a group of anthropologists demonstrating a rain-dance. As Miss Bogan remarked in the case of Baudelaire, when poets put new wine in old bottles, the bottles become new, too. This, I suppose, is my main objection to Dr. Williams's talk; he lays all the stress on structural reforms and inventions, as if structure were a practically separable thing, instead of talking about the need of a perpetual revolution of the entire sensibility, in the incessant task of achieving relations to the always changing face of reality. To this latter purpose I have seen sonnets, villanelles, inversions, and all that Dr. Williams reprehends do great services in the last few years, and when this is so, one cannot say that the poets have surrendered to traditional forms. They have taken them over, rather.

*Beginning in 1952, I have tried from time to time
to put Molière's verse-comedies into English pentameter couplets, and have now published three
translations, each with a brief introduction. Those
introductions, which I group together here, will
be more readily understood if the reader has some
familiarity with the plays. I have incorporated
many things I learned from scholarship, criticism,
and the conversation of friends—far more than
could be acknowledged without clutter; yet these
pieces also express a translator's hard-earned
sense of the plays and are, I trust, sufficiently
my own.*

INTRODUCTIONS TO MOLIÈRE

The Misanthrope (1955)

The idea that comedy is a ritual in which society's
laughter corrects individual extravagance is particularly inapplicable to *The Misanthrope*. In this play,
society itself is indicted, and although Alceste's criti-
cisms are indiscriminate, they are not unjustified. The
fact is that falseness and intrigue are everywhere on
view; the conventions enforce a routine dishonesty,
justice is subverted by influence, love is over-
whelmed by calculation, and these things are accepted, even by the best, as "natural." The cold vanity of Oronte, Acaste, and Clitandre, the malignant
hypocrisy of Arisnoé, the insincerity of Célimène,
are to be taken as exemplary of the age, and Philinte's
philosophic tolerance will not quite do in response
to such a condition of things. The honest Éliante is
the one we are most to trust, and this is partly because she sees that Alceste's intransigence *A quelque
chose en soy de noble & d'héroïque.*
But *The Misanthrope* is not only a critique of soci-

282

ety; it is also a study of impurity of motive in a critic of society. If Alceste has a rage for the genuine, and he truly has, it is unfortunately compromised and exploited by his vast, unconscious egotism. He is a jealous friend (*Je veux qu'on me distingue*), and it is Philinte's polite effusiveness toward another which prompts his attack on promiscuous civility. He is a jealous lover, and his "frankness" about Oronte's sonnet owes something to the fact that Oronte is his rival, and that the sonnet is addressed to Célimène. Like many humorless and indignant people, he is hard on everybody but himself, and does not perceive it when he fails his own ideal. In one aspect, Alceste seems a moral giant misplaced in a trivial society, having (in George Eliot's phrase) "a certain spiritual grandeur ill-matched with the meanness of opportunity"; in another aspect, he seems an unconscious fraud who magnifies the petty faults of others in order to dramatize himself in his own eyes.

He is, of course, both at once: but the two impressions predominate by turns. A victim, like all around him, of the moral enervation of the times, he cannot consistently be the Man of Honor—simple, magnanimous, passionate, decisive, true. It is his distinction that he is aware of that ideal, and that he can fitfully embody it; his comic flaw consists in a Quixotic confusion of himself with the ideal, a willingness to distort the world for his own self-deceptive and histrionic purposes. Paradoxically, then, the advocate of true feeling and honest intercourse is that the one character most artificial, most out of touch, most in danger of that nonentity and solitude which all, in the chattery, hollow world of this play, are fleeing. He must play-act continually in order to believe in his own existence, and he welcomes the fact or show of injustice as a dramatic cue. At the close of the play, when Alceste has refused to appeal his lawsuit and has spurned the hand of Célimène, one cannot escape the suspicion that his indignation is in great part instrumental, a desperate means of counterfeiting an identity.

Martin Turnell (whose book *The Classical Moment* contains a fine analysis of *The Misanthrope*) observes that those speeches of Alceste which ring most false are, as it were, parodies of "Cornelian *tirade*." To duplicate this parody-tragic effect in English it was clearly necessary to keep the play in verse, where it would be possible to control the tone more sharply, and to recall our own tragic tradition. There were other reasons, too, for approximating Molière's form. The constant of rhythm and rhyme was needed, in the translation as in the original, for bridging great gaps between high comedy and farce, lofty diction and ordinary talk, deep character and shallow. Again, while prose might preserve the thematic structure of the play, other "musical" elements would be lost, in particular the frequently intricate arrangements of balancing half-lines, lines, couplets, quatrains, and sestets. There is no question that words, when dancing within such patterns, are not their prosaic selves, but have a wholly different mood and meaning.

Consider, finally, two peculiarities of the dialogue of the play: redundancy and logic. When Molière has a character repeat essentially the same thing in three successive couplets, it will sometimes have a very clear dramatic point; but it will always have the intention of stabilizing the idea against the movement of the verse, and of giving a specifically rhetorical pleasure. In a prose rendering, these latter effects are lost, and the passage tends to seem merely prolix. As for logic, it is a convention of *The Misanthrope* that its main characters can express themselves logically, and in the most complex grammar; Molière's dramatic verse, which is almost wholly free of metaphor, derives much of its richness from argumentative virtuosity. Here is a bit of logic from Arsinoé:

> *Madame, l'Amitié doit sur tout éclater*
> *Aux choses qui le plus nous peuvent importer:*
> *Et comme il n'en est point de plus grande importance*
> *Que celles de l'Honneur et de la Bienséance,*
> *Je viens par un avis qui touche vostre honneur*
> *Témoigner l'amitié que pour vous a mon Coeur.*

In prose it might come out like this: "Madam, friendship should most display itself when truly vital matters are in question: and since there are no things more vital than decency and honor, I have come to prove my heartfelt friendship by giving you some advice which concerns your reputation." Even if that were better rendered, it would still be plain that Molière's logic loses all its baroque exuberance in prose; it sounds lawyerish; without rhyme and verse to phrase and emphasize the steps of its progression, the logic becomes obscure, like Congreve's, not crystalline and followable, as it was meant to be.

For all these reasons, rhymed verse seemed to me obligatory. The choice did not preclude accuracy, and what follows is, I believe, a line-for-line verse translation quite as faithful as any which have been done in prose. I hasten to say that I am boasting only of patience; a translation may, alas, be faithful on all counts and still lack quality.

One word about diction. This is a play in which

French aristocrats of 1666 converse about their special concerns, and employ the moral and philosophical terms peculiar to their thought. Not all my words, therefore, are strictly modern; I had for example to use "spleen" and "phlegm"; but I think that I have avoided the zounds sort of thing, and that at best the diction mediates between then and now, suggesting no one period. There are occasional vulgarities, but for these there is precedent in the original, Molière's people being aristocrats and therefore not genteel.

If this English version is played or read aloud, the names should be pronounced in a fashion *roughly* French, without nasal and uvular agonies. Damon should be *dah-MOAN*, and for rhythmic convenience Arsinoé should be *ar-SIN-oh-eh*.

Tartuffe (1963)

There may be people who deny comedy the right to be serious, and think it improper for any but trivial themes to consort with laughter. It would take people of that kind to find in *Tartuffe* anything offensive to religion. The warped characters of the play express an obviously warped religious attitude, which is corrected by the reasonable orthodoxy of Cléante, the wholesomeness of Dorine, and the entire testimony of the action. The play is not a satire on religion, as those held who kept it off the boards for five years. Is it, then, a satire on religious hypocrisy, as Molière claimed in his polemical preface of 1669?

The play speaks often of religious hypocrisy, displays it in action, and sometimes seems to be gesturing toward its practitioners in seventeenth-century French society. Tartuffe is made to recommend, more than once, those Jesuitical techniques for easing the conscience which Pascal attacked in the *Provincial Letters*. Cléante makes a long speech against people who feign piety for the sake of preferment or political advantage. And yet no one in the play can be said to be a religious hypocrite in any representative sense. Tartuffe may at times suggest or symbolize the slippery casuist, or the sort of hypocrite denounced by Cléante, but he is not himself such a person. He is a versatile parasite or confidence man, with a very long criminal record, and to pose as a holy man is not his only *modus operandi:* we see him, in the last act, shifting easily from the role of saint to that of hundred-percenter. As for the other major characters who might quality, Madame Pernelle is simply a nasty bigot, while the religious attitudes of her son Orgon are, for all their underlying corruption, quite sincere.

Tartuffe is only incidentally satiric; what we experience in reading or seeing it, as several modern critics have argued, is not a satire but a "deep" comedy in which (1) a knave tries to control life by cold chicanery, (2) a fool tries to oppress life by unconscious misuse of the highest values, and (3) life, happily, will not have it.

Orgon, the central character of the play, is a rich bourgeois of middle age, with two grown children by his first wife. His second wife, Elmire, is attractive, young, and socially clever. We gather from the maid Dorine that Orgon has until lately seemed a good and sensible man, but the Orgon whom we meet in Act I, Scene 4 has become a fool. What has happened to him? It appears that he, like many another middle-aged man, has been alarmed by a sense of failing powers and failing authority, and that he has compensated by adopting an extreme religious severity. In this he is comparable to the aging coquette described by Dorine, who "quits a world which fast is quitting her," and saves face by becoming a censorious prude.

Orgon's resort to bigotry has coincided with his discovery of Tartuffe, a wily opportunist who imposes upon him by a pretense of sanctity, and is soon established in Orgon's house as honored guest, spiritual guide, and moral censor. Tartuffe's attitude toward Orgon is perfectly simple: he regards his benefactor as a dupe, and proposes to swindle him as badly as he can. Orgon's attitude toward Tartuffe is more complex and far less conscious. It consists, in part, of an unnatural fondness or "crush," about which the clear-sighted Dorine is explicit:

> He pets and pampers him with love more tender
> Than any pretty mistress could engender. . . .

It also involves, in the strict sense of the word, idolatry: Orgon's febrile religious emotions are all related to Tartuffe and appear to terminate in him. Finally, and least consciously, Orgon cherishes Tartuffe because, with the sanction of the latter's austere precepts, he can tyrannize over his family and punish them for possessing what he feels himself to be losing: youth, gaiety, strong natural desires. This punitive motive comes to the surface, looking like plain sadism, when Orgon orders his daughter to:

> Marry Tartuffe, and mortify your flesh!

Orgon is thus both Tartuffe's victim and his unconscious exploiter; once we apprehend this, we can better understand Orgon's stubborn refusal to see Tartuffe for the fraud he is.

When Orgon says to Cléante,

> My mother, children, brother and wife could die,
> And I'd not feel a single moment's pain,

he is parodying or perverting a Christian idea which derives from the Gospels and rings out purely in Luther's "A Mighty Fortress is Our God":

> Let goods and kindred go,
> This mortal life also. . . .

The trouble with Orgon's high spirituality is that one cannot obey the First Commandment without obeying the Second also. Orgon has withdrawn all proper feeling from those about him, and his vicious fatuity creates an atmosphere which is the comic equivalent of *King Lear's*. All natural bonds of love and trust are strained or broken; evil is taken for good; truth must to kennel. Cléante's reasonings, the rebellious protests of Damis, the entreaties of Mariane, and the mockeries of Dorine are ineffectual against Orgon's folly; he must see Tartuffe paw at his wife, and hear Tartuffe speak contemptuously of him, before he is willing to part with the sponsor of his spiteful piety. How little "religion" there has been in Orgon's behavior, how much it has arisen from infatuation and bitterness, we may judge by his indiscriminate outburst in the fifth act:

> Enough, by God! I'm through with pious men!
> Henceforth I'll hate the whole false brotherhood,
> And persecute them worse than Satan could.

289

By the time Orgon is made to see Tartuffe's duplicity, the latter has accomplished his swindle, and is in a position to bring about Orgon's material ruin. It takes Louis XIV himself to save the day, in a conclusion which may seem both forced and flattering, but which serves (as Jacques Guicharnaud has noted) to contrast a judicious, humane, and forgiving ruler with the domestic tyrant Orgon. The King's moral insight is Tartuffe's final undoing; nevertheless there is an earlier scene in which we are given better assurance of the invincibility of the natural and sane. I refer to Tartuffe's first conversation with Elmire, in which passion compels the hypocrite recklessly to abandon his role. What comes out of Tartuffe in that scene is an expression of helpless lust, couched in an appalling mixture of the languages of gallantry and devotion. It is not attractive; and yet one is profoundly satisfied to discover that, as W. G. Moore puts it, "Tartuffe's human nature escapes his calculation." To be flawlessly monstrous is, thank heaven, not easy.

In translating *Tartuffe* I have tried, as with *The Misanthrope* some years ago, to reproduce with all possible fidelity both Molière's words and his poetic form. The necessity of keeping verse and rhyme, in such plays as these, was argued at some length in an introduction to the earlier translation, and I shall not repeat all those arguments here. It is true that *Tartuffe* presents an upper-bourgeois rather than a courtly milieu; there is less deliberate wit and elegance than in the dialogue of *The Misanthrope*, and consequently there is less call for the couplet as a conveyor of epigrammatic effects. Yet there are such effects in *Tartuffe*, and rhyme and verse are required here for other good reasons: to play out the long speeches with clarifying emphasis, and at an assimilable rate; to couple farcical sequences to passages of greater weight and resonance; and to give a purely formal pleasure, as when balancing verse-patterns support the "ballet" movement of the close of Act II. My convictions being what they are, I am happy to report what a number of productions of *The Misanthrope* translation have shown: that contemporary audiences are quite willing to put up with rhymed verse on the stage.

A Note to the Harvest Edition of The Misanthrope *and* Tartuffe (1965)

There are one or two things I would like to say to those who will be using this edition of *The Misanthrope* and *Tartuffe* as a script. These translations have had the good luck to be performed, a number of times, in New York, regional, and university theaters, and also on radio and on television. The best of the stage productions have repeatedly proved what the fact of radio production would suggest: the verbal sufficiency of Molière's serious comedies. What the plays are about, what the characters think, feel, and do, is clearly and amply presented in the dialogue, so that a mere reading-aloud of the lines, without any effort at performance, can provide a complete, if austere, experience of the work.

I do not mean to say that there are no open questions in either play. To what extent do Philinte and Cléante, in their reasonable yet ineffectual speeches, express the playwright's view of things? Is Célimène incorrigibly trivial, or is she in process of developing a moral sensitivity, a capacity for love? Is it possible that Tartuffe possesses, in his real and underlying nature, a kind of balked religious yearning? And what on earth does Elmire see in Orgon? These are questions that director and actor may, and indeed must, decide; but it will be found that Molière's comedy, because it is so thoroughly "written," resists the overextension of any thesis. The actor or director who insists on a stimulatingly freakish interpretation will find himself engaged in deliberate misreading and willful distortion, and the audience will not be deceived.

In short, trust the words. Trust the words to convey the point and persons of the comedy, and trust them also to be sufficiently entertaining. A fussy anxiety on the part of the director, whereby the dialogue is hurried, cut, or swamped in farcical action, is the commonest cause of failure in productions of Molière. To such want of confidence in the text we owe the occasional presentation of the fops, Acaste and Clitandre, as flouncingly epicene, or the transformation of Tartuffe's two interviews with Elmire into a couple of wrestling bouts. In the first case the characters are falsified for the sake of an easy laugh, and cease to be legitimate rivals to Alceste for the hand of Célimène; in the second case, a real quality of Tartuffe's–his lustfulness–is manifested, but at the cost of making his great speeches seem redundant and pointlessly nuanced. The cost is too great, and once again the audience, though it may consent to laugh, will not be satisfied.

The introductions to the original editions still say what I think, and I shall let them stand. Were I to revise them, each would contain a qualification of my claim to accuracy. The translation of *The Misanthrope* does not fully reproduce the formulaic preciosity with which some of the characters speak of love. In translating *Tartuffe,* I have not always captured Madame Pernelle's way of slipping into old-fashioned and inelegant speech, or Mariane's of parroting the rhetoric of artificial romances. My excuse for these deficiencies is that, while echoes of an unchanging scripture or liturgy are readily duplicated, as in the speeches of Tartuffe, a translation that seeks to avoid a "period" diction cannot easily find equivalents for such quirks and fads of language as I have mentioned.

The School for Wives (1971)

As Dorante says in the *Critique de l'École des femmes,* a comic monster need not lack all attractive qualities. Arnolphe, the hero of Molière's first great verse comedy, is a forty-two-year-old provincial bourgeois whom it is possible to like, up to a point, for his coarse heartiness and his generosity with money. He is, however, a madman, and his alienation is of a harmful and unlovable kind. What ails him is a deep general insecurity, which has somehow been focused into a specific terror of being cuckolded. In fear of that humiliation, he has put off marriage until what, for the seventeenth century, was a very ripe age; meanwhile, he has buttressed his frail vanity by gloating over such of his neighbors as have been deceived by their wives. He has, furthermore, become the guardian of a four-year-old child, Agnès, with a view to shaping her into his idea of a perfect bride, and for thirteen years has had her trained to be docile and ignorant. It is his theory, based upon much anxious observation, that a stupid wife will not shame her husband by infidelity. As the play begins,

Arnolphe is about to marry Agnès and achieve a double satisfaction: he will quiet his long trepidation by marrying safely, and he will have the prideful pleasure of showing the world how to rig an infallible alliance. It goes without saying that poor, stultified Agnès is not his object but his victim.

Arnolphe, then, is one of Molière's coercers of life. Like Tartuffe, he proposes to manipulate the world for his own ends, and the play is one long joke about the futility of selfish calculation. Agnès is guileless; her young man, Horace, is a rash bumbler who informs his rival of all that he does and means to do; yet despite Arnolphe's mature canniness, and his twenty years' pondering and plotting, he loses out to a *jeune innocente* and a *jeune écervelé*. Why? There is much high talk in the play, especially from Arnolphe, of cruel destiny, fate, and the stars, and this contributes, as J. D. Hubert has noted, to an effect of "burlesque tragedy"; it is not implacable fate, however, but ridiculous chance which repeatedly spoils Arnolphe's designs. And indeed, the plans of other characters, even when benign, meet constantly with the fortuitous: if Horace achieves his goal, it is certainly not because his blundering intrigues have mastered circumstance; and though Oronte and Enrique accomplish the premeditated union of their children, *le hasard* has already brought the pair together. The play seems to assert that any effort to impose expectations on life will meet with surprises, and that a narrow, rigid, and inhumane demand will not be honored by Nature.

The plot of *L'École des femmes* has often been criticized for its unlikelihood. Doubtless Molière was careless of the fact, since, as W. G. Moore has written, "The plot is not the main thing at all. . . . The high points of the play are not the turning points of the action; they are moments when the clash of youth and age, of spontaneity and automatism, takes shape in speech and scene." And yet it may not be too much to say that the absurdity of the plot is expressive, that it presents us with the world as Arnolphe is bound to experience it. To an obsessed man, the world will be full of exasperating irrelevancies: in this case, a dead kitten, a ribbon, the inopportune chatter of a notary. Similarly, a man who has for years left nothing to chance in the prosecution of a maniacal plan, and who encounters difficulties on the very eve of success, will experience the world as a chaos of disruptive accidents, a storm of casualty: in this case, an old friend's son will by chance gain the affections of Arnolphe's intended; in repeated chance meetings he will subject Arnolphe, whose new title he chances not to know, to tormenting confidences; Oronte and Enrique will chance to arrive in town on what was to have been Arnolphe's wedding day, and will reveal the true identity of the young woman whom Arnolphe once chanced to adopt. It is all too much, for Arnolphe and for us, and in the last-minute breathless summary of Enrique's story, delivered by Chrysalde and Oronte in alternating couplets, Molière both burlesques a species of comic dénouement and acknowledges the outrageousness of his own. At the same time, for this reader, the gay arbitrariness of the close celebrates a truth which is central to the comic vision—that life will not be controlled, but makes a fluent resistance to all crabbèd constraint. The most triumphant demonstration of life's (or Nature's) irrepressibility occurs within Arnolphe himself, when, after so many years of coldly exploiting Agnès for his pride's sake, he becomes vulnerably human by falling in love with her.

Spontaneity versus automatism, life's happy refusal to conform to cranky plans and theories: such terms describe the play for me. Some, however, may wish to be less general, and to discern here a thesis play about, say, education. This comedy is, indeed, permeated with the themes of instruction and learning. Arnolphe has Agnès minimally educated, so that she will have no attractive accomplishments; the nuns teach her to pray, spin, and sew (and somehow, though it is against her guardian's orders, she also learns to read). In Act III, Arnolphe himself becomes her teacher, or, rather, her priest, and with repeated threats of hell-fire informs her that the function of a wife is to live wholly for her husband, in absolute subjection. *The Maxims of Marriage*, which Agnès is then given to study, are likened by Arnolphe to the rules which a novice must learn on entering a convent; and very like they are, counseling as they do a cloistered and sacrificial life devoted to the worship of one's husband. Arnolphe's whole teaching is that the purpose of marriage is to preserve the husband's honor, which is like saying that the purpose of dancing is not to break a leg; and his whole education of Agnès is intended to incapacitate her for adultery by rendering her spiritless and uninteresting. There are moments, I think, when other characters burlesque Arnolphe as educator: the manservant Alain, informing Georgette in Act II, Scene 2 that "womankind is . . . the soup of man," caricatures his master's attitude toward women, as well as his patronizing pedagogical style; and the notary, torrentially instructing Arnolphe in contract law, resembles in his pedantic formulae the Arnolphe of the smug thesis, the airtight plan, and the *Maxims*.

Much else in the play might be seen as extending the motif of instruction: Arnolphe rehearsing or drilling his servants; Chrysalde lecturing Arnolphe on the temperate view of cuckoldry; Arnolphe schooling himself in the causes of marital disaster, being guided by a Greek who counseled Augustus, or advising Oronte on the use of paternal power. But what is more surely pertinent, and stands in opposition to Arnolphe's kind of schooling, is the transformation of Horace and Agnès by that *grand maître*, Love. When we first meet him, Horace is a pretty-boy very full of himself and quite capable of seducing Agnès, but by the fifth act he has come to esteem and cherish her, and had "rather die than do her any wrong." Agnès, awakened by love to her own childish ignorance and dependence, proceeds like Juliet to develop gumption and resourcefulness, and discovers a wit which is the more devastating because of her continuing simplicity.

The play is full of "education"; granted. But it cannot convincingly be interpreted as a thesis play *about* education. What can Molière be said to advocate? Latin for women? The inclusion of love in the curriculum? Clearly Molière had a low opinion of Agnès's convent schooling, which was rather standard for the age; what really interests him, however, is not the deficiencies of such schooling but Arnolphe's ill-intended use of them. Similarly, Molière is concerned not with religion but with Arnolphe's selfish and Orgon-like abuse of it, his turning it into a bludgeon. Nor does he comment on parental authority in itself, but, rather, on Arnolphe's attempt to exploit it for his own ends. It will not do, in short, for the contemporary reader or director to inject this play with Student Unrest or Women's Liberation, or to descry in it a Generation Gap. That way lies melodrama.

Any director of this English version will have to solve for himself certain problems of interpretation and staging, but I shall say what I think. It is my own decided opinion that Chrysalde is *not* a cuckold, and that Arnolphe's second speech in Act I, Scene 1 is a bit of crude and objectionable ribbing. Chrysalde's discourses about cuckoldry should be regarded, I think, both as frequently dubious "reasoning" and as bear-baiting; a good actor would know where to modulate between them. Arnolphe's distaste for fuss and sophistication is likely to impress some as an endearing quality, but I do not see it so; rather, it is of a piece with the man's anxiety to prove himself superior to a society whose ridicule he fears, and like the "honesty" of the *Misanthrope's* Alceste, it entails posturing and bad faith. Finally, there is the fact that much of the slapstick in the plot—the throwing of the brick, Horace's tumble from the ladder—occurs off stage, and that the on-stage proceedings consist in fair part of long speeches. I should be sorry to see any director right this apparent imbalance by introducing too much pie-throwing and bottom-pinching of his own invention. Once again, Dorante gives Molière's point of view: the long speeches, he says, "are themselves actions," involving incessant ironic *interplay* between speakers and hearers. To take the most obvious example, Horace's addresses to Arnolphe are rendered wonderfully "busy" by the fact that he does not know he is addressing M. De la Souche, that Arnolphe cannot enlighten him, and that Arnolphe must continually struggle to conceal his glee or anguish. To add any great amount of farcical "business" to such complex comedy would be to divert in an unfortunate sense.

This translation has aimed at a thought-for-thought fidelity, and has sought in its verse to avoid the metronomic, which is particularly fatal on the stage: I have sometimes been very limber indeed, as in the line "He's the most hideous Christian I ever did see." For a few words or phrases I am indebted to earlier English versions in blank verse or prose.

These grateful remarks were made in Chicago, in 1996, when I was given the T. S. Eliot Award.

REGARDING FORM

For this very welcome and unexpected award, I thank the Ingersoll Foundation and all concerned. When I was in high school, there were certain books that I carried around in order to impress people with my literariness. One was the *Collected Poems of Hart Crane*, whom I didn't altogether understand, but whose words made me dizzy. Another was a slender book of James Joyce's poems; the poems inside it were melodious, conventional, and easy to understand, but the book's cover gave other people the impression that I was reading an author both difficult and scandalous. A third book that I carried with me like a sword or attribute was T. S. Eliot's *Collected Poems of 1935*. The book was physically delectable; it was bound in blue, and its pages were crisp and creamy like hearts of lettuce; it was a kind of transcendental sandwich, and though I didn't understand all the poems in it, I did consume them. It seems to me that the books I used for purposes of ostentation were in fact well-chosen, for I was truly drawn to them, and when I was through showing off by their means, I went on to know them better and better. What I first loved in Eliot was his mastery of tone and of changes of tone, his power to marshal various voices, and his ability, in such a poem as "Sweeney Among the Nightingales," to take a form suggestive of light verse and be savagely serious in it. I still admire all those things, though for me Eliot has come to be above all the poet of that great poem of spiritual struggle, "Ash Wednesday." It is an especial honor to receive a prize which bears his name.

Because I am generally accounted a formalist poet, I should like to say something this afternoon about form and order and the making of order. The other day, a man I didn't know came up to me and said, "I saw your latest poem in the *New Yorker*. What a pleasure to read iambic pentameter again!" I thanked him, and was glad to have met a reader who, after several decades of free verse ascendancy, could still recognize a meter. At the same time I hoped that he did not, as some do, nostalgically confuse formal poetry with conservatism, law and order, and the old fashioned virtues and verities. The fact is that iambic pentameter is in itself meaningless, and belongs to no age or party; it is simply an instrument, like a number 2 pencil, and as such can be used either well or badly.

In life, of course, there are many forms which are meaningful in themselves and of great value. I think, for instance, of good manners. Some of my college students of the 1960's, believing themselves to be naturally good and loving, rejected good manners along with certain other things, such as attractive dress and correct grammar, which they believed to be artificial. That was a sad mistake. Manners are no more coercive than a dance step is coercive, and indeed they are liberating: seating ladies and opening doors for people, and writing thank-you notes to grandmother, are acts of compliance with a code, but they also facilitate social dealings and the growth and expression of true kindness. The forms of religion can also be benignly enabling. Eleanor Clark, when living in Italy, found herself drawn toward the Roman Church, and she asked an Italian Catholic friend how she could best find out whether Catholicism was for her. The friend said, "Go to Mass. Kneel when the others kneel. Do and say what the others do and say. Ultimately you will have a Catholic experience." Similarly T. S. Eliot, at one stage of his religious quest, reversed St. Paul by valuing the letter above the spirit. On the American stage, we are familiar with so-called "Studio" acting, in which the actor creates the role by going deep into his own subjectivity; but there is another kind of theatre in which performances are shaped externally by the director in accordance with his knowledge of the play. I am told that Herman Shumlin would sometimes address an actor in such terms as these: "Take two steps forward, raise your eyebrows, hold out your hands, and say the line." That may sound brutal, but Edmund Burke would understand and approve, and I am sure that many actors have learned by such means what their characters were feeling.

So, there are forms and outward disciplines which may be enhancing and enlarging. The world is also full, as we know, of dismal routines and of oppressions large and small. People who, like me, visited the Soviet Union in the pre-Gorbachev days, may not have encountered the gulag, but they did encounter much wariness and protective dishonesty, and they were able to see how a tyrannical government trivializes most of its citizens. When people are powerless, when they dare not think for themselves and have no say in anything, they are too readily reduced to mean material concerns–to envying the neighbor's fur hat and trying to wangle a better television. All order, alas, is not good; it wasn't quite enough for Mussolini to make the trains run on time; and I think of a French man of letters who, recalling the Vichy regime and its apologists, observed that no people have ever raised a monument to Order.

Which brings me back to poetry. Toward the end of his poem, "The Idea of Order at Key West," Wallace Stevens exclaims, "Oh! Blessed rage for order," and what he is celebrating there is the power of art to create imaginative unities in which both the spirit and the objective world are fully and truly expressed. Such unities of vision, in which self and world meet at the full, are the great forms which poetry achieves, and which formal techniques like rhyme and meter merely serve to implement. When poetry does not bring "the whole soul of man into activity," as Coleridge says it must, or when it does violence to outward reality, it fails, and here is a well-known little poem of Stevens' about a poetic failure. It is called *Anecdote of the Jar*.

> I placed a jar in Tennessee,
> And round it was, upon a hill.
> It made the slovenly wilderness
> Surround that hill.
>
> The wilderness rose up to it,
> And sprawled around, no longer
> wild.
> The jar was round upon the
> ground
> And tall and of a port in air.
>
> It took dominion everywhere.
> The jar was gray and bare.
> It did not give of bird or bush,
> Like nothing else in Tennessee.

That jar declares itself to be the center of a circle, and thus organizes the wilderness of Tennessee; but it does so in such a way as to nullify the wild birds and bushes, while asserting its own sterile dominion. What the jar accomplishes is not an imaginative interplay between jar and wilderness, but an imposition of itself; a tyranny; it is a little pre-Gorbachev Kremlin of a jar, and Stevens elsewhere sums the matter up by saying, "A violent order is a disorder."

There are various ways in which poetry can leave things out and thus be less than itself–through distortions of propaganda, for instance, through the omissions of sentimentality, through the evasions of timidity. At its best, poetry has always confronted our sorrows and said the names of our fears, and I want to offer a modest but genuine example of that–a poem by the mid-nineteenth-century English writer Charles Kingsley, the author of *Westward Ho!*

> When all the world is young, lad,
> And all the trees are green;
> And every goose a swan, lad,
> And every lass a queen;
> Then hey for boot and horse, lad,
> And round the world away:
> Young blood must have its course,
> lad,
> And every dog his day.
> When all the world is old, lady,
> And all the trees are brown;
> And all the sport is stale, lad,
> And all the wheels run down,
> Creep home and take your place
> there
> The spent and maimed among;
> God grant you find one face there
> You loved when all was young!

What that says is pretty awful: it says that we begin life full of adventurous energy and romance, and end in weariness, disillusion, and lonely infirmity. Those assertions may not be universally true, but they have some painful pertinence to everyone, and so one might ask why such a grim message is wittily conveyed in clever rhymes and a rollicking ballad meter. Is Kingsley sugar-coating a bitter pill? I don't think so. For one thing, the jaunty ballad rhythms are appropriate to the youthful vigor and zest evoked in the first stanza, and the same rhythms are poignantly slowed as the poem saddens. For another thing, the poem's breezy movement reflects the high morale that poetry always has when it faces up to depressing or dreadful truths. Auden, in his elegy for Yeats, urges poets to

Sing of human unsuccess
In a rapture of distress,

and there is indeed a sort of rapture in any line of verse which articulately braves the darker areas of our experience. A recent magazine article about Yevgeny Kissim spoke of music as a way of mastering bad noises; poetry, which aspires to the fullest possible consciousness, masters bad thoughts by uttering them perfectly. I think that Shakespeare must have rejoiced when he got our fears of the grave into one horrible line: "To lie in cold obstruction and to rot."

I seem to have come round, now, to talking about meter and rhyme and verse-forms as they may further the utterance of a poem. The founders of the free verse movement (people like Ford and Pound and Williams) envisioned it as a kind of recess period—a

306

"formless interim," as Williams put it–after which poetry would return to a fresh formality. Unfortunately, the free verse experiment, like most experiments, became institutionalized, and has dragged on for most of this century, producing a certain number of triumphs and a lot of dreary minced prose. As a result, there are many writers and readers who don't understand what meter is and how it works. They imagine that Pound was correct in his foolish statement that metrical verse is metronomic; they suppose that words in a metrical stanza are like soldiers doing close order drill and striving for a maximum of mechanical regularity.

That's not how it is at all. A metrical form–the pentameter, for instance–is an underlying paradigm or model which we never hear, though a line like Tennyson's "the woods decay, the woods decay and fall" may come near conforming to that silent model. What one does in writing a metrical poem is to outrage the paradigm, to counterpoint the unheard model with the rhythms of emotion or description or dramatic speech. The result is that those rhythms, underlined by variance from the tidy norm, are heightened, strong, and definite in a way that the rhythms of prose or free verse can never be. Enjambment–the spilling-over of one line into the next–is also an expressive violation of the norm, because the tidy pentameter norm wants us to pause at the end of every five-foot measure; when we don't, when we brush aside that pause and plunge into the next line, we do it in support of the poem's meaning, emphasizing perhaps some impetuous emotion or some sustained and headlong action. If one were describing in verse a ninety-yard broken-field run for a touchdown, a good bit of enjambment would be called for.

Rhyme, together with the other sound-effects of a poem, can cast a musical spell, and that music is best when most attuned to the larger purposes of the poem. There are many other ways, as well, in which rhyme can be functional: it can serve to emphasize important words; it can make important linkages between key words; it can demarcate the stages of an argument; it can help a witty statement to close with a bang; by the dense repetition of a few sounds, it can orchestrate obsession or abiding grief, as in Robert Frost's poem "Bereft." Some of the things rhyme can do for a poem are almost too subtle to talk about. For instance, when two lines rhyme, and one of the rhyme-words has more force than the other, the disparity can tell us in what tone or tones those lines should be read. I put in evidence the first four lines of a Gerard Manley Hopkins sonnet, a sonnet that's full of spiritual anguish:

> No worst, there is none. Pitched
> past pitch of grief,
> More pangs will, schooled at
> forepangs, wilder wring.
> Comforter, where, where is your
> comforting?
> Mary, mother of us, where is your
> relief?

"Wring" is a strong rhyme-word, and "comforting," in the next line, rhymes very weakly with it. If I am not mistaken, we are thereby instructed to read that whole line about the absence of the Holy Spirit–"Comforter, where, where is your comforting?"–in a weak, spiritless, and broken way.

Now I want to move toward saying a little about

those traditional verse forms which were bequeathed to us by the masters–by those whom Yeats addresses as "sages standing in God's holy fire." When a formal poet feels a poem coming on, he reaches into the tool-box of traditional means and picks out a meter which seems likely to suit his hazily emerging thought; he tentatively decides whether or not the services of rhyme will be needed; he tries to foresee whether the argument of his poem will want to be paragraphed into stanzas; and then he gets going– knowing, of course, that as his poem finds its voice he may change his mind about what devices will further it. Many formal poems, nowadays, are constructed in that ad hoc fashion, and they sometimes arrive at rhyme-schemes and stanza patterns which are quit without precedent or name. On the other hand, the poet has a splendid resource in all those tested verse-forms which have been handed down to us: the couplet, the canzone, the Spenserian stanza, the rondeau, the sonnet, and so on. These various structures have something of that benign, enabling character which I ascribed to good manners, but with the difference that they are all optional, and should only be used when they are peculiarly appropriate to some incipient utterance. Robert Frost once said something like this: that if you feel like saying something for about eight lines, and then qualifying or unsaying it for six lines or so, you are probably about to write a Petrarchan sonnet. That is the way it should happen: the beginning poem, as it materializes, should choose the form whose logic will provide it with precision, economy, and power.

Every form has its particular logic and capabilities; if an epigram is on the tip of one's tongue, it should probably find utterance in a smartly rhyming couplet or quatrain, and it would be pointless folly to try to inflate it into a sonnet. There are certain reiterative forms, like the villanelle and sestina, which are designed to accommodate the mind's hashing and rehashing of a subject; if sestinas and villanelles ruminate to some purpose, they can be splendid; but if they are not driven by a strong need to turn some subject over and over, if they amount to no more than the fulfilling of a tricky pattern, then they are vacuous and interminable.

Lest I be interminable, let me call a halt to all this technical talk. I hope to have made it clear that I have no interest in form for form's sake. The meter-using poets of my generation would surely say the same, as would the excellent younger formalists who are now occupying the field: I could mention Timothy Steele, Mary Jo Salter, Emily Grosholz, Dana Gioia, R. S. Gwynn, and many another. All these would join me, I believe, in agreeing with Ralph Waldo Emerson, who said that "it is not meters, but a meter-making argument that makes a poem."

As for this sort of prize-giving occasion, I think it is a truly benign form, and once again I express my thanks.

This lecture was first given at the Library of Congress in 1959, to celebrate the 150th birthday of Edgar Allan Poe. The sixth paragraph, as I now see, does not sufficiently distinguish the function of poetry, in Poe's aesthetic, from that of prose fiction; and my new book, The Catbird's Song, is a little more accurate about Poe's attitude toward Prince Prospero. But otherwise I stand by what follows.

THE HOUSE OF POE

A few weeks ago, in the *New York Times Book Review,* Saul Bellow expressed impatience with the current critical habit of finding symbols in everything. No self-respecting modern professor, Mr. Bellow observed, would dare to explain Achilles' dragging of Hector around the walls of Troy by the mere assertion that Achilles was in a bad temper. That would be too drearily obvious. No, the professor must say that the circular path of Achilles and Hector relates to the theme of circularity which pervades *The Iliad.*

In the following week's *Book Review,* a pedantic correspondent corrected Mr. Bellow, pointing out that Achilles did not, in Homer's *Iliad,* drag Hector's body around the walls of Troy; this perhaps invalidates the Homeric example, but Mr. Bellow's complaint remains, nevertheless, a very sensible one. We are all getting a bit tired, I think, of that laboriously clever criticism which discovers mandalas in Mark Twain, rebirth archetypes in Edwin Arlington Robinson, and fertility myths in everybody.

Still, we must not be carried away by our impatience, to the point of demanding that no more symbols be reported. The business of the critic, after all, is to divine the intention of the work, and to interpret the work in the light of that intention; and since some writers are intentionally symbolic, there is nothing for it but to talk about their symbols. If we speak of Melville, we must speak of symbols. If we speak of Hawthorne, we must speak of symbols. And as for Edgar Allan Poe, whose sesquicentennial year we are met to observe, I think we can make no sense about him until we consider his work–and in particular his prose fiction–as deliberate and often brilliant allegory.

Not everyone will agree with me that Poe's work has an accessible allegorical meaning. Some critics, in fact, have refused to see any substance, allegorical or otherwise, in Poe's fiction, and have regarded his tales as nothing more than complicated machines for saying "boo." Others have intuited undiscoverable meanings in Poe, generally of an unpleasant kind: I recall one Freudian critic declaring that if we find Poe unintelligible we should congratulate ourselves, since if we *could* understand him it would be proof of our abnormality.

It is not really surprising that some critics should think Poe meaningless, or that others should suppose his meaning intelligible only to monsters. Poe was not a wide-open and perspicuous writer; indeed, he was a secretive writer both by temperament and by conviction. He sprinkled his stories with sly references to himself and to his personal history. He gave his own birth day of January 19 to his character William Wilson; he bestowed his own height and color of eye on the captain of the phantom ship in *Ms. Found in a Bottle*; and the name of one of his heroes, Arthur Gordon Pym, is patently a version of his own. He was a maker and solver of puzzles, fascinated by codes, ciphers, anagrams, acrostics, hieroglyphics, and the Kabbala. He invented the detective story. He was fond of aliases; he delighted in accounts of swindles; he perpetrated the famous Balloon Hoax of 1844; and one of his most characteristic stories is entitled *Mystification*. A man so devoted to concealment and deception and unraveling and detection might be expected to have in his work what Poe himself called "undercurrents of meaning."

And that is where Poe, as a critic, said that meaning belongs: not on the surface of the poem or tale, but below the surface as a dark undercurrent. If the meaning of a work is made overly clear–as Poe said in his *Philosophy of Composition*–if the meaning is brought to the surface and made the upper current of the poem or tale, then the work becomes bald and prosaic and ceases to be art. Poe conceived of art, you see, not as a means of giving imaginative order to earthly experience, but as a stimulus to unearthly visions. The work of literary art does not, in Poe's view, present the reader with a provisional arrangement of reality; instead, it seeks to disengage the reader's mind from reality and propel it toward the ideal. Now, since Poe thought the function of art was to set the mind soaring upward in what he called "a wild effort to reach the Beauty above," it was important to him that the poem or tale should not have such definiteness and completeness of meaning as might contain the reader's mind within the work. Therefore Poe's criticism places a positive value on the obscuration of meaning, on a dark suggestiveness, on a deliberate vagueness by means of which the reader's mind may be set adrift toward the beyond.

Poe's criticism, then, assures us that his work does have meaning. And Poe also assures us that this neaning is not on the surface but in the depths. If we accept Poe's invitation to play detective, and commence to read him with an eye for submerged meaning, it is not long before we sense that there are meanings to be found, and that in fact many of Poe's stories, though superficially dissimilar, tell the same tale. We begin to have this sense as we notice Poe's repeated use of certain narrative patterns; his repetition of certain words and phrases; his use, in story after story, of certain scenes and properties. We notice, for instance, the recurrence of the spiral or vortex. In *Ms. Found in a Bottle*, the story ends with a plunge into a whirlpool; the *Descent into the Maelström* also concludes in a water vortex; the house of Usher, just before it plunges into the tarn, is swaddled in a whirlwind; the hero of *Metzengerstein*, Poe's first published story, perishes in " a whirlwind of chaotic fire"; and at the close of *King Pest*, Hugh Tarpaulin is cast into a puncheon of ale and disappears "amid a whirlpool of foam." That Poe offers us so many spirals or vortices in his fiction, and that they should always appear at the same terminal point in their respective narratives, is a strong indication that the spiral had some symbolic value for Poe. And it did: What the spiral invariably represents in any tale of Poe's is the loss of consciousness, and the descent of the mind into sleep.

I hope you will grant, before I am through, that to find spirals in Poe is not so silly as finding circles in Homer. The professor who finds circles in Homer does so to the neglect of more important and more provable meanings. But the spiral or vortex is a part of that symbolic language in which Poe said his say, and unless we understand it, we cannot understand Poe.

But now I have gotten ahead of myself, and before I proceed with my project of exploring one area of Poe's symbolism, I think I had better say something about Poe's conception of poetry and the poet. Poe conceived of God as a poet. The universe, therefore, was an artistic creation, a poem composed by God. Now, if the universe is a poem, it follows that one proper response to it is aesthetic, and that God's creatures are attuned to Him in proportion as their imaginations are ravished by the beauty and harmony of his creation. Not to worship beauty, not to regard poetic knowledge as divine, would be to turn one's back on God and fall from grace.

The planet Earth, according to Poe's myth of the cosmos, has done just this. It has fallen away from God by exalting the scientific reason above poetic intuition, and by putting its trust in material fact rather than in visionary knowledge. The Earth's inhabitants are thus corrupted by rationalism and materialism; their souls are diseased; and Poe sees this disease of the human spirit as having contaminated physical nature. The woods and fields and waters of Earth have thereby lost their first beauty, and no longer clearly express God's imagination; the landscape has lost its original perfection of composition, in proportion as men have lost their power to perceive the beautiful.

Since Earth is a fallen planet, life upon Earth is necessarily a torment for the poet: neither in the human sphere nor in the realm of nature can he find fit objects for contemplation, and indeed his soul is oppressed by everything around him. The rationalist mocks at him; the dull, prosaic spirit of the age damps his imaginative spark; the gross materiality of the world crowds in upon him. His only recourse is to abandon all concern for Earthly things, and to devote himself as purely as possible to unearthly visions, in hopes of glimpsing that heavenly beauty which is the thought of God.

Poe, then, sees the poetic soul as at war with the mundane physical world; and that warfare is Poe's fundamental subject. But the war between soul and world is not the only war. There is also warfare within the poet's very nature. To be sure, the poet's nature was not always in conflict with itself. Prior to his earthly incarnation, and during his dreamy childhood, Poe's poet enjoyed a serene unity of being; his consciousness was purely imaginative, and he knew the universe for the divine poem that it is. But with his entrance into adult life, the poet became involved with a fallen world in which the physical, the factual, the rational, the prosaic are not escapable. Thus compromised, he lost his perfect spirituality, and is now cursed with a divided nature. Though his imagination still yearns toward ideal beauty, his mortal body chains him to the physical and temporal and local; the hungers and passions of his body draw him toward external objects, and the conflict of conscience and desire degrades and distracts his soul; his mortal senses try to convince him of the reality of a material world which his soul struggles to escape; his reason urges him to acknowledge everyday fact, and to confine his thought within the prison of logic. For all these reasons it is not easy for the poet to detach his soul from earthly things, and regain his lost imaginative power–his power to commune with that supernal beauty which is symbolized, in Poe, by the shadowy and angelic figures of Ligeia, and Helen, and Lenore.

These, then, are Poe's great subjects: first, the war

between the poetic soul and the external world; ond, the war between the poetic soul and the ear self to which it is bound. All of Poe's major stc are allegorical presentations of these conflicts, and everything he wrote bore somehow upon them. How does one wage war against the external world?? And how does one release one's visionary soul from the body, and from the constraint of the reason? These may sound like difficult tasks; and yet we all accomplish them every night. In a subjective sense–and Poe's thought is wholly subjective–we destroy the world every time we close our eyes. If esse est percipi, as Bishop Berkeley said–if to be is to be perceived–then when we withdraw our attention from the world in somnolence or sleep, the world ceases to be. As our minds move toward sleep, by way of drowsiness and reverie and the hypnagogic state, we escape from consciousness of the world, we escape from awareness of our bodies, and we enter a realm in which reason no longer hampers the play of the imagination: we enter the realm of dream.

Like many romantic poets, Poe identified imagination with dream. Where Poe differed from other romantic poets was in the literalness and absoluteness of the identification, and in the clinical precision with which he observed the phenomena of dream, carefully distinguishing the various states through which the mind passes on its way to sleep. A large number of Poe's stories derive their very structure from this sequence of mental states: *Ms. Found in a Bottle,* to give but one example, is an allegory of the mind's voyage from the waking world into the world of dreams, with each main step of the narrative symbolizing the passage of the mind from one state to another–from wakefulness to reverie, from reverie to the hypnagogic state, from the hypnagogic state to the deep dream. The departure of the narrator's ship from Batavia represents the mind's withdrawal from the waking world; the drowning of the captain and all but one of the crew represents the growing solitude of reverie; when the narrator is transferred by collision from a real ship to a phantom ship, we are to understand that he has passed from reverie, a state in which reality and dream exist in a kind of equilibrium, into the free fantasy of the hypnagogic state. And when the phantom ship makes its final plunge into the whirlpool, we are to understand that the narrator's mind has gone over the brink of sleep and descended into dreams.

What I am saying by means of this example is that the scenes and situations of Poe's tales are always concrete representations of states of mind. If we bear in mind Poe's fundamental plot–the effort of the poetic soul to escape all consciousness of the world in dream–we soon recognize the significance of certain scenic or situational motifs which turn up in story after story. The most important of these recurrent motifs is that of *enclosure* or *circumscription*; perhaps the latter term is preferable, because it is Poe's own word, and because Poe's enclosures are so often more or less circular in form. The heroes of Poe's tales and poems are violently circumscribed by whirlpools, or peacefully circumscribed by cloud-capped Paradisal valleys; they float upon circular pools ringed in by steep flowering hillsides; they dwell on islands, or voyage to them; we find Poe heroes also in coffins, in the cabs of balloons, or hidden away in the holds of ships; and above all we find them sitting alone in the claustral and richly-furnished rooms of remote and mouldering mansions.

Almost never, if you think about it, is one of Poe's heroes to be seen standing in the light of common day; almost never does the Poe hero breathe the air that others breathe; he requires some kind of envelope in order to be what he is; he is always either enclosed or on his way to an enclosure. The narrative of William Wilson conducts the hero from Stoke Newington to Eton, from Eton to Oxford, and then to Rome by way of Paris, Vienna, Berlin, Moscow, Naples, and Egypt: and yet, for all his travels, Wilson seems never to set foot out-of-doors. The story takes place in a series of rooms, the last one locked from the inside.

Sometimes Poe emphasizes the circumscription of his heroes by multiple enclosures. Roderick Usher dwells in a great and crumbling mansion from which, as Poe tells us, he has not ventured forth in many years. This mansion stands islanded in a stagnant lake, which serves it as a defensive moat. And beyond the moat lies the Usher estate, a vast barren tract having its own peculiar and forbidding weather and atmosphere. You might say that Roderick Usher is defended in depth; and yet at the close of the story Poe compounds Roderick's inaccessibility by having the mansion and its occupant swallowed up by the waters of the tarn.

What does it mean that Poe's heroes are invariably enclosed or circumscribed? The answer is simple: circumscription, in Poe's tales, means the exclusion from consciousness of the so-called real world, the world of time and reason and physical fact; it means the isolation of the poetic soul in visionary reverie or trance. When we find one of Poe's characters in a remote valley, or a claustral room, we know that he is in the process of dreaming his way out of the world.

Now, I want to devote the time remaining to the consideration of one kind of enclosure in Poe's tales: the mouldering mansion and its richly-furnished rooms. I want to concentrate on Poe's architecture and decor for two reasons: first, because Poe's use of architecture is so frankly and provably allegorical that I should be able to be convincing about it; second, because by concentrating on one area of Poe's symbolism we shall be able to see that his stories are allegorical not only in their broad patterns, but also in their smallest details.

Let us begin with a familiar poem, *The Haunted Palace*. The opening stanzas of this poem, as a number of critics have noted, make a point-by-point comparison between a building and the head of a man. The exterior of the palace represents the man's physical features; the interior represents the man's mind engaged in harmonious imaginative thought.

> In the greenest of our valleys,
>   By good angels tenanted,
> Once a fair and stately palace–
>   Radiant palace–reared its head.
>
> In the monarch Thought's dominion,
>   It stood there!
> Never seraph spread a pinion
>   Over fabric half so fair!
>
> Banners yellow, glorious, golden,
>   On its roof did float and flow
> (This–all this–was in the olden
>   Time long ago),
> And every gentle air that dallied,
>   In that sweet day,

Along the ramparts plumed and
pallid,
    A wingéd odor went away.

Wanderers in that happy valley,
    Through two luminous win
    dows, saw
Spirits moving musically
    To a lute's well-tunéd law,
Round about a throne where, sitting,
    Porphyrogene,
In state his glory well befitting,
    The ruler of the realm was seen.

And all in pearl and ruby glowing
    Was the fair palace door,
Through which came flowing, flow-
    ing, flowing,
    And sparkling evermore,
A troop of Echoes, whose sweet duty
    Was but to sing,
In voices of surpassing beauty,
    The wit and wisdom of their
king.

I expect you observed that the two luminous windows of the palace are the eyes of a man, and that
the yellow banners on the roof are his luxuriant blond
hair. The "pearl and ruby" door is the man's mouth—
ruby representing red lips, and pearl representing
pearly white teeth. The beautiful Echoes which issue from the pearl and ruby door are the poetic ut-
terances of the man's harmonious imagination, here
symbolized as an orderly dance. The angel-guarded
valley in which the palace stands, and which Poe
describes as "the monarch Thought's dominion," is
a symbol of the man's exclusive awareness of exalted

and spiritual things. The valley is what Poe elsewhere called "that evergreen and radiant paradise which the true poet knows . . . as the limited realm of his authority, as the circumscribed Eden of his dreams."

As you all remember, the last two stanzas of the poem describe the physical and spiritual corruption of the palace and its domain, and it was to this part of the poem that Poe was referring when he told a correspondent, "By the 'Haunted Palace' I mean to imply a mind haunted by phantoms—a disordered brain." Let me read you the closing lines:

> But evil things, in robes of sorrow,
> Assailed the monarch's high estate.
> (Ah, let us mourn!—for never morrow
> Shall dawn upon him, desolate!)
> And round about his home the glory
> That blushed and bloomed,
> Is but a dim-remembered story
> Of the old time entombed.
>
> And traveller, now, within that valley,
> Through the red-litten windows see
> Vast forms that move fantastically
> To a discordant melody,
> While, like a ghastly rapid river,
> Through the pale door
> A hideous throng rush out forever,
> And laugh—but smile no more.

The domain of the monarch Thought, in these final stanzas, is disrupted by civil war, and in consequence everything alters for the worse. The valley becomes barren, like the domain of Roderick Usher; the eye-like windows of the palace are no longer "luminous," but have become "red-litten"–they are like the bloodshot eyes of a madman or a drunkard. As for the mouth of our allegorized man, it is now "pale" rather than "pearl and ruby," and through it come no sweet Echoes, as before, but the wild laughter of a jangling and discordant mind.

The two states of the palace–before and after–are, as we can see, two states of mind. Poe does not make it altogether clear why one state of mind has given way to the other, but by recourse to similar tales and poems we can readily find the answer. The palace in its original condition expresses the imaginative harmony which the poet's soul enjoys in early childhood, when all things are viewed with a tyrannical and unchallenged subjectivity. But as the soul passes from childhood into adult life, its consciousness is more and more invaded by the corrupt and corrupting external world: it succumbs to passion, it develops a conscience, it makes concessions to reason and to objective fact. Consequently, there is civil war in the palace of the mind. The imagination must now struggle against the intellect and the moral sense; finding itself no longer able to possess the world through a serene solipsism, it strives to annihilate the outer world by turning in upon itself; it flees into irrationality and dream; and all its dreams are efforts both to recall and to simulate its primal, unfallen state.

The Haunted Palace presents us with a possible key to the general meaning of Poe's architecture; and this key proves, if one tries it, to open every building in Poe's fiction. Roderick Usher, as you will remember, declaims *The Haunted Palace* to the visitor who tells his story, accompanying the poem with wild improvisations on the guitar. We are encouraged, therefore, to compare the palace of the poem with the house of the story; and it is no surprise to find that the Usher mansion has "vacant eye-like windows," and that there are mysterious physical sympathies between Roderick Usher and the house in which he dwells. The House of Usher is, in allegorical fact, the physical body of Roderick Usher, and its dim interior is, in fact, Roderick Usher's visionary mind.

The House of Usher, like many edifices in Poe, is in a state of extreme decay. The stonework of its facade has so crumbled and decomposed that it reminds the narrator, as he puts it, "of the specious totality of old woodwork which has rotted for long years in some neglected vault." The Usher mansion is so eaten away, so fragile, that it seems a breeze would push it over; it remains standing only because the atmosphere of Usher's domain is perfectly motionless and dead. Such is the case also with the "time-eaten towers that tremble not" in Poe's poem *The City in the Sea;* and likewise the magnificent architecture of *The Domain of Arnheim* is said to "sustain itself by a miracle in mid-air." Even the detective Dupin lives in a perilously decayed structure: the narrator of *The Murders in the Rue Morgue* tells how he and Dupin dwelt in a "time-eaten and grotesque manion, long deserted through superstitions into which we did not enquire, and tottering to its fall in a retired and desolate portion of the Faubourg St. Germain." (Notice how, even when Poe's buildings are situated in cities, he manages to circumscribe them with a protective desolation.)

We must now ask what Poe means by the extreme and tottering decay of so many of his structures. The answer is best given by reference to *The Fall of the House of Usher*, and in giving the answer we shall arrive, I think, at an understanding of the pattern of that story.

The Fall of the House of Usher is a journey into the depths of the self. I have said that all journeys in Poe are allegories of the process of dreaming, and we must understand *The Fall of the House of Usher* as a dream of the narrator's, in which he leaves behind him the waking, physical world and journeys inward toward his *moi intérieur*, toward his inner and spiritual self. That inner and spiritual self is Roderick Usher.

Roderick Usher, then, is a part of the narrator's self, which the narrator reaches by way of reverie. We may think of Usher, if we like, as the narrator's imagination, or as his visionary soul. Or we may think of him as a state of mind which the narrator enters at a certain stage of his progress into dreams. Considered *as a state of mind*, Roderick Usher is an allegorical figure representing the hypnagogic state.

The hypnagogic state, about which there is strangely little said in the literature of psychology, is a condition of semi-consciousness in which the closed eye beholds a continuous procession of vivid and constantly changing forms. These forms sometimes have color, and are often abstract in character. Poe regarded the hypnagogic state as the visionary condition *par excellence*, and he considered its rapidly shifting abstract images to be—as he put it—"glimpses of the spirit's outer world." These visionary glimpses, Poe says in one of his *Marginalia*, "arise in the soul . . . only . . . at those mere points of time where the confines of the waking world blend with those of the world of dreams." And Poe goes on to say: "I am aware of these 'fancies' only when I am upon the very brink of sleep, with the consciousness that I am so."

Roderick Usher enacts the hypnagogic state in a number of ways. For one thing, the narrator describes Roderick's behavior as inconsistent, and characterized by constant alternation: he is alternately vivacious and sullen; he is alternately communicative and rapt; he speaks at one moment with "tremulous indecision," and at the next with "energetic concision" of an excited opium-eater. His conduct resembles, in other words, that wavering between consciousness and sub-consciousness which characterizes the hypnagogic state. The trembling of Roderick's body, and the floating of his silken hair, also bring to mind the instability and underwater quality of hypnagogic images. His improvisations on the guitar suggest hypnagogic experience in their rapidity, changeableness, and wild novelty. And as for Usher's paintings, which the narrator describes as "pure abstractions," they quite simply are hypnagogic images. The narrator says of Roderick, "From the paintings over which his elaborate fancy brooded, and which grew, touch by touch, into vaguenesses at which I shuddered the more thrillingly because I shuddered without knowing why–from these paintings (vivid as their images now are before me) I would in vain endeavor to educe more than a small portion which should lie within the compass of merely written words." That the narrator finds Roderick's paintings indescribable is interesting, because in that one of the Marginalia from which I have quoted, Poe asserts that the only things in human experience which lie "beyond the compass of words" are the visions of the hypnagogic state.

Roderick Usher stands for the hypnagogic state,

which as Poe said is a teetering condition of mind occurring "upon the very brink of sleep." Since Roderick is the embodiment of a state of mind in which *falling*–falling asleep–is imminent, it is appropriate that the building which symbolizes his mind should promise at every moment to fall. The House of Usher stares down broodingly at its reflection in the tarn below, as in the hypnagogic state the conscious mind may stare into the subconscious; the house threatens continually to collapse because it is extremely easy for the mind to slip from the hypnagogic state into the depths of sleep; and when the House of Usher does fall, the story ends, as it must, because the mind, at the end of its inward journey, has plunged into the darkness of sleep.

We have found one allegorical meaning in the tottering decay of Poe's buildings; there is another meaning, equally important, which may be stated very briefly. I have said that Poe saw the poet as at war with the material world, and with the material or physical aspects of himself; and I have said that Poe identified poetic imagination with the power to escape from the material and the materialistic, to exclude them from consciousness and so subjectively destroy them. Now, if we recall these things, and recall also that the exteriors of Poe's houses or palaces, with their eye-like windows and mouth-like doors, represent the physical features of Poe's dreaming heroes, then the characteristic dilapidation of Poe's architecture takes on sudden significance. The extreme decay of the House of Usher–a decay so extreme as to approach the atmospheric–is quite simply a sign that the narrator, in reaching that state of mind which he calls Roderick Usher, has very nearly dreamt himself free of his physical body, and of the material world with which that body connects him.

This is what decay or decomposition mean everywhere in Poe; and we find them almost everywhere. Poe's preoccupation with decay is not, as some critics have thought, an indication of necrophilia; decay in Poe is a symbol of visionary remoteness from the physical, a sign that the state of mind represented is one of almost pure spirituality. When the House of Usher disintegrates or dematerializes at the close of the story, it does so because Roderick Usher has become all soul. *The Fall of the House of Usher*, then, is not really a horror story; it is a triumphant report by the narrator that it is possible for the poetic soul to shake off this temporal, rational, physical world and escape, if only for a moment, to a realm of unfettered vision.

We have now arrived at three notions about Poe's typical building. It is set apart in a valley or a sea or a waste place, and this remoteness is intended to express the retreat of the poet's mind from worldly consciousness into dream. It is a tottery structure, and this indicates that the dreamer within is in that unstable threshold condition called the hypnagogic state. Finally, Poe's typical building is crumbling or decomposing, and this means that the dreamer's mind is moving toward a perfect freedom from his material self and the material world. Let us now open the door–or mouth–of Poe's building and visit the mind inside.

As we enter the palace of the visionary hero of *The Assignation*, or the house of Roderick Usher, we find ourselves approaching the master's private chamber by way of dim and winding passages, or a winding staircase. There is no end to dim windings in Poe's fiction: there are dim and winding woods paths, dim

and winding streets, dim and winding watercourses–
and, whenever the symbolism is architectural, there
are likely to be dim and winding passages or stair-
cases. It is not at all hard to guess what Poe means
by this symbol. If we think of waking life as domi-
nated by reason, and if we think of the reason as a
daylight faculty which operates in straight lines, then
it is proper that reverie should be represented as an
obscure and wandering movement of the mind.
There are other, and equally obvious meanings in
Poe's symbol of dim and winding passages: to grope
through such passages is to become confused as to
place and direction, just as in reverie we begin to lose
any sense of locality, and to have an infinite freedom
in regard to space. In his description of the huge old
mansion in which William Wilson went to school,
Poe makes this meaning of winding passages very
plain:

> But the house!–how quaint an old
> building was this!–to me how
> veritable a palace of enchantment!
> There was no end to its windings–
> to its incomprehensible subdivi-
> sions. It was difficult, at any given
> time, to say with certainty upon
> which of its two stories one hap-
> pened to be. From each room to
> every other there were sure to be
> found three or four steps either in
> ascent or descent. Then the lateral
> branches were innumerable–
> inconceivable–and so returning in
> upon themselves, that our most
> exact ideas in regard to the whole
> mansion were not very far differ-

ent from those with which we
pondered on infinity.

Dim windings indicate the state of reverie; they
point toward that infinite freedom in and from space
which the mind achieves in dreams; also, in their
curvature and in their occasional doubling-back, they
anticipate the mind's final spiralling plunge into
unconsciousness. But the immediate goal of reverie's
winding passages is that magnificent chamber in
which we find the visionary hero slumped in a chair
or lolling on an ottoman, occupied in purging his
consciousness of everything that is earthly.

Since I have been speaking of geometry–of straight
lines and curves and spirals–perhaps the first thing
to notice about Poe's dream-rooms is their shape. It
has already been said that the enclosures of Poe's tales
incline to a curving or circular form. And Poe himself, in certain of his essays and dialogues, explains
this inclination by denouncing what he calls "the
harsh mathematical reason of the schools," and complaining that practical science has covered the face
of the earth with "rectangular obscenities." Poe quite
explicitly identifies regular angular forms with everyday reason, and the circle, oval, or fluid arabesque
with the otherworldly imagination. Therefore, if we
discover that the dream-chambers of Poe's fiction are
free of angular regularity, we may be sure that we
are noticing a pointed and purposeful consistency
in his architecture and décor.

The ball-room of the story *Hop-Frog* is circular. The
Devil's apartment in *The Duc de l'Omelette* has its corners "rounded into niches," and we find rounded
corners also in Poe's essay *The Philosophy of Furni-
ture*. In *Ligeia*, the bridal chamber is a pentagonal tur-

ret-room; however, the angles are concealed by sarcophagi, so that the effect is circular. The corners of
Roderick Usher's chamber are likewise concealed,
being lost in deep shadow. Other dream-rooms are
either irregular or indeterminate in form. For example, there are seven rooms of Prince Prospero's
imperial suite in *The Masque of the Red Death*. As Poe
observes, "in many palaces . . . such suites form a
long and straight vista"; but in Prince Prospero's
palace, as he describes it, "the apartments were so
irregularly disposed that the vision embraced but
little more than one at a time. There was a sharp turn
at every twenty or thirty yards, and at each turn a
novel effect." The turret-room of *The Oval Portrait* is
not defined as to shape; we are told, however, that it
is architecturally "bizarre," and complicated by a
quantity of unexpected nooks and niches. Similarly,
the visionary's apartment in *The Assignation* is described only as dazzling, astounding and original in
its architecture; we are not told in what way its di-
mensions are peculiar, but it seems safe to assume
that it would be a difficult room to measure for wall-
to-wall carpeting. The room of *The Assignation*, by
the way–like that of *Ligeia*–has its walls enshrouded
in rich figured draperies which are continually agitated by some mysterious agency. The fluid shifting
of the figures suggests, of course, the behavior of
hypnagogic images; but the agitation of the draperies would also produce a perpetual ambiguity of architectural form, and the effect would resemble that
which Pevsner ascribes to the interior of San Vitale
in Ravenna: "a sensation of uncertainty [and] of a
dreamlike floating."

Poe, as you see, is at great pains to avoid depicting
the usual squarish sort of room in which we spend

much of our waking lives. His chambers of dream either approximate the circle–an infinite form which is, as Poe somewhere observes, "the emblem of Eternity"–or they so lack any apprehensible regularity of shape as to suggest the changeableness and spatial freedom of the dreaming mind. The exceptions to this rule are few and entirely explainable. I will grant, for instance, that the iron-walled torture-chamber of *The Pit and the Pendulum* portrays the very reverse of spatial freedom, and that it is painfully angular in character, the angles growing more acute as the torture intensifies. But there is very good allegorical reason for these things. The rooms of *Ligeia* or *The Assignation* symbolize a triumphantly imaginative state of mind in which the dreamer is all but free of the so-called "real" world. In *The Pit and the Pendulum*, the dream is of quite another kind; it is a nightmare state, in which the dreamer is imaginatively impotent, and can find no refuge from reality, even in dream. Though he lies on the brink of the pit, on the very verge of the plunge into unconsciousness, he is still unable to disengage himself from the physical and temporal world. The physical oppresses him in the shape of lurid graveyard visions; the temporal oppresses him in the form of an enormous and deadly pendulum. It is altogether appropriate, then, that this particular chamber should be constricting and cruelly angular.

But let us return to Poe's typical room, and look now at its furnishings. They are generally weird, magnificent, and suggestive of great wealth. The narrator of "The Assignation," entering the hero's apartment, feels "blind and dizzy with luxuriousness, and looking about him he confesses, "I could not bring myself to believe that the wealth of any subject in Europe could have supplied the princely magnificence which burned and blazed around." Poe's visionaries are, as a general thing, extremely rich; the hero of *Ligeia* confides that, as for wealth, he possesses "far more, very far more, than ordinarily falls to the lot of mortals"; and Ellison, in *The Domain of Arnheim*, is the fortunate inheritor of 450 million dollars. Legrand, in *The Gold Bug*, with his treasure of 450 thousand, is only a poor relation of Mr. Ellison; still, by ordinary standards, he seems sublimely solvent.* (*Actually, Legrand's treasure amounted to "a million and a half dollars," of which "four hundred and fifty thousand dollars" were in coin. R.W.)

Now, we must be careful to take all these riches in an allegorical sense. As we contemplate the splendor of any of Poe's rooms, we must remember that the room is a state of mind, and that everything in it is therefore a thought, a mental image. The allegorical meaning of the costliness of Poe's decor is simply this: that his heroes are richly imaginative. And since imagination is a gift rather than an acquisition, it is appropriate that riches in Poe should be inherited or found, but never earned.

Another thing we notice about Poe's furnishings is that they are eclectic in the extreme. Their richness is not the richness of Tiffany's and Sloan's, but of all periods and all cultures. Here is a partial inventory of the fantastic bridal-chamber in *Ligeia*: Egyptian carvings and sarcophagi; Venetian glass; fretwork of a semi-Gothic, semi-Druidical character; a Saracenic chandelier; Oriental ottomans and candelabra; an Indian couch; and figured draperies with Norman motifs. The same defiance of what interior decorators once called "keeping" is found in the apartment of the visionary hero of *The Assignation*, and one of the hero's speeches hints at the allegorical meaning of his jumbled decor:

> To dream [says the hero of *The Assignation*]–to dream has been the business of my life. I have therefore framed for myself, as you see, a bower of dreams. In the heart of Venice could I have erected a better? You behold around you, it is true, a medley of architectural embellishments. The chastity of Ionia is offended by antediluvian devices, and the sphynxes of Egypt are outstretched upon carpets of gold. Yet the effect is incongruous to the timid alone. Proprieties of place, and especially of time, are the bugbears which terrify mankind from the contemplation of the magnificent.

That last sentence, with its scornful reference to "proprieties of place, and . . . time," should put us in mind of the first stanza of Poe's poem *Dream-Land*:

> By a route obscure and lonely,
> Haunted by ill angels only,
> Where an Eidolon, named NIGHT,
> On a black throne reigns upright,
> I have reached these lands but
> newly
> From an ultimate dim Thule–
> From a wild weird clime that lieth,
> sublime,
> Out of SPACE–out of TIME.

In dream-land, we are "out of SPACE–out of TIME," and the same is true of such apartments or "bowers of dreams" as the hero of *The Assignation* inhabits. His eclectic furnishings, with their wild juxtapositions of Venetian and Indian, Egyptian and Norman, are symbolic of the visionary soul's transcendence of spatial and temporal limitations. When one of Poe's dream-rooms is not furnished in the fashion I have been describing, the idea of spatial and temporal freedom is often conveyed in some other manner; Roderick Usher's library, for instance, with its rare and precious volumes belonging to all times and tongues, is another concrete symbol of the timelessness and placelessness of the dreaming mind.

We have spoken of the winding approaches to Poe's dream-chambers, of their curvilinear or indeterminate shape, and of the rich eclecticism of their furnishings. Let us now glance over such matters as lighting, sound-proofing, and ventilation. As regards lighting, the rooms of Poe's tales are never exposed to the naked rays of the sun, because the sun belongs to the waking world and waking consciousness. The narrator of *The Murders in the Rue Morgue* tells how he and his friend Dupin conducted their lives in such a way as to avoid all exposure to sunlight. "At the first dawn of the morning," he writes, "we closed all the massy shutters of our old building; lighting a couple of tapers which, strongly perfumed, threw out only the ghastliest and feeblest of rays. By the aid of these we then busied our souls in dreams. . . ."

In some of Poe's rooms, there simply are no windows. In other cases, the windows are blocked up or shuttered. When the windows are not blocked or shuttered, their panes are tinted with a crimson or leaden hue, so as to transform the light of day into a lurid or ghastly glow. This kind of lighting, in which the sun's rays are admitted but transformed, belongs to the portrayal of those half-states of mind in which dream and reality are blended. Filtered through tinted panes, the sunlight enters certain of Poe's rooms as it might enter the half-closed eyes of a day-dreamer, or the dream-dimmed eyes of someone awakening from sleep. But when Poe wishes to represent that deeper phase of dreaming in which visionary consciousness has all but annihilated any sense of the external world, the lighting is always artificial and the time is always night.

Flickering candles, wavering torches, and censers full of writhing varicolored flames furnish much of the illumination of Poe's rooms, and one can see the appropriateness of such lighting to the vague and shifting perceptions of the hypnagogic state. But undoubtedly the most important lighting-fixture in Poe's rooms—and one which appears in a good half of them—is the chandelier. It hangs from the lofty ceiling by a long chain, generally of gold, and it consists sometimes of a censer, sometimes of a lamp, sometimes of candles, sometimes of a glowing jewel (a ruby or a diamond), and once, in the macabre tale *King Pest*, of a skull containing ignited charcoal. What we must understand about this chandelier, as Poe explains in his poem *Al Aaraaf*, is that its chain does not stop at the ceiling: it goes right on through the ceiling, through the roof, and up to heaven. What comes down the chain from heaven is the divine power of imagination, and it is imagination's purifying fire which flashes or flickers from the chandelier. That is why the immaterial and angelic Ligeia makes her reappearance directly beneath the chandelier; and that is why Hop-Frog makes his departure for dream-land by climbing the chandelier-chain and vanishing through the sky-light. The dreaming soul, then, has its own light–a light more spiritual, more divine, than that of the sun. And Poe's chamber of dream is autonomous in every other respect. No breath of air enters it from the outside world: either its atmosphere is dead, or its draperies are stirred by magical and intramural air-currents. No earthly sound invades the chamber: either it is deadly still, or it echoes with a sourceless and unearthly music. Nor does any odor of flower or field intrude: instead, as Poe tells in *The Assignation*, the sense of smell is "oppressed by mingled and conflicting perfumes, reeking up from strange convolute censers."

The point of all this is that the dreaming psyche separates itself wholly from the bodily senses–the "rudimental senses," as Poe called them. The bodily senses are dependent on objective stimuli–on the lights and sounds and odors of the physical world. But the sensuous life of dream is self-sufficient and immaterial, and consists in the imagination's God-like enjoyment of its own creations.

I am reminded, at this point, of a paragraph of Santayana's, in which he describes the human soul as it was conceived by the philosopher Leibniz. Leibniz, says Santayana, assigned

> a mental seat to all sensible objects.
> The soul, he said, had no windows
> and, he might have added, no
> doors; no light could come to it
> from without; and it could not
> exert any transitive force or make
> any difference beyond its own
> insulated chamber. It was a camera

obscura, with a universe painted on its impenetrable walls. The changes which went on in it were like those in a dream, due to the discharge of pent-up energies and fecundities within it. . . .

Leibniz's chamber of the soul is identical with Poe's chamber of dream: but the solipsism which Leibniz saw as the normal human condition was for Poe an ideal state, a blessed state, which we may enjoy as children or as preexistent souls, but can reclaim in adult life only by a flight from everyday consciousness into hypnagogic trance.

The one thing which remains to be said about Poe's buildings is that the cellars or catacombs, whenever they appear, stand for the irrational part of the mind; and that is so conventional an equation in symbolic literature that I think I need not be persuasive or illustrative about it. I had hoped, at this point, to discuss in a leisurely way some of the stories in which Poe makes use of his architectural properties, treating those stories as narrative wholes. But I have spoken too long about other things; and so, if you will allow me a few minutes more, I shall close by commenting briskly on two or three stories only.

The typical Poe story occurs within the mind of a poet; and its characters are not independent personalities, but allegorical figures representing the warring principles of the poet's divided nature. The lady Ligeia, for example, stands for that heavenly beauty which the poet's soul desires; while Rowena stands for that earthly, physical beauty which tempts the poet's passions. The action of the story is the dreaming soul's gradual emancipation from earthly attachments–which is allegorically expressed in the slow dissolution of Rowena. The result of this process is the soul's final, momentary vision of the heavenly Ligeia. Poe's typical story presents some such struggle between the visionary and the mundane; and the duration of Poe's typical story is the duration of a dream.

There are two tales in which Poe makes an especially clear and simple use of his architectural symbolism. The first is an unfamiliar tale called *The System of Dr. Tarr and Prof. Fether*, and the edifice of that tale is a remote and dilapidated madhouse in southern France. What happens, in brief, is that the inmates of the madhouse escape from their cells in the basement of the building, overpower their keepers, and lock them up in their own cells. Having done this, the lunatics take possession of the upper reaches of the house. They shutter all the windows, put on odd costumes, and proceed to hold an uproarious and discordant feast, during which there is much eating and drinking of a disgusting kind, and a degraded version of Ligeia or Helen does a strip-tease. At the height of these festivities, the keepers escape from their cells, break in through the barred and shuttered windows of the dining-room, and restore order.

Well: the madhouse, like all of Poe's houses, is a mind. The keepers are the rational part of that mind, and the inmates are its irrational part. As you noticed, the irrational is suitably assigned to the cellar. The uprising of the inmates, and the suppression of the keepers, symbolizes the beginning of a dream, and the mad banquet which follows is perhaps Poe's least spiritual portrayal of the dream-state: this dream, far from being an escape from the physical, consists exclusively of the release of animal appetites–as dreams sometimes do. When the keepers break in the windows, and subdue the revellers, they bring with them reason and the light of day, and the wild dream is over.

The Masque of the Red Death is a better-known and even more obvious example of architectural allegory. You will recall how Prince Prospero, when his dominions are being ravaged by the plague, withdraws with a thousand of his knights and ladies into a secluded, impregnable and windowless abbey, where after a time he entertains his friends with a costume ball. The weird decor of the seven ballrooms expresses the Prince's own taste, and in strange costumes of the Prince's own design the company dances far into the night, looking, as Poe says, like "a multitude of dreams." The festivities are interrupted only by the hourly striking of a gigantic ebony clock which stands in the western-most room; and the striking of this clock has invariably a sobering effect on the revellers. Upon the last stroke of twelve, as you will remember, there appears amid the throng a figure attired in the blood-dabbled grave-clothes of a plague-victim. The dancers shrink from him in terror. But the Prince, infuriated at what he takes to be an insolent practical joke, draws his dagger and pursues the figure through all of the seven rooms. In the last and westernmost room, the figure suddenly turns and confronts Prince Prospero, who gives a cry of despair and falls upon his own dagger. The Prince's friends rush forward to seize the intruder, who stands now within the shadow of the ebony clock; but they find nothing there. And then, one after the other, the thousand revellers fall dead of the Red Death, and the lights flicker out, and Prince Prospero's ball is at an end.

In spite of its cast of one thousand and two, *The Masque of the Red Death* has only one character. Prince Prospero is one-half of that character, the visionary half; the nameless figure in grave-clothes is the other, as we shall see in a moment. More than once, in his dialogues or critical writings, Poe describes the earth-bound, time-bound rationalism of his age as a *disease*. And that is what the Red Death signifies. Prince Prospero's flight from the Red Death is the poetic imagination's flight from temporal and worldly consciousness into dream. The thousand dancers of Prince Prospero's costume ball are just what Poe says they are—"dreams" or "phantasms," veiled and vivid creatures of Prince Prospero's rapt imagination. Whenever there is a feast, or carnival, or costume ball in Poe, we may be sure that a dream is in progress.

But what is the gigantic ebony clock? For the answer to that, one need only consult a dictionary of slang: we call the human heart a *ticker*, meaning that it is the clock of the body, and that is what Poe means here. In sleep, our minds may roam beyond the temporal world, but our hearts tick on, binding us to time and mortality. Whenever the ebony clock strikes, the dancers of Prince Prospero's dream grow momentarily pale and still, in half-awareness that they and their revel must have an end; it is as if a sleeper should half-awaken, and know that he has been dreaming, and then sink back into dreams again.

The figure in blood-dabbled grave-clothes, who stalks through the terrified company and vanishes in the shadow of the clock, is waking, temporal consciousness, and his coming means the death of dreams. He breaks up Prince Prospero's ball as the keepers in *Dr. Tarr and Prof. Fether* break up the revels of the lunatics. The final confrontation between Prince Prospero and the shrouded figure is like the terrible final meeting between William Wilson and his double. Recognizing his adversary as his own worldly and mortal self, Prince Prospero gives a cry of despair which is also Poe's cry of despair: despair at the realization that only by self-destruction could the poet fully free his soul from the trammels of this world.

Poe's aesthetic, Poe's theory of the nature of art, seems to me insane. To say that art should repudiate everything human and earthly, and find its subject-matter at the flickering end of dreams, is hopelessly to narrow the scope and function of art. Poe's aesthetic points toward such impoverishments as *poésie pure* and the abstract expressionist movement in painting. And yet, despite his aesthetic, Poe is a great artist, and I would rest my case for him on his prose allegories of psychic conflict. In them, Poe broke wholly new ground, and they remain the best things of their kind in our literature. Poe's mind may have been a strange one; yet all minds are alike in their general structure; therefore we can understand him, and I think that he will have something to say to us as long as there is civil war in the palaces of men's minds.